# Focus Group Methodology

# Focus Group Methodology

## Principles and Practice

Pranee Liamputtong

Los Angeles | London | New Delhi
Singapore | Washington DC

SAGE Publications Ltd
1 Oliver's Yard
55 City Road
London EC1Y 1SP

SAGE Publications Inc.
2455 Teller Road
Thousand Oaks, California 91320

SAGE Publications India Pvt Ltd
B 1/I 1 Mohan Cooperative Industrial Area
Mathura Road
New Delhi 110 044

SAGE Publications Asia-Pacific Pte Ltd
33 Pekin Street #02-01
Far East Square
Singapore 048763

**Library of Congress Control Number: 2010931532**

**British Library Cataloguing in Publication data**

A catalogue record for this book is available from the British Library

ISBN 978-1-84787-908-0
ISBN 978-1-84787-909-7 (pbk)

Typeset by C&M Digitals (P) Ltd, Chennai, India
Printed by MPG Books Group, Bodmin, Cornwall
Printed on paper from sustainable resources

To my children:

Zoe Sanipreeya Rice and Emma Inturatana Rice

# CONTENTS

# ABOUT THE AUTHOR

**Pranee Liamputtong** is a medical anthropologist and holds a position of Personal Chair in Public Health at the School of Public Health, La Trobe University, Melbourne, Australia.

Pranee has a particular interest in issues relating to cultural and social influences on childbearing, childrearing and women's reproductive and sexual health. She has undertaken many research projects with immigrant women in Australia and women in Southeast Asia. Pranee has published numerous books and a large number of papers in these areas. Her recent books in the health area include: *The journey of becoming a mother amongst women in northern Thailand* (Lexington Books, 2007); *Community, health and population* (Oxford University Press, 2008); and *Infant feeding practices: A cross-cultural perspective* (Springer, 2010). She is editing a series of books on HIV/AIDS for Springer including two upcoming books: *Motherhood and HIV/AIDS: A cross-cultural perspective,* and *Stigma, discrimination and HIV/AIDS: A cross-cultural perspective.*

Pranee is a qualitative researcher and has also published several methods books. Her most recent ones include: *Researching the vulnerable: A guide to sensitive research methods* (Sage, 2007); *Qualitative research methods*, 3rd edition (Oxford University Press, 2009); *Performing qualitative cross-cultural research* (Cambridge University Press, 2010); and *Research methods in health: Foundations for evidence-based practice* (Oxford University Press, 2010).

# PREFACE

Focus group methodology has been used for a long time in marketing research, but it is only in the last decade or so that it has started to gain popularity as a research method within the health and social sciences. Focus group interviews are now employed extensively. A review of online databases in social science in 1994 alone shows that over 100 papers utilising focus groups as a method appeared in refereed journals. A content analysis of the materials from Sociological Abstracts over the past decade indicates that more than 60 per cent of research employing focus groups was done in combination with other research methods. However, self-contained focus group research has gradually become more common in recent years.

In this book, I demonstrate that the focus group methodology is not new. It can be traced back to the year 1926 when Emory Bogardus described group interviews in social science research. The methodology was also used during the Second World War when Robert Merton employed the method to examine people's reactions to wartime propaganda and the effectiveness of training materials for the soldiers. In the same period, the methodology was introduced into marketing research. Since then, focus groups have been popular and used extensively in the applied social sciences. The methodology has started to gain popularity in research relating to different social groups and in cross-cultural and development research. The main argument for using this methodology in this context is the collective nature, which may suit people who cannot articulate their thoughts easily, and which provides collective power to marginalised people. Hence, we have seen more articles dedicated to the use of focus groups in different social and cultural groups. Additionally, the Internet has become a site and source of data collection for many health and social science researchers. We have begun to witness more virtual focus groups in recent times. However, to my knowledge, there is not a single book that includes all of the issues mentioned above. In this volume, I propose to bridge the main gap in the literature.

This book includes discussions relating to the use of focus group methodology in the health and social sciences. I cover both theoretical and practical aspects of research using the focus group methodology. I also include detailed suggestions on how to adapt focus groups in diverse social and cultural settings and with different groups of people including vulnerable and marginalised populations and in cross-cultural research. The volume also includes a chapter on virtual focus groups, a new trend and innovative means of conducting focus groups in the health and social sciences. It is essential that a book like this needs to provide discussions on how to manage and make sense of focus group data. These issues are also included in this book.

In each chapter, I integrate the following features: chapter objectives, chapter summaries, case examples, tutorial exercises and sources of further reading. Case examples are drawn from a wide selection of extended empirical studies in the United States, United Kingdom, Canada, Australia and other English-speaking and non-English-speaking countries. I also use simple language that students and novice researchers are able to follow easily.

The book is aimed at students and interested researchers. It is particularly pertinent to postgraduate students who are carrying out research as part of their degrees, and who are interested in qualitative focus group methodology. The book is useful for researchers who wish to have a basic understanding of focus groups and need to adopt the methodology to suit the exigencies and circumstances of their research in different social and cultural settings. It can also be used as a textbook for both undergraduates and postgraduate in health sciences, medical sciences, social work, anthropology, sociology, cross-cultural and development studies since it contains simple research methodology for the students to follow and many case examples for illustrating the points.

In bringing this book to life, I owe my gratitude to many people. First, I thank Patrick Brindle, the Senior Acquisition Editor of Sage Publications in London, who believes in the virtue of this book and contracted me to write it. I thank him wholeheartedly. I wish to thank Rosemary Oakes, my dearest friend, who diligently read through, commented and edited my chapters before I submitted the book. She sacrificed much of her time to assist me with the final touches to this book. Rosemary's help is greatly appreciated. My thanks also go to several of my PhD students and colleagues including Dusanee Suwankhong for helping to check references, and Carolyn Weston, Danielle Couch and Helen Rawson who helped edit some chapters in this volume. I also want to express my thanks to David Hodge, Editorial Assistant of Sage, who not only worked with me on the book cover and production of the book, but also provided valuable feedback in the revision of the manuscript. I am grateful to the Development Editor, Stuart Mitchell, who provided valuable comments during the revision of the manuscript. Last, I thank my two daughters, Zoe Sanipreeya Rice and Emma Inturatana Rice, for putting up with my busy writing tasks.

Pranee Liamputtong
Melbourne, March 2010

# 1
# FOCUS GROUP METHODOLOGY:
## Introduction and History

## CHAPTER OBJECTIVES

In this chapter you will learn about:

- An introduction to the focus group method
- The nature of focus group research
- Why the focus group is used in the health and social sciences
- Some criticisms about the focus group methodology
- History and development of focus group methodology
- Focus groups employed in market research and social research
- Virtual focus groups

## INTRODUCING THE FOCUS GROUP METHODOLOGY

| | |
|---|---|
| Fezile: | From rape you get AIDS. |
| Gugu: | AIDS is rape. |
| Researcher: | What's rape? |
| Nokulunga: | When an older person calls you and does bad things to you. |
| Mlondi: | A person grabs you when you are going to the shops and then does bad things to you. |
| Nontobeko: | When he's doing bad things to you … he puts his penis in you with force. |

Focus group interview with young African children aged between seven and eight in a working class township context of KwaDabeka, Greater Durban, South Africa. (Bhana 2009: 596)

The quote above is taken from a study by Deevia Bhana (2009) in her research on how HIV and AIDS are interpreted and made meaningful by seven- and eight-year-old South African children. Her work shows that children's understandings of HIV and AIDS are constructed through many social processes and these processes frame their responses to the disease. This was carried out via focus group methodology. Fundamentally, as the quote above presents, the methodology offers the researchers 'a way of listening to people and learning from them' (Morgan 1998: 9).

Focus group methodology can be traced back to Emory Bogardus, who in 1926 described group interviews in his social psychological research to develop social distance scale (Wilkinson 2004). Over the past century or so, focus groups have been used for many purposes. In particular, the US military (see Merton 1987), Marxist revolutionaries (see Freire 1970/1993), literacy activists (see Kozol 1985) and feminist activists (see Madriz 2003) have adopted the focus group methodology as a means to allow them to advance their causes and concerns (see Chapter 2 in this volume).

Despite the fact that focus groups were initially developed as an academic research method, since the 1950s they have become more synonymous with market research (Munday 2006). However, the focus group methodology has now been regaining more popularity among academic researchers in the health and social sciences. Many of these researchers have been developing the methodology and steering it to suit their research needs.

The more recent popularity of focus groups in qualitative research in the health and social sciences is reflected in an increased number of papers and books. The reason that focus groups have become popular in recent years is partly because they are seen as the methodology which can provide results quickly (Kroll et al. 2007). It is perceived as a methodology which can generate complex information at low cost and with the minimum amount of time. It can also be used with a wide range of people and groups in different settings. However, this claim has been contested by several writers on focus groups (see Wilkinson 2004) and as readers will see in later chapters, the focus group methodology is not as cheap, easy and quick as has been claimed.

Focus groups have started to gain popularity in research relating to different social groups and in cross-cultural and development research. The main argument for using them in this context is their collective nature. This may suit people who cannot articulate their thoughts easily and provide collective power to marginalised people. Hence, we have seen more articles dedicated to the use of focus groups in different social and cultural groups. However, there is not a single book that includes such topics. This is the main gap in the literature that I propose to fill with this volume.

According to David Morgan (2002), a prominent focus group researcher, there are two broad types of focus groups: a structured approach which is employed more in market research; and a less rigid and structured approach which has emerged from focus group research in the social sciences. In marketing research, the moderators need to be visible and take an active role in the group. They perform focus groups for the satisfaction of their clients because they are usually employed to seek some specific answers for their clients. Hence, more interaction is likely to occur between the moderators and the participants. Additionally, discussion between the participants will be minimal and they are likely to answer the set questions posed by the moderators (see also Stewart et al. 2009). On the other hand, in the less structured approach to focus groups which is commonly adopted in social science research, the participants are encouraged to talk to each other instead of answering the moderators' questions. Hence, the moderators primarily aim to facilitate discussion, rather than to direct it. The aim of focus groups in social science research is to understand the participants' meanings and interpretations. Morgan (2002) argues that, depending on the research topic and theoretical approach, both approaches can be adopted within the social sciences. However, in this book, I advocate the less structured focus groups in the social sciences as I base my discussion on the social construction of knowledge and praxis/practices, as readers will see later on in this chapter and throughout the volume. In this chapter, I will focus on the importance of the focus group methodology, its history, and its benefits and limitations.

## THE NATURE OF FOCUS GROUP METHODOLOGY

At the simplest level, a focus group is an informal discussion among a group of selected individuals about a particular topic (Wilkinson 2004). There are many potential focus group scenarios, for example women who are waiting to see their health care providers in a family planning clinic discussing contraception; adolescent girls sprawled over tables in a classroom to share stories about sexual harassment in schools; and a group of family members gathered around the TV in their living room and discussing their favourite movies (Wilkinson 2004). A focus group, as a research method, 'involved more than one participant per data collection session' (Wilkinson 2004: 271). As such, the focus group methodology is sometimes referred to as a focus group interview, a group interview, or a group depth interview.

Broadly speaking, focus groups are 'collective conversations', which can be small or large (Kamberelis & Dimitriadis 2008: 375). Focus groups are group discussions which are arranged to examine a specific set of topics (Kitzinger 2005). The group is focused because 'it involves some kind of collective activity' (Kitzinger 2005: 56), for example debating a specific set of social or health issues, reflecting on common perspectives or experiences, or discussing a health or welfare campaign. The primary aim of a focus group is to describe and understand meanings and interpretations of a select group of people to gain an understanding of a specific issue from the perspective of the participants of the group (Liamputtong 2009).

Methodologically, focus group interviews involve a group of 6–8 people who come from similar social and cultural backgrounds or who have similar experiences or concerns. They gather together to discuss a specific issue with the help of a moderator in a particular setting where participants feel comfortable enough to engage in a dynamic discussion for one or two hours. Focus groups do not aim to reach consensus on the discussed issues. Rather, focus groups 'encourage a range of responses which provide a greater understanding of the attitudes, behavior, opinions or perceptions of participants on the research issues' (Hennink 2007: 6).

A successful focus group discussion relies heavily on 'the development of a permissive, non-threatening environment within the group' where the participants can feel comfortable to discuss their opinions and experiences without fear that they will be judged or ridiculed by others in the group (Hennink 2007: 6). Focus group discussions are more akin to natural social interaction among participants. Thus, the environment of focus groups may be more comfortable and enjoyable for the research participants (Jowett & O'Toole 2006; Liamputtong 2009).

A focus group is not simply a means for obtaining accounts of individuals. Rather, it is 'a means to set up a negotiation of meanings through intra- and inter-personal debates' (Cook & Crang 1995: 56). In conceptual terms then, focus groups are situated between individual interviews where only one respondent is involved in a considerably structured setting and participant observation where many participants are involved in a relatively unstructured of 'natural' setting (Conradson 2005).

The focus group method is different from group interviews since group interactions are treated explicitly as 'research data' (Ivanoff & Hultberg 2006: 125). The participants are chosen because they are able to provide valuable contributions to the research questions. The discussion between participants provides the researchers with an opportunity to hear issues which may not emerge from their interaction with the researchers alone. The interaction among the participants themselves leads to more emphasis on the points of view of the participants than those of the researchers (Gaiser 2008).

Focus group interviews allow group dynamics and help the researcher capture shared lived experiences, accessing elements that other methods may not be able to reach. Focus groups permit researchers to uncover aspects of understanding that often remain hidden in the more conventional in-depth interviewing method. Group work is an inviting method for researchers who are working from 'power-sensitive' theoretical perspectives including feminism and postmodernism. The methodology may reduce the imbalance in power relationships between the researcher and participants that grants the researcher the 'authoritative voice', an issue that most feminist and postmodern researchers are concerned about. Instead, focus groups 'create data from multiple voices' (Madriz 2003).

Focus groups put control of the interaction into the hands of the participants rather than the researcher. The interaction between participants themselves substitutes for their exchange with the researcher, and this gives more prominence to the points of view of the respondents. Focus groups provide an opportunity for researchers to listen to local voices. A focus group is a research tool that gives a 'voice' to the research participant by giving him or her an opportunity to define what is relevant and important to understand his or her experience. In this way, the focus group methodology allows researchers to pay attention to the needs of those who have little or no societal voice.

The strengths of the focus group methodology are that the researchers are provided with a great opportunity to appreciate the way people see their own reality and hence 'to get closer to the data' (Ivanoff & Hultberg 2006: 126). The methodology allows the intended individuals and groups to be more involved in the research project. As such, it is likely that the research will meet their needs.

A focus group interview has several important features:

- It enables in-depth discussions and involves a relatively small number of people.
- It is focused on a specific area of interest that allows participants to discuss the topic in greater detail.
- Interaction is a unique feature of the focus group interview. Indeed, this characteristic distinguishes the method from the individual in-depth interview. It is based on the

idea that group processes assist people to explore and clarify their points of view. Such processes tend to be less accessible in an individual interview. This group interaction has been termed 'the group effect' by recent writers on focus groups (see Carey & Smith 1994; Barbour 2007; Stewart et al. 2007; Davidson et al. 2010).

- A moderator, who is often also the researcher, introduces the topic and assists the participants to discuss it, encouraging interaction and guiding the conversation. The moderator plays a major role in obtaining good and accurate information from the focus groups. There can be more than one moderator facilitating and moderating in one focus group.
- The participants usually have shared social and cultural experiences (such as age, social class, gender, ethnicity, religion and educational background) or shared particular areas of concern (such as divorce, marriage, motherhood, childbirth, infant feeding, childhood immunisation, diarrhoea, nutrition, mental health, contraception, STDs, or living with HIV/AIDS).

## WHY FOCUS GROUPS?

Focus group methodology is useful in exploring and examining what people think, how they think, and why they think the way they do about the issues of importance to them without pressuring them into making decisions or reaching a consensus. According to Jenny Kitzinger (2005: 57), a well-known focus group researcher, the focus group methodology is an 'ideal' approach for examining the stories, experiences, points of view, beliefs, needs and concerns of individuals. The methodology is especially valuable for permitting the participants to develop their own questions and frameworks as well as to seek their own needs and concerns in their own words and on their own terms. Group work allows the researchers to access different communication forms which people use in their day-to-day interaction, and these include joking, arguing, teasing and recapturing past events. Being able to gain access to diverse forms of communication is valuable since it may not be possible, or can be difficult, to capture the knowledge and attitudes of individuals by asking them to respond to more direct questions as in positivist science such as surveys and questionnaires. The forms of communication that people use in their everyday life 'may tell us *as much*, if not *more*' (Kitzinger 2005: 58) about their knowledge and experience. As such, focus groups permit researchers to enter the world of the participants which other research methods may not be able to do. Focus groups are likely to reveal diverse understandings which often are difficult to access by more orthodox methods of data collection. The methodology also allows the researchers to explore individuals' diverse perspectives since focus groups function within the social network of groups. Crucially then, focus groups discover 'how accounts are articulated, censured, opposed, and changed through social interaction and how this relates to peer communication and group norms' (Kitzinger 2005: 58).

As a research method, focus groups are valuable in two main perspectives (Conradson 2005). They offer the researchers a means of obtaining an understanding (insight) of a wide range of views that people have about a specific issue as well as how they interact and discuss the issue. A focus group, for example, could be used to find out how consumers perceive health care and services, both in terms of their own opinions and in relation to others. For example, how individuals who live in urban areas see health care in comparison with those who live in rural settings (Conradson 2005).

A focus group interview is a useful research tool when the researcher does not have a depth of knowledge about the participants. Focus groups provide rich and detailed information about feelings, thoughts, understandings, perceptions and impressions of people in their own words. The focus group methodology is a flexible research tool because the methodology can be applied to elicit information from any topic, from diverse groups of people and in diverse settings (Stewart et al. 2009).

Focus groups are valuable for obtaining in-depth understandings of the numerous interpretations of a particular issue of the research participants. Focus groups permit researchers to search for the reasons why particular views are held by individuals and groups. The methodology also provides insight into the similarities and differences of understandings held by people. If carried out appropriately, the methodology enables researchers to examine how such understandings differ by social groups, such as social class, age, gender, ethnicity, profession and so on (Conradson 2005). This is the reason why focus groups are particularly suitable for exploring issues 'where complex patterns of behaviour and motivation are evident, where diverse views are held' (Conradson 2005: 131).

As such, focus groups offer possibilities for researchers to explore 'the gap between what people say and what they do' (Conradson 2005: 131). In a Western society, for example, when people are surveyed about their opinions regarding waste recycling, many would suggest that it has significant environmental merits. However, the actual practice of recycling is not always correlated with what they say. People believe that recycling is a good idea, but they actually recycle very little (Conradson 2005). Why is this so? The focus group methodology is a useful approach for exploring this difference. An individual may be reluctant to discuss this contradiction during an in-depth interview where the main dynamic occurs primarily between researcher and the participant. But in a focus group setting, where the interactions occur between the participants themselves rather than with the researcher, the participants are likely to be more open about the divergence and the reason why this might be. The focus group setting also provides the researcher with opportunities to follow up the comments and to cross-check with the participants in a more interactive manner than a questionnaire or individual interview can offer.

Focus groups allow multiple lines of communication. For people who find one-on-one and face-to-face interaction 'intimidating' or 'scary', the group interview may offer them 'a safe environment where they can share ideas, beliefs, and attitudes in the company of people from the same socioeconomic, ethnic, and gender backgrounds' (Madriz 2003: 364). Focus groups are ideal for many people from ethnic minority groups. For instance, in their study on the views of health services with Negev Bedouin Arabs, Jeffrey Borkan and others (2000: 209) suggest that focus groups offer 'an enjoyable forum for interaction' among respondents and permit some data quality control because 'extreme views are often muted or marginalized by the majority'. They also offer the respondents the possibility for connecting with others and the continuous establishment of opinions during the group sessions. See Chapter 8 in this volume.

Focus groups have been used to 'give a voice' to marginalised groups such as ethnic minority groups, poor women and men, or people affected by stigmatised illnesses such as HIV/AIDS. They enable researchers, policy-makers and others to 'listen' to people who may have little chance otherwise to express their viewpoints about their health and other needs (Madriz 1998; 2003; Liamputtong 2007; 2010a). In early HIV/AIDS research, Joseph and others (1984) employed focus groups as a means of understanding gay and bisexual men who were perceived as at risk, yet whose health behaviour and needs were not well understood by researchers or the public. The voice of marginalised groups is essential in participatory action research where the participants play an active role in the research process (Liamputtong 2007; 2009; 2010a). Thus, focus groups are used extensively in this type of qualitative research as a basis for empowering marginalised people (see Chapter 7 in this volume).

Focus group methodology is adopted widely in the field of development in a cross-cultural context, especially in eliciting community viewpoints and understanding community dynamics (Lloyd-Evans 2006). Recently, there has been a move towards more participatory research approaches which seek to 'redress issues of unequal power, positionality and Eurocentricity', which may happen when field research is undertaken in non-Western contexts (Lloyd-Evans 2006: 153; see Peek & Fothergill 2009; Liamputtong 2010a). The focus group methodology has become 'one of the main processes for engendering public participation and facilitating the use of non-verbal techniques'. Focus groups provide a more rapid and fruitful way for working with communities than other methods such as in-depth interviewing or ethnographic methods can (Lloyd-Evans 2006: 153–154). See Chapter 8 in this volume.

One of the great advantages of the focus group methodology is its ability to cultivate people's responses to events as they evolve (Barbour 2007). In some situations, research can be carried out quickly. For example, Elizabeth Black and Philip Smith (1999) undertook their focus group research in a timely manner following the death of Princess Diana. They observed that women comprised 80 per cent of the signatories in books of condolence. Hence, three separate focus groups were held with Australian women of different age groups and social backgrounds and were conducted within three weeks of her death and funeral. Black and Smith (1999: 263) argued that: 'The death of Princess Diana set in train a series of official and popular responses … Mass media accounts of Princess Diana's purportedly extraordinary appeal are speculative, lack methodological foundation, and fail to give adequate consideration to potential variability in responses to her life and death.' Focus groups were seen as an appropriate method which would enable Black and Smith to timely explore popular understandings of Diana.

Similarly, Lori Peek and Alice Fothergill (2009: 34) carried out a longitudinal study of children's experiences in the aftermath of Hurricane Katrina. About a month after Katrina had devastated the US Gulf Coast, in October 2005, they travelled to Louisiana to explore how the disaster had affected the lives, relationships and schooling of children, how children themselves were doing in order to assist their own recovery, and what attempts were being made by adults to help the children cope. In this study, they undertook seven focus groups as part of the larger project. One focus group had a group of young children, with ages ranging from three to nine years. Three were carried out with adolescents who were enrolled in middle school. One was organised with four mothers who had been evacuated to a Baptist church shelter in Baton

Rouge. Two focus groups of elementary teachers from three schools in New Orleans were also carried out. Most of the focus groups with the adults were undertaken in October 2005. But the focus groups with the children and adolescents were conducted in May 2007. See also the study conducted by Ali Ardalan and colleagues (2010) with older people in the aftermath of the Bam earthquake in Iran in 2003.

## SOME CRITICISMS ABOUT THE FOCUS GROUP METHODOLOGY

Like any other research methods, focus groups do not suit all research aims and there have been times when they were found to be inappropriate or problematic. For example, focus group discussions may not be sufficiently in depth to allow the researchers to gain a good understanding of the participants' experiences. In addition, the participants may not actively take part in group discussion. A focus group researcher, Janet Smithson (2008: 361), contends that some research topics are unsuitable for focus group environments. For example, topics which are seen as too personal (such as living with HIV/AIDS, sexuality, infertility, financial status, divorce, domestic violence and abortion) may be better carried out by other methods such as individual interviews. In institutional contexts (such as the workplace or schools), people may be reluctant to express their opinions or discuss their personal experiences in front of colleagues. If the objective of the research is to generate in-depth personal narratives such as the experience of infertility or illness, focus groups may not be appropriate. And for topics where people have strong or opposing opinions, there may be some difficulties associated with the use of this method. Nevertheless, these difficulties or problems really depend on the questions asked and the dynamics of the groups. And some unexpected and very interesting discussions which are seen as problematic in some focus group topics may emerge (see Jowett & O'Toole 2006, for example).

Often, focus groups are criticised for only offering a shallower understanding of an issue than those obtained from individual interviews (Hopkins 2007; Krueger & Casey 2009). In a focus group discussion, personal information and experiences may not be discussed. Peter Hopkins' (2007) own qualitative research project about the life and times of young Muslim men living in Scotland showed that they revealed personal experiences of racism during individual interviews far more than they did in focus group discussions.

In some focus groups, certain personalities of the participants (such as dominant and aggressive personalities) may influence the group discussion (Hollander 2004; Krueger & Casey 2009; see Chapter 5 in this volume). Also, the social context of focus groups has a significant influence on 'issues of disclosure, social conformity and desirability' (Hopkins 2007: 530; see also Hollander 2004). In some focus groups, due to the presence of some group members, the participants may feel too intimidate to speak. In other situations, they may simply conform to the dominant ideas present in the group. As such, the quality of data generated will be affected by the characteristics and context of the focus groups.

David Morgan (1997: 17) suggests that the simplest way that researchers can be confident whether focus groups are appropriate for a research project or not is 'to ask how actively and easily the participants would discuss the topic of interest'. If the researchers suspect that there may be serious barriers to active and easy interaction, they should review some of the detailed procedures described by other researchers who have dealt with the issue. If there are still problems, perhaps the researchers need to look for a more suitable method.

It is often perceived that a focus group interview provides greater numbers of participants than in-depth interviews (Willis et al. 2009). In health research in particular, 'quick and easy' focus groups with opportunistic participants are a popular means of tapping into people's values, beliefs, perceptions and experiences. Indeed, this perception has prompted some cost-conscious contracting organisations to specify that their preferred method is the focus group interview. Willis and colleagues are concerned that this 'overuse of impressionistic focus group' research may impair the value of the methodology. This will lead to the perception that 'focus groups are an easy but low-level research approach, rather than a method capable of providing high quality evidence when well designed and well conducted' by funding agencies and health journals (2009: 132).

## HISTORY OF THE FOCUS GROUP METHODOLOGY

Focus group methodology has been adopted by social science researchers for a long time, but it was not made visible by the earlier field researchers. Bronislaw Malinowski, one of the leaders in cultural anthropology, wrote in his diaries about group conversations among native Trobriand Islanders but did not explicitly depict the specifications of these group interviews in his report (Frey & Fontana 1993). Similarly, in his *Street corner society* (1943; 1955), William Foote Whyte employed group interviews with gang members in Boston, but did not explicitly credit the use of group interviews as his unique research tool (Madriz 2003: 366).

The visible use of focus group interviews in the social sciences can be traced back to 1941 when Paul Lazarfeld and Robert Merton, who worked at Columbia University, employed the method to examine the impact of media on people's attitudes towards the involvement of the United States in World War II (Merton & Kendall 1946). Lazarfeld and Merton invited groups of individuals to listen and respond to radio programmes which were designed to boost morale for the war effort (Merton 1987). Originally, the participants were asked to push buttons to indicate their responses, positively or negatively, to the radio programmes. However, this type of data did not help them to answer why the participants responded as they did. It became clear that this method was not sufficient to understand 'the complexity of the respondents' views' (Conradson 2005: 131). In their subsequent studies, an alternative approach for carrying out these group-based interviews was developed. More attention was given to the unstructured and qualitative aspects of the participants' views as expressed in their own words. Hence, focus groups were used as forums for permitting the participants to articulate the reasons for their responses. The details of this method entitled 'The focused interview' (Merton & Kendall 1946) were published in the *American Journal of Sociology*, which has now become a classic paper (Conradson 2005). Although Lazarfeld and Merton used focus groups as qualitative research strategy, they were used in exploratory ways as a means to generate new questions which could be used to develop new quantitative strategies or to complement the more quantitative results of their research (Madriz 2003: 366).

However, Lazarfeld and Merton's research efforts have created the use of the focus group methodology as qualitative enquiry in two main ways. First, to capture individuals' responses in real space and time and in the context of face-to-face interactions. Second, the use of focused interview themes and prompts which are relevant and important to the researchers and the research topics for generating data in the face-to-face interactions (Madriz 2003: 391).

Because of the interest in the in–depth interviewing method and due to the fact that sociologists rarely employed focus group interviews in their research, the influence of Merton and Kendall's focused interview on academic research at that time was short-lived. Within the social sciences in the United States in the 1950s, the focused interview 'faded into relative obscurity' (Conradson 2005: 130). Nevertheless, the focused interview method received growing attention within the commercial world. In the 1960s, numerous companies started to use focus groups as their market research strategies. Thomas Greenbaum is the leader in the development and dissemination of the focus group method in the commercial world. Focus group suites are located on entire floors of Manhattan office blocks and are complete with recording facilities and moderators which can be accommodated for any research projects (Conradson 2005). Within market research, focus groups have been used mainly to explore consumer preferences for commercial products (Kroll et al. 2007).

---

**FOCUS GROUPS IN MARKET RESEARCH: CASE STUDY**

On 23 April 1985, the Coca-Cola Company introduced a new product, called New Coke, which turned out to be one of the greatest misjudgements in the marketing world. Not only was New Coke introduced, but also the old one, on which the corporation had been massively built, was removed from sale. As it turned out, New Coke was a failure and consumers demanded the return of the old Coke. This disaster might have been prevented from happening if the company had paid closer attention to the information generated from focus group research which the company had authorised prior to the launch of New Coke. In 1982 and 1983, focus group research was carried out in different parts of the United States. The consumer participants were presented with a vignette where a new formula of a certain product had been introduced and local consumers had given their favourable responses towards the new formula. The participants were then asked how they themselves would feel if that product arrived at their local areas and replaced the old one. But when the replacement of Coke was discussed, the participants expressed their antagonistic feelings towards the idea. When the consumers were tested by tasting the formula, the results showed that they liked New Coke. However, they were not asked how they would feel if the old Coke was dropped from market shelves. The results from the focus groups clearly showed the consumers' negative responses, but the chief executive officer of the Coca-Cola Company was determined to press ahead. And his assistant, who worked closely with the company carrying out the focus groups, decided to follow the determination of the CEO (Bryman 2008: 474; see also Pendergrast 1993; Greising 1998).

It was only in the 1980s that focus groups re-emerged as a distinct research methodology in the health and social sciences (Conradson 2005: 130). When it did re-emerge, 'it was no longer wed to – or used in the service of – predominantly quantitative-oriented research' (Kamberelis & Dimitriadis 2008: 391). Since then, focus groups have been popular and used extensively in several disciplines. Many social scientists and other professionals have found this qualitative approach very useful. Political scientists, for example, employed focus groups to examine the public perceptions of political candidates and their opinions on particular political issues (Madriz 2003; Gaiser 2008). Gamson published a noted study in *Talking politics* (1992) that relied on a form of the focus group methodology for its data collection. During President Ronald Reagan's administration in the 1980s, focus groups were adopted to learn about the perceptions of relations between the United States and the Soviet Union and their citizens (Stewart et al. 2007). In the UK, focus groups were used by the New Labour government to examine British opinions about health spending, education policy and military action. The aim was to explore 'a better understanding of the multiple and sometimes conflicting perspectives held by the public on particular issues' (Conradson 2005: 130).

Focus groups have also found their place in the assessment of public health and strategies and campaigns for preventive health care (Kroll et al. 2007). In the early 1980s, focus groups were introduced in the health area through studies of knowledge, attitudes and practices of contraception (Folch-Lyon & Trost 1981; Stycos 1981). John Knodel and colleagues (1984; Knodel et al. 1987) used focus groups to elicit information about the transition of fertility in Thailand. With the AIDS epidemic, focus groups were used as a first step to overcome the limited knowledge of researchers about the gay community (see Joseph et al. 1984). Health educators have also used the methodology. Basch (1987), for example, employed it to improve the effectiveness of intervention programmes in public health. In more recent times, focus groups have been popularly employed in public health research (see Willis et al. 2009).

Focus groups have been used historically by Marxist revolutionaries, literacy activists and three waves of feminist scholar–activists in order to raise the consciousness of oppressed people. In his work on the *Pedagogy of the oppressed* (1970/1993), Paulo Freire established focus groups, what he calls 'study circles', as a way to work with vulnerable individuals in their 'lived realities' in order to empower them to change their worlds from their marginalised positions within society. Jonathan Kozol (1985) similarly used 'study circles' to elicit information and empower oppressed groups in his literacy programmes in New York City. Both Freire and Kozol adopted focus groups for imagining and enacting the emancipatory political possibilities of collective work (see also Chapter 2 in this volume).

The use of focus groups is becoming increasingly popular among feminist researchers. The focus group methodology resembles feminist research practice ideals (see Madriz 2000; Strange et al. 2003; Wilkinson 1999; 2004; Munday 2006; see also Chapter 2 in this volume). They have been effectively used by feminist academics such as Ann Oakley and Esther Madriz. With the influence of feminist research and increased movement towards qualitative research methods, focus groups have now become very visible in different disciplines (Gaiser 2008).

## FOCUS GROUPS, MARKET RESEARCH AND SOCIAL RESEARCH

As I pointed out earlier in the chapter, focus groups are adopted differently in market research and the social sciences. Often, the practices in market research are not suitable for conducting social science research. Focus groups practising in market research fall within the positivist paradigm; that is, they are very rigidly structured and highly controlled as in most quantitative methods (Munday 2006). The aim of focus groups in market research is to obtain perspectives and opinions on new products from the perspectives of the consumer participants (Morgan & Krueger 1993). Hence, the researchers need skilful moderating skills in order to generate 'objective facts' about the perceptions, attitudes and opinions of the participants in the group.

However, social researchers explore different kinds of research data from the processes of focus groups and hence require different research skills for the management of the focus groups and data analysis from those of market researchers (Kitzinger 2005; Munday 2006; Barbour 2007). But as Morgan (1993) and Kitzinger and Barbour (1999) note, the model of the focus group method in market research seems to dominate as an accepted norm. This has created certain presumptions as to how focus groups should be carried out. And these have resulted in the limitation of the use of focus group methodology in qualitative research within academia. Often, social science researchers feel that they must adhere to 'the rules' of focus groups in market research, which are not necessarily appropriate for academic research. Many focus group researchers have warned of this danger. In order to use the focus group methodology successfully in the social sciences, it is crucial for researchers to 'break away' from common presumptions which derive from the market research about how focus groups should be practised (Munday 2006: 90). This book touches on these issues in the chapters that follow.

## VIRTUAL FOCUS GROUPS

More than ever before in human existence, we are now able not only to reach out to other human beings, but also to gain knowledge rapidly through new global technologies such as computers and the Internet. As our lives and societies are being transformed by innovative technology, there are new ways for qualitative researchers to collect the data. I argue that, as researchers, we must engage in 'the fourth revolution' in 'the production of knowledge' (Murray 1995: 11), which is essential for our understanding of the intersection of language, society and technology. Qualitative researchers cannot ignore electronic communication as a research tool. We are 'saturated in technologies', and 'Internet technologies have the potential to shift the ways in which qualitative researchers collect, make sense of, and represent data'. This is particularly so for social scientists who are concerned with understanding different aspects of collective human behaviour.

A qualitative method which takes advantage of new technology is the use of the Internet to carry out focus groups, and this is known as virtual focus groups or online focus groups (Hughes & Lang 2004; Liamputtong 2009). Online focus groups have received increasing popularity in recent years, not only in market research, but also in the fields of health, social science and educational research (Mann & Stewart 2000; Liamputtong 2006; Fielding et al. 2008; Gaiser 2008). This trend stems primarily from several pragmatic advantages which the Internet can offer. The most attractive aspects of virtual focus groups include the reduction in costs and time of research fieldwork, the feasibility of bringing together individuals who are located in geographically dispersed areas, the availability of a complete record of the discussion without the need for transcription, and the anonymity secured by the research setting (Mann & Stewart 2000; Liamputtong 2006).

Similar to the development of orthodox focus groups, market research adopted virtual focus groups much earlier than research in the academic area (Robson & Williams 2005). Additionally, as a means for carrying out academic research, computer-mediated communications were cultivated in other methods before being taken up by the focus group method. In the second half of the 1990s, online surveys were popularly used, as were covert observation and collection of online discussions, which provide a swift and viable means of collecting rich data. The virtual focus group method and its applications, benefits and limitations are presented in Chapter 7 of this volume.

## CONCLUSION

In this chapter, I have introduced the focus group methodology which has become popularly employed in the health and social sciences. The nature and main features of a focus group have been discussed. This was followed by the history of focus groups and some discussions on the differences between focus group practised in market and social science research. In this chapter, I also introduced virtual or online focus groups.

Readers can now see that the focus group methodology offers many advantages to health and social science researchers. Many researchers have adopted the methodology in their research and continue to point to the benefits of the method in different disciplines. However, for some researchers, its use is not without difficulties. It is likely that the methodology will continue to be on the horizon of discussion in the years to come.

## TUTORIAL ACTIVITIES

1 In Raymond Macdonald and Graeme Wilson's focus group research concerning the perceptions of jazz music and lifestyle with Scottish jazz professionals (2005: 398), they claimed that 'if jazz is to be seen as a socially generated music, then social understandings of it should be examined; if you create the music in a group, it is worth asking a group about it. Focus group interviewing was therefore adopted as methodology.' You are about to commence your work as a research assistant in an art department. You are asked to develop a research proposal to examine

the social and professional identities of young artists. Will the focus group allow you to explore these issues? How will it provide the answers that you wish to explore? Discuss.

2 As a student undertaking a course in evidence-based practice, you are required to find the best evidence using empirical research to find answers about housing issues and the needs of older people from low-socioeconomic backgrounds. You need to consider the best method which allows the potential participants to interact so that they can find their collective voices which are seldom heard. Is the focus group methodology the best approach you can use? Discuss in detail.

## FURTHER READING

Barbour, R. (2007). *Doing focus groups*. London: Sage.

Bloor, M., Frankland, J., Thomas, M., & Robson, K. (2001). *Focus groups in social research*. Thousand Oaks, CA: Sage.

Hennink, M.M. (2007). *International focus group research: A handbook for the health and social sciences*. Cambridge University Press: Cambridge.

Johnson, A. (1996). 'It's good to talk': The focus group and the sociological imagination. *The Sociological Review* 44(2), 517–536.

Jowett, M., & O'Toole, G. (2006). Focusing researchers' minds: Contrasting experiences of using focus groups in feminist qualitative research. *Qualitative Research* 6(4), 453–472.

Kitzinger, J. (1994a). The methodology of focus groups: The importance of interaction between research participants. *Sociology of Health and Illness* 16(1), 103–121.

Krueger, R.A., & Casey, M.A. (2009). *Focus groups: A practical guide for applied research*, 4th edition. Thousand Oaks, CA: Sage.

Morgan, D.L. (2002). Focus group interviewing. In J.F. Gubrium & J.A. Holstein (eds.), *Handbook of interviewing research: Context & method* (pp. 141–159). Thousand Oaks, CA: Sage.

Stewart, D.W., Shamdasani, P.N., & Rook, D.W. (2007). *Focus groups: Theory and practice*, 2nd edition. Thousand Oaks, CA: Sage.

Wilkinson, S. (2004). Focus groups: A feminist method. In S.N. Hesse-Biber & M.L. Yaiser (eds.), *Feminist perspectives on social research* (pp. 271–295). New York: Oxford University Press.

# 2
# FOCUS GROUP METHODOLOGY:
# Theory and Ethics

## CHAPTER OBJECTIVES

In this chapter you will learn about:

- Theoretical frameworks on which focus group research can be based
- Ethical issues in focus group research

In this chapter, I provide discussions on two important issues in focus group research. First, I introduce theoretical frameworks on which the focus group method can be situated. I will discuss three different theoretical frameworks, including symbolic interactionism, feminism and critical pedagogical practice. Second, ethical issues concerning both conventional focus group and virtual focus group methods will be introduced.

## THEORETICAL FRAMEWORKS

It is crucial that focus group research is situated within some theoretical frameworks. It is the responsibility of researchers to create 'theoretically convincing stories', to borrow a term from William Miller and Benjamin Crabtree (2005: 626), by providing a strong rationale for their focus group research based on an informed knowledge of a theoretical framework (see also Avis 2003; Liamputtong 2009; Willis et al. 2009). The theoretical framework will shape our research question and contribute to the choice of our method and interpretation of the data (Dew 2007). It is essential for focus group researchers to have a good understanding of the theoretical position so that they are able to 'interpret data sensibly and with insight, and not simply interpret data in the light of preconceptions and prejudice – and so potentially perpetrate unsatisfactory or inappropriate understandings of the phenomenon of interest' (Dew 2007: 433).

Focus group methodology is a key research approach where interpretive, political and pedagogical enquiries 'intersect and interanimate' (Kamberelis & Dimitriadis 2008: 397). In what follows, I will introduce these three intersections which underpin most focus groups in the social sciences by introducing three theoretical frameworks on which the focus group methodology can be situated: symbolic interactionism, feminism and critical pedagogical practice.

## Symbolic Interactionism

Feminist researchers Michelle Fine and Susan Gordon (1989: 159) write that:

> If you really want to know either of us, do not put us in a laboratory, or hand us a survey, or even interview us separately alone in our homes. Watch me (MF) with women friends, my son, my father, my niece, or my mother and you will see what feels most authentic to me.

This statement clearly points to the essence of interaction among the participants, as well as the interaction between the researcher and the participants in a focus group.

Symbolic interactionism is a framework which greatly emphasises the essence of meaning and interpretation as crucial human processes. Individuals 'create shared meanings through their interactions, and those meanings become their reality' (Patton 2002: 112). According to Alan Bryman (2008: 476), the focus group methodology allows the researchers to examine the ways in which people collectively understand an issue of concern and then construct meanings around it. Symbolic interactionism postulates that individuals do not carry out the process of making sense of social phenomena in isolation. Rather, the process occurs in discussion and interaction with others. Symbolic interactionism is concerned with 'the subjective meaning individuals attribute to their activities and their environments' (Flick 2006: 66). This methodology is grounded in an understanding that individuals construct their perceptions and meanings as a result of their interaction with others. Focus groups represent the processes in which people construct meanings collectively in their everyday life. Hence, symbolic interactionism provides a central tenet of the theoretical position on which the focus group method is based (Bryman 2008: 476).

Historically and recently, symbolic interactionism has played a prominent role in the focus group methodology. This theoretical framework characterises the position of theory and practice within the Chicago School of sociology in the United States. Symbolic interactionism is closely associated with George Herbert Mead (1934) and Herbert Blumer (1938; 1969). A number of prominent sociologists including Anselm Strauss, Barney Glaser, Norman Denzin, Howard Becker, and many others adopt symbolic interactionism in their research. In the 1970s, the methodological position of symbolic interactionism of Blumer (1969) had a paramount impact on the methodological discussions among social science researchers (Flick 2006).

According to prominent sociologist Herbert Blumer (1969), there are three premises of the symbolic interactionist approach. First, individuals behave towards things based on the meanings that the things have for them. Second, the meaning of things is acquired through the social interaction that they have with others. And third, these meanings are managed and changed through an interpretive process that individuals employ in dealing with the things they experience (see also Denzin 1995; Patton 2002; Angrosino 2007). For Uwe Flick (2006: 67), these three premises suggest that research should begin with the idea that there are 'different ways in which individuals invest objects, events, experiences … with meaning'. And 'the reconstruction of such subjective viewpoints becomes the instrument for analysing social worlds'.

These three premises led Blumer to argue that only qualitative enquiry is the appropriate means for understanding how individuals see, understand and interpret their world. He suggested that it is 'only through close contact and direct interaction with people in open-minded, naturalistic inquiry and inductive analysis could the symbolic interactionist come to understand the symbolic world of the people being studied' (Patton 2002: 112). Blumer was among the first few sociologists who used group discussion and interview methods with key informants in their research. Blumer (1969: 41) believed strongly that 'a small number of individuals, brought together as a discussion or resource group, is more valuable many times over than any representative sample'. He carefully recruited a group of well-informed people and invited them to act as a 'panel of experts' on the phenomenon he wished to study. They were experts who provided the researchers with insider perspectives of the concerned phenomenon (Patton 2002). As we have witnessed, focus groups have now become prominent methods and widely adopted in qualitative enquiry. Nowadays, symbolic interactionism continues to have a prominent influence on qualitative research. It has been adopted extensively by researchers in sociology, anthropology, psychology, health and education (Willis 2007; Angrosino 2007; Peek & Fothergill 2009).

Focus group interviews are particularly important since they permit the researchers 'to witness one of the most important processes for the social sciences – social interaction' (Madriz 2003: 372). In focus group interviews, researchers can see directly how the participants take part in discussion, share ideas, views and experiences, and may even argue with others in the group. Essentially, this engagement leads to 'the socially constructed interactional experiences', which a prominent qualitative researcher, Norman Denzin (1989), refers to as 'interpretive interactionism'. The number of players (participants) involved in focus groups leads to a more dynamic discussion process and hence facilitates the social construction of meaning (Holstein & Gubrium 1995). The group interaction contributes to the creation of 'shared stocks of knowledge' (Holstein & Gubrium 1995: 71), and hence forms an essential part of the research. This shared stock of knowledge is particularly essential for marginalised people in that it permits 'the process of writing history and culture together' (Madriz 2003: 373). For marginalised people, who have often been ignored in research, this writing is particularly essential since it helps to demolish 'the walls of silence' which have masked their 'triple and overlapping marginality'. For women of colour, for example, this triple marginality includes being female, of colour and often poor (Madriz 2003: 73).

Human experience is built and organised within particular social contexts. Individuals make collective sense, negotiate meanings and elaborate their identities through the process of social interaction with others (Wilkinson 2004). In a focus group, participants are not individuals who act in isolation. Rather, they belong to a social group whose members interact with each other. In itself, the focus group is 'a social context' (Wilkinson 2004: 276). The social context of focus groups offers the researchers opportunities to explore the way individuals participate in constructing meanings, and the ways their views are formed, articulated and changed in their exchange with others (Wilkinson 2004). In focus group discussions, people constantly negotiate and renegotiate meanings (Kitzinger 1994b). People bring in their diverse 'individual experiences' and try to make 'collective sense' of them (Wilkinson 2004: 277). The process of collective sense-making takes place through their interactions with others in the focus group.

The focus group researcher Richard Krueger (1988: 44) refers to individuals as 'social creatures' who 'interact with others'. Through this interaction, they make their own decisions about things after they hear other people's comments and discuss the issues with other people around them. Focus groups 'tap into' the authentic communication processes that people engage in their everyday life, such as joking, teasing, boasting, arguing, disagreeing, challenging and persuading (Wilkinson 2004: 274). Robin Jarrett (1993: 194) tells us that in her focus groups with low-income young women it felt like having 'rap sessions with friends'. The atmosphere in the focus group 'was exuberantly boisterous' and 'frank in language'. In her research about menstruation with young people in school, Kathryn Lovering (1995: 16) found that the focus group discussions offered a 'naturalistic conversational exchange' context. This appeared in the forms of embarrassment and giggling. These features are the expressions that people commonly display in their interaction with others when talking about embarrassing and sensitive issues like menstruation.

The social context of focus groups provides the researchers with the opportunity to directly witness the co-construction of meaning through the interactions of participants in the group. The data generated from the interactive nature of focus groups offers 'insights' which would not be accessible without the group context (Wilkinson 2004: 278). This can be seen in the 'over-dinner group' in Pat MacPherson and Michelle Fine's study (1995: 188–189) when participants elaborated on the meaning of racial identities. In this focus group, when Janet, who is a Korean American, used the term 'African Americans', she was challenged by Shermika:

| Shermika: | I don't consider myself no African American. |
| Janet: | That's the acceptable politically correct … |
| Shermika: | I'm full American, I've never been to Africa. |
| Janet: | Are you black or wh[ite] … African American? (Sorry.) |
| Shermika: | I'm neither one. |
| Michelle: | What racial group do you consider yourself? |
| Shermika: | Negro. Not black, not African American. That's just like saying all white people come from Europe. Why don't you call 'em European American? |

According to Sue Wilkinson (2004: 279), in the context of a challenge from a group member, Shermika emphasised her identity (as 'full American' and as 'Negro'). The challenge from Janet also led Shermika to express her reasons for the label choice of her identity ('I've never been to Africa'). Without an interaction with others in the group, Michelle (the researcher) might not fully appreciate the racial identity that Shermika has constructed about herself.

## Feminism

Within feminist methodology, women and their concerns are the centre of investigation. The ultimate deliberateness of feminist research is to 'capture women's lived experiences in a respectful manner that legitimates women's voices as sources of knowledge' (Campbell & Wasco 2000: 783; Angrosino 2007). A feminist researcher, Barbara Pini (2002: 340), contends that one of the most important attempts of feminist researchers is to make research political; that is, 'to change women's lives, both at a personal level and a societal level'. Therefore, feminist researchers endeavour to conduct research which aims for 'women's emancipation'. Liz Stanley (1990: 15) puts it bluntly that the point of doing feminist research is 'to change the world, not only to study it'. Feminist research must be 'research *for* women' instead of 'research *on* women' (Pini 2002: 341, original emphases; see also Harding 1987; Edwards 1990; Stanley & Wise 1990). Additionally, feminist research aspires to undertake research which is beneficial for women, not only about women.

Feminist researchers, over the last few decades, have explored how a feminist stance could have an impact on the research process (Robinson 2009). Mary Maynard and June Purvis (1994: 1) call this attempt 'the dynamics of actually doing research in the field'. Feminist researchers have produced research methods which allow them to unveil women's existences in ways that 'move on the agenda of explaining the process of the marginalization and exclusion of women' (Robinson 2009: 263). Doing feminist research is to witness resistance. Hence, feminist research opposes research methods which are the products of objective research aimed at measuring women, like those used in positivist science (Allen & Walker 1992; Madriz 2003; Angrosino 2007; Reiger & Liamputtong 2010). Feminist research aspires to qualitative enquiry which is less structured and more flexible than that of the positivist science (Pini 2002; Robinson 2009; Hesse-Biber & Leavy 2010). It takes the position that, due to the standardised nature of positivist science, much of what occurs to individuals and groups involved in the research, including the researcher and the researched, remains 'unsaid and unanalysed' (Allen & Walker 1992: 201).

Feminist researchers attempt to develop and employ research methods which can access the everyday lives of women as well as the particularities of their lives (Madriz 2003). The focus group methodology facilitates this process (Robinson 2009). As Esther Madriz, a well-known feminist focus group researcher, suggests (2003: 375), the interaction that occurs in a focus group 'accentuates empathy and commonality of experiences and fosters self-disclosure and self-validation. Communication among women can be an awakening experience and an important element in the consciousness-raising process.' Interaction in focus groups authenticates the women's own problematic experiences and permits them to build on the views, thoughts and feelings of other women. Being known that their own experiences are similar to those of other women, or sharing similar views with others, contributes to their realisation that their experiences and opinions are tangible and legitimate. This in turn helps to raise women's consciousness that their problematic experiences are not individual but structural, and that they are also shared by many others.

Many qualitative feminist researchers promote the focus group methodology for research with women (see Jarrett 1993; Madriz 1997; 1998; 2003; Wilkinson 1998;

2004; Pini 2002; Pollack 2003; Hyams 2004; Robinson 2009). In her research on how popular culture influences women's constructions of sex, Frances Montell (1999: 44) argues that the focus group methodology provides feminist scholars with the opportunity to undertake research which is 'consciousness raising and empowering'. Sue Wilkinson (1998; 1999) suggests similarly. Both Montell and Wilkinson claim that focus groups offer opportunities for researchers to reduce the 'hierarchical research relationship' and produce 'situated and localized knowledge' about women's lives (Pini 2002: 341). According to Barbara Pini (2002: 341–342), the prominent character of the focus group method, the group interaction, offers further benefits to feminist scholars. Within the group interaction, 'there is potential … for power relationships to be more greatly diffused, for knowledge to be collectively constructed, and for empowerment, as participants challenge, question, critique, and learn from each other'.

In Barbara Pini's work (2002: 339) with rural farm women's involvement in the sugar industry in the far north of Queensland, Australia, she argues that participation in focus group research allows women to make 'what is invisible to many women visible; it enabled connections to be made between individual and collective experiences; it facilitated challenges to dominant beliefs; and it provided space for discussion and reflexivity about gender issues'. She also suggests that focus group methodology has the potential to empower research participants. This quality should be of interest to researchers who aspire not only to reduce or abandon the hierarchy between the researcher and the participants in research relationships, but also to produce contextualised and situated knowledge which contributes to social and political changes.

Some feminist researchers have pointed to the importance of using the focus group methodology in research with women of lower socioeconomic status, particularly women of colour (Jarrett 1993; Madriz 1998; 2003; Toner 2009). Women of colour experience 'a triple subjugation' which is based on gender, race and class oppression (Collins 1986; Benmayor 1991; Espiritu 1997; Madriz 1997; 2003; Toner 2009). Feminist researchers must consider such subjugation in the selection of research methods for examining women's lives. But not all methods are sensitive and appropriate for women, and particularly for women of colour, who may feel ambivalent or unsafe about discussing their personal lives with the researchers (Madriz 2003: 370). The focus group method allows women of colour to share ideas, thoughts, experiences and feelings with other women (see also Chapter 8 in this volume).

Esther Madriz (2003: 371) contends that focus group methodology is more suitable than other research approaches for 'shattering a colonizing discourse in which images of research subjects as the Other are constantly reproduced'. She argues that focus groups reduce the 'self-other distance' in many ways. First, due to the multiple voices of the participants, the control of the researcher (moderator) is reduced, as the researcher has less power over a group than over an individual. Second, the control of the researcher over the interview process is decreased due to the more unstructured feature of the focus group interview guide (see Chapter 5). Last, a focus group entails not only 'vertical interaction' (interaction between the researcher and the participants), but also 'horizontal interaction' among the participants in the focus group.

According to feminist methodology, the process of research is as important as its outcome. The process of participating in a focus group, which requires the participants to interact and share with others, allows their collective voice to emerge. Instead of emphasising the voice of an individual, focus groups focus on the collective voice as there is more than one participant in a group (Madriz 2003). The methodology allows individuals to freely express their points of view, and this encourages the group members to speak up.

Feminist researchers are greatly concerned about the role of the researcher and the moral dilemmas inherent in an interviewing situation. These dilemmas are alleviated by the focus group method simply because the method allows multiple lines of communication which generate 'safe spaces' for discussion with others who share lived experiences or face similar problems (Madriz 2003; Ahmad et al. 2009). Madeleine Jowett and Gill O'Toole (2006: 467) provide a good example of this point. They argue that despite the fact that feminism has become known and practised by many researchers and lay people, nowadays it is still difficult for young women to find a 'safe space' to discuss the 'taboo' subject of feminism. The focus group project that Jowett carried out with young British women (cited in Jowett & O'Toole 2006: 467) created a safe space for women to explore this prohibited topic:

Sarah:      God, feminism's never mentioned today is it?! I mean you never hear people talking about it, not out and around. Well I never have.

Kirsten:    The thing is, if you mention feminism today, people think you're mad! It's like: 'feminism – uuuh' [Mimics sharp intake of breath] And if you say you're a feminist, it's like: 'Oh – my – God: a feminist?!!!'

The young women in this study also commented that being able to come together in a focus group and discuss issues about feminism and inequality in women provided them with a 'fresh and novel experience' as they felt safe to speak up about a culturally prohibited topic. Almost all the young women (22 out of 26) volunteered to participate in a further focus group. This was not something that Jowett had anticipated. Many women also offered their homes for further focus group meetings.

Additionally, focus groups lessen the control that the researcher has during the data collection process. According to Sue Wilkinson (2004: 279), the numbers of participants which simultaneously interact in the group shift the balance of power away from the researcher. Since a focus group provides the scope for 'a relatively free-flowing and interactive exchange of views', the power of the researcher over the research participants and the research process is minimised (Madriz 2003; Robinson 2009). Jowett and O'Toole (2006: 455) contend that focus groups offer the potential to 'subvert and problematize epistemic authority'. And as the authority of the researcher is decentred in the research process, it provides women with safe spaces to articulate their own lives and struggles with others. As such, focus groups permit women to connect with each other and share their individual experiences. The collective nature of the groups empowers the participants and legitimates their voices and experiences (Madriz 2003; Hyams 2004). Collectively then, women are able to 'reclaim their humanity' in a supporting environment of focus groups (Madriz 2000: 843; Kamberelis & Dimitriadis 2008: 383).

Similar to the work of Paulo Freire and Jonathan Kozol (see below), focus group work situated within a feminist framework recognised the 'constitutive power of *space* and *place*' (Kamberelis & Dimitriadis 2008: 386). Typically, feminist focus groups are organised in familiar locations and settings such as kitchens, living rooms, dining rooms, classrooms, church basements, women's shelters and sometimes even a bedroom. In their five years of ethnographic research exploring the lived experiences of 25 women living with HIV/AIDS in Ohio, Patti Lather and Chris Smithies (1997) used focus groups as the main data collection method. Often, focus groups were held at birthday parties, baby showers, picnics, holiday get-togethers, hospital rooms and funerals. Janice Radway, in her pioneering research on the reading practices of romance novel enthusiasts which resulted in a book *Reading the romance* (1991), used focus groups as a means to collect data. Her focus groups were conducted in and around a local bookstore. Her participants included the store owner and a group of 42 women who were regular romance readers and frequently visited the store. Conducting focus groups in a familiar space helps to decrease the power of the researcher, and hence reduce 'the possibilities of "Otherization" of the research participants' (Madriz 2003: 374). This is what cross-cultural researchers tend to use in their focus group research (see Hennink 2007; see also Chapter 8 in this volume). Often, focus groups are organised under a tree or in someone's house and participants sit cross-legged on a mat on the floor.

As a qualitative method, focus groups tremendously benefit social researchers who are interested in constructing new knowledge about social research and accommodating social change (Madriz 2003). Focus groups provide opportunities for researchers to listen to the multiple voices of the marginalised people 'as constructors and agents of knowledge' (Fine 1994: 75) and 'as agents of social change' (Madriz 2003: 372).

## Dialogic Focus Groups: Critical Pedagogical Practice

The work of Paulo Freire in Brazil and Jonathan Kozol in New York clearly shows the use of focus groups as pedagogical tools or positions. They illustrate how 'collective critical literacy practices' (Kamberelis & Dimitriadis 2008: 378) could be employed by oppressed people to speak about local politics and express their concerns about social justice. Similar to the feminist framework (outlined above), it is important to note that Freire and Kozol work '*with* people and not *on* them'. Freire and Kozol employ focus groups for 'imagining and enacting the emancipator political possibilities of collective work' (Kamberelis & Dimitriadis 2008: 378). Primarily, Freire and Kozol aim to use 'literacy ... to mobilize oppressed groups to work against their oppression through praxis' (p. 383).

Freire's famous book *Pedagogy of the oppressed* (1970/1993) can be perceived not only as a social theory and philosophy, but also as an educational tool and a research methodology. The objective of education, as Freire suggests, is to allow individuals to 'name the world' and to realise that 'we are all "subjects" of our own lives and narratives, not "objects" in the stories of others' (Kamberelis & Dimitriadis 2008: 378). What Freire advocates (to name the world and to realise that we are all 'subjects' of our own lives and narratives) is very much like the positions that we take in qualitative enquiry, including the focus group method. And to me, the 'objects' in the stories of others mean what positivist scientists do to their participants; that is, by measuring people or comparing them to others in research which often makes certain groups more marginalised because they would or could not do as well as the others. Freire strongly encourages individuals to realise that we, as humans, are fundamentally responsible for the making and transformation of our situations and realities together. This, to me, is what the focus group methodology is all about and what it allows us to do (see the section on feminism given above and Chapter 7 on collective testimony in this volume). Freire contends that those who do not take this position, or who want to control and oppress others, are 'committing a kind of epistemic "violence"' (Kamberelis & Dimitriadis 2008: 378).

To assist oppressed people to imagine lives beyond their oppression, Freire invests a lot of time in communities in order to understand the interest of community members, their concerns and assets so that he can compile comprehensive sets of what he refers to as 'generative words'. He uses these words to start literacy learning. In turn, literacy learning allows oppressed people to begin their social and political activism (deployed in the service of social and political activism). The 'generative words' are then used in conjunction with pictures (drawings) which represented them. Both the 'generative words' and the pictures are then critically examined by the oppressed people to uncover how the meanings and effects of these words operated in their daily lives. He also encourages oppressed people to carry out research on how their meanings and their effects worked, or could work, differently in diverse social and political contexts. Primarily, Freire believes that these activities would assist oppressed people to have more control of their words and be able to use them to change the economic, material and ideological conditions of their lives. Freire's literacy programmes are constructed so that oppressed people's critical consciousness (which he calls 'conscientisation') could be cultivated. He encourages oppressed people to 'engage in "praxis" or critical reflection inextricably linked to political action in the real world' (Kamberelis & Dimitriadis 2008: 379).

Freire strongly believes that through conscientisation and praxis, people are able to change the conditions of their lives for the better. He refers to this as 'human agency'. This human agency, although limited, would be powerful enough to make it possible for people to change their own selves and their situations for the better. In order to proclaim such agency, Freire argues, people need to 'emerge from their unconscious engagements with the world, reflect on them, and work to change them' (Kamberelis & Dimitriadis 2008: 379).

Within Freirean pedagogies, the process of emancipation could only be done with the collective effort of oppressed people. And this collective effort could be achieved through the power of dialogue (talk/discussion). Dialogue, for Freire, is referred to collective action or reflection. Importantly, the production and use of generative words and the realisation of conscientisation are carried out in the locally situated 'study circles' (or focus groups). The aim of the educator (or facilitator) within these study circles is to allow people to share their lived experiences, to construct realities and transform them. According to George Kamberelis and Greg Dimitriadis (2008: 380), the work of Freire is seen by many critical educators and social science researchers as an important social movement in the educational field. The intensive group activities of these movements have also offered a model for focus group research. Following the framework of 'study circles' developed by Freire, focus groups can also be undertaken in innovative ways so that knowledge about oppressed and marginalised people can be constructed (see the section on focus groups and community-based participatory research (CBPR) in Chapter 6 of this volume).

Freirean pedagogies have a powerful influence on several educationally oriented social movements in the United States. Jonathan Kozol drew on Freire's emancipatory work for research and wrote *Illiterate America* (1985). Similar to Freire, Kozol's literacy programmes in New York City were based on the real lived experiences of the people with whom he worked to develop dialogic collectives about leadership in programme planning. Kozol (1985: 106) contends that there is a marked difference between telling people about any programme which has already been developed and in which they are offered the choice to join or to ignore, or to invite them to help in the creation of the plan. He tells us that some of the best ideas which he has learned have emerged from discussion groups held within the neighbourhoods. He argues that people will be more likely to take part in a programme in which they or their neighbours have been invited to take part in planning, particularly when the ideas they have offered have been adopted rather than merely 'heard'. This is precisely what qualitative research, including the focus group method, offers.

Like Freire, Kozol prescribes working in study circles (or focus groups) as key educational environments and tools. Kozol (1985: 108) tells us:

> I have come to be convinced that groups of six or seven learners and one literacy worker represent an ideal unit of instruction for this plan. The presence of a circle of [a] half-dozen friends or neighbours helps to generate a sense of common cause and to arouse a sense of optimistic ferment that is seldom present in the one-to-one encounter.

The composition of such groups is dynamic enough to provide opportunities for the construction of successful histories. By learning in groups, Kozol (1985: 109) contends, individuals will be able to produce group leaders. As these leaders are selected out of their ranks by group members, they will continue to be susceptible to criticism and correction. However, because of their own position and shared lived experiences, they are also in an ideal position to unveil realities and encourage others in the group.

Similar to the feminist framework (see above), Kozol recognises the significance of space as a crucial aspect of the decentring activity in the study circles (or focus groups). He proposes that study circles rarely occur in formal sites like public schools and other institutions. Rather, they should be held in unofficial settings such as people's apartments, recreation centres, church basements, and so on. These spaces signify the commitment of educated (intellectual) workers to working with marginalised groups in order to help these people to be responsible for their own existences and struggles.

Following 'intellectual workers' such as Freire and Kozol, dialogic focus groups have always been adopted by social researchers who advocate social transformation in oppressed and marginalised communities and groups (Pini 2002). Raymond Padilla (1993: 158) contends that the important role of the researchers engaging in dialogical focus group research is to facilitate the production of knowledge by the research participants themselves. His project with Hispanic students in a US community college aiming to overcome barriers to success was based on the theoretical framework of Paulo Friere. As part of a project concerning political freedom, cultural autonomy and liberation from oppressive economic and social conditions, Padilla employed focus groups as a 'dialogical method' to empower the participants to transform their own lives. The project intended that: 'By critically examining through dialogue the problematic aspects of their own lives, the [participants] are able to gain the critical understanding that is necessary to identify viable alternatives to existing social arrangements and to take appropriate actions to change and improve their own lives' (Padilla 1993: 154).

## FOCUS GROUP METHODOLOGY AND ETHICS

Ethical issues have become an essential aspect of research, more so in qualitative research and the focus group methodology due to the nature of close interaction and relationship between the researcher and the participants as well as the unstructured and unpredictable nature of the methods. Ethics is a set of moral principles which aims to prevent the research participants from being harmed by the researcher and the research process. It is crucial that researchers take their ethical responsibilities seriously (Israel & Hay 2006; Liamputtong, 2007; 2009; Ramcharan 2010).

According to Clifford Christians (2008), codes of ethics comprise informed consent, deception, privacy and confidentiality, and accuracy. In this section, due to space limits, I will focus only on confidentiality and issues concerning risk and harm in focus group research. For more information regarding codes of ethics and other ethical issues including informed consent, see Beauchamp and Childress (2001), Gabard and Martin (2003), Israel and Hay (2006); Berglund (2007), Liamputtong (2007; 2009; 2010a) and Ramcharan (2010).

### Ethics and Conventional Focus Groups

Confidentiality aims to conceal the true identity of the participants (Israel & Hay 2006; Christians 2008; Ramcharan 2010). Based on the principle of respect for autonomy (Beauchamp & Childress 2001), individuals should have the right to 'maintain secrets, deciding who knows about them' (Israel & Hay 2006: 78). When the participants reveal their private world to the researchers, they must make sure that their private world is protected as much as possible. However, the main ethical concern with using the focus group method is that there is more than one research participant in a group at a time. The researcher cannot ensure that all discussions in the group will remain totally confidential (Smithson 2008; Willis et al. 2009). It is useful to commence the focus group with a list of 'dos' and 'don'ts' (Smithson 2008: 361). For example, the researchers must ask the participants to respect the confidences of all group members and not to repeat what is said outside the group (Smith 1995). This, however, cannot be totally guaranteed. The researchers can ensure their own confidentiality, but cannot promise that other participants will do the same. This can become problematic, particularly for focus groups in institutional settings, such as in workplaces and health care services.

Whether the group is composed of strangers or familiar faces, individuals may feel uncomfortable about discussing their concerns in a group context (Smithson 2008).

In particular, when discussing sensitive topics, group members may sometimes not respond sensitively to personal disclosures of others. When this occurs, the moderator may have to move the discussion in another direction or change the topic. And this can create some problems with the data collected.

Another common concern which has been raised about focus groups is that participants who take part in some areas of research may reveal personal and intimate details about their lives and these people can be vulnerable in many ways (Pini 2002). In the process of talking in great depth with the participants, the discussions may include information concerning their illegal or deviant activities or highly personalised matter, which could have grave consequences for the lives and reputations of these people if it becomes known publicly. Also, the participants may reveal more than they should and may later become uncomfortable about their over-disclosure (see Smith 1995). This often occurs in focus groups which follow the framework within feminist research which emphasises 'participation, reciprocity, voice and equalisation of the research relationship' (Pini 2002: 348). The researchers should warn the participants about the possibility that such disclosure may happen (Smith 1995).

In some focus groups which are conducted in small communities, the confidentiality of the participants or others may be compromised by the fact that people tend to know about each other. This was an issue in Barbara Pini's own research in the far north of Queensland (2002: 348). When two women were criticising a specific Canegrower leader, they were interrupted by another woman who said, 'You are talking about my brother. My brother John is in Canegrowers.' Pini had no knowledge about this connection. One of the participants then said, 'Well there you go. My husband says that I'm going to get myself in trouble in this district talking about people and not knowing who's who.'

Confidentiality is extremely important with some groups, particularly those who are marginalised and stigmatised in the society (Israel & Hay 2006; Liamputtong 2007; 2010a). The most disturbing and unethical damage in research occurs when the participants are harmed by the disclosure of their private world. According to the principle of non-maleficence, researchers have a responsibility to ensure the physical, emotional and social well-being of their research participants (Ramcharan 2010). Researchers must make sure that the participants will not be adversely affected by participating in research (Liamputtong 2007; Dickson-Swift et al. 2008; Liamputtong 2010a).

In research involving sensitive issues (see Chapter 7), distress and emotional harm may occur (Liamputtong 2007; Padgett 2008). In participating in focus group research, the participants may bring up painful memories of their life events and may become emotionally distressed. If this happens during and after their participation, the researchers need to develop some strategies to assist them. A common strategy is to provide the participants with a list of social and welfare workers such as counsellors or psychologists from whom they may seek help if needed.

Carey Smith (1995) suggests several strategies for running focus groups on sensitive issues:

- The moderator needs to observe the stress levels of participants and be well prepared to intervene if necessary.
- It may be better to run a small group rather than a group with too many participants.

- It is essential to have a debriefing session after the focus group so that the participants can talk about their reactions to the discussion.
- It may also be desirable to have a co-researcher with clinical experience present during the focus group so that the 'comfort level' of the participants can be monitored.

Ethical issues concerning focus groups involving children deserve some mention here. Focus group research with children can give rise to ethical issues which may not occur in other research methods (Hennessy & Heary 2005; Gibson 2007). Similar to the points I have made above, there are two reasons for this. First, disclosures by children are shared with not just the researcher but all group members. Second, when running a focus group with children, it is possible that group discussions can lead to strong emotional reactions among the children (Hennessy & Heary 2005; Goodman & Evans 2006; Gibson 2007). This is another crucial matter that researchers must seriously take into consideration. It is not possible for the researcher to ensure that the children will not be discontented or hurt by the comments of others or become upset in a group situation (Gibson 2007). Although these ethical concerns are important for all focus group research with children, they are especially significant when working with children on sensitive topics, such as parental separation/divorce or sexual behaviour. The researchers should pay particular attention to these issues (Hennessy & Heary 2005). Since the risks of disclosure of personal information outside the group setting are high, the composition of a group must be given particular attention. For example, a group composed of children who do not know each other and are unlikely to meet again because they do not live near one another might be organised in preference to a group with familiar faces. This strategy would help to reduce the chance that personal disclosure could become widely known in the neighbourhood or among peer groups (Hennessy & Heary 2005).

The researchers have the responsibility to find ways which can protect the children in focus groups (Hennessy & Heary 2005; Gibson 2007). As part of the introduction to the focus group, the moderator may inform the children that it is all right to discuss the topics in general but not to give details and not to identify what any individual member has said. It is important too that the researchers need to discuss with the children the meaning of disclosure and confidentiality in focus group research (Gibson 2007). The ongoing consenting process can be a place to stress these issues.

## Ethics and Virtual Focus Group

In this section, I will focus my discussions on the following two issues, which are more relevant to the conduct of virtual focus group research: confidentiality and risks to participants. Confidentiality is more problematic in online research than conventional research. Data collected online can have multiple risks (Mann & Stewart 2000; Liamputtong 2006; Gaiser & Schreiner 2009). Despite the fact that researchers may promise confidentiality in the way the data is used, they cannot provide a guarantee to their participants that the information will not be accessed by others (Mann & Stewart 2000). Researchers need to be cautious about assuring their participants of confidentiality (Im & Chee 2006; Gaiser 2008). The researchers can simply make clear to potential participants that total confidentiality may not be ensured (Mann & Stewart 2000). However, they could inform the participants that every precaution within their power will be taken to maintain confidentiality in their research projects. Similarly, Ted Gaiser (2008: 295), a well-known online focus group researcher, suggests that researchers have a responsibility to make clear to their participants the nature of online anonymity. Participants may think that 'a simple promise of anonymity means just that: that they are anonymous'. But online communications may be traceable and accessible at different times both during and after the research project. The partici-pants must be informed that 'best attempts do not directly equate with actual ano-nymity'. However, the researchers are still ethically required to make attempts to ensure confidentiality as best they can.

As in social science qualitative research, a researcher may make use of pseudonyms as a means of preserving the identities of participants in virtual focus group research reports or other publications. Real names, user names, domain names and signatures can be adjusted to disguise the true identity of the participants (Im & Chee 2003; Flicker et al. 2004; Couch & Liamputtong 2007; 2008). For example, real names can be replaced with 'nicknames', or 'pseudonyms'. In the online focus group research conducted by Fiona Stewart and colleagues (1998), participants' names include for example 'Red Beijing, Red Australia, Yellow Beijing'.

Another way to protect the confidentiality of participants is not to cite their direct quotes in subsequent publications, even though their names or personal information have been changed or removed (Liamputtong 2006). The identity of the person who provides the quote can be identified by a powerful search engine, such as Google, as it can retrieve the original message which includes the email address of the person (Eysenbach & Till 2001; Pitts 2004). If this occurs, then surely the confidentiality of the participant is breached. If the researchers need to use the direct words of the participants, they should be informed clearly about the potential consequences, and explicit consent to use their quotes must be given (Eysenbach & Till 2001).

Researchers may not be able to protect participants who stray into dangerous zones in cyberspace. People may think that the Internet is an uncensored, unpoliced environment and they may be more willing to tell other online users about their use of illegal drugs or crimes they have committed (Coomber 1997; Gaiser 2008). In conventional focus groups, the researchers are able to warn the participants, turn off the interview tape or decline to transcribe the sensitive parts. But these cannot be done in online focus groups. Even if the researcher attempts to delete the message on the screen, a total deletion is not possible.

In online focus groups, participants may come across harassment and abuse (Mann & Stewart 2000; Moloney et al. 2003). Harassment and abuse among research partici-pants may be prevented by making it clear to all participants about netiquette and the need to respect confidentiality in research. The moderator may have some influ-ence on this and needs to be able to control the groups. Conducting focus groups through the conferencing site can also prevent outsiders' harassment and abuse as only the researched participants can access the conference site. In addition, all par-ticipants should be told not to share the information outside the researched groups. Such harassment and abuse can also occur within Internet communities. The group members may post messages that attack other individuals or groups, contain sexual overtones, and violate community tenets (Flicker et al. 2004).

Deception is easily performed in online communication. Often, the deception emerges on the part of the participants as it is difficult to tell if they are telling the truth or who they actually are (Mann & Stewart 2000; Gaiser 2008; Markham 2008). How do we know if our participants are actually females presenting the intimate sexual encounters that we are researching? We cannot be sure about this. The deception will have a great impact not only on the researchers, but also among the researched participants themselves. What can researchers do to prevent these things that I have identified? It is the ethical responsibility of researchers at least to ensure that the potential participants are aware of the public nature of online communications prior to giving out consent forms and during the study (Mann & Stewart 2000; Gaiser 2008).

## CONCLUSION

A theoretical framework provides 'ways of seeing' for the conduct of qualitative research (Morgan 1996: 12). Focus group researchers too must defend the adoption of their methods based on an appropriate theoretical framework (Liamputtong 2009; Willis et al. 2009). Qualitative researchers, including focus group researchers, should pay great attention to the role that theory plays in their research: 'research cannot be conducted without the conscious or unconscious use of underlying theory' (Mertz & Anfara 2006: 190). It is the task of focus group researchers to consider carefully which theory is more useful and suitable for their research projects.

In this chapter, I have suggested several theoretical frameworks on which the focus group methodology is grounded. I have pointed out that if we situate our focus group method within the framework of symbolic interactionism, feminism and critical pedagogical practice, we will carry out our focus group research differently from market research which is based on 'positivism, behaviourism and empiricism' (Johnson 1996: 517; Pini 2002; see also Chapter 1 in this volume). It is essential for social science researchers who are committed to feminist and praxis research to make a 'paradigmatic shift' (Johnson 1996: 525) in the use of focus groups, which has been adopted in market research. This move will allow us to engage in what Jonathan Murdoch and Andy Pratt (1993: 423) refer to as a 'new recipe', which 'disrupts the traditional power relations between researchers and participants, emphasises localised and lived knowledge, encourages and facilitates self-reflexivity, and invites social and political change' (Pini 2002: 349).

Second, as in any qualitative approach, the ethical issues are paramount in focus group research. Focus group researchers must be responsible for the ethical conduct of their research. They need to ensure that their research participants will not be harmed and exploited. They need to consider the means by which they are able to assist their participants if any harm comes to them. It is crucial to remember that we, as researchers, ask our participants to take part in our research. We have intruded into their lives and hence we have the utmost responsibility to safeguard their health and well-being.

## TUTORIAL ACTIVITIES

1 As an honours student in the social science area, you must carry out some minor research to fulfil your programme. You wish to examine how young men in your local area who are of low socioeconomic status construct their self-identity. You decide to use the focus group methodology in your research. Which theoretical framework would you base your focus group research on? What are the reasons for your theoretical choice?

2 You wish to conduct a focus group project using both conventional and virtual methods. You need to present your proposal to a research panel and apply for ethical clearance from your university. What are the ethical issues that you must carefully consider in defending that your project is ethically conducted?

## FURTHER READING

Christians, C.G. (2008). Ethics and politics in qualitative research. In N.K. Denzin & Y.S. Lincoln (eds.), *The landscape of qualitative research*, 3rd edition (pp. 185–220). Thousand Oaks, CA: Sage.

Hyams, M. (2004). Hearing girls' silences: Thoughts on the politics and practices of a feminist method of group discussion. *Gender, Place & Culture* 11(1), 105–119.

Israel, M., & Hay, I. (2006). *Research ethics for social scientists: Between ethical conduct and regulatory compliance*. London: Sage.

Johnson, A. (1996). 'It's good to talk': The focus group and the sociological imagination. *The Sociological Review* 44(2), 517–536.

Jowett, M., & O'Toole, G. (2006). Focusing researchers' minds: Contrasting experiences of using focus groups in feminist qualitative research. *Qualitative Research* 6(4), 453–472.

Kamberelis, G., & Dimitriadis, G. (2008). Focus groups: Strategic articulations of pedagogy, politics, and inquiry. In N.K. Denzin & Y.S. Lincoln (eds.), *Collecting and interpreting qualitative materials*, 3rd edition (pp. 375–402). Thousand Oaks, CA: Sage.

Madriz, E. (2003). Focus groups in feminist research. In N.K. Denzin & Y.S. Lincoln (eds.), *Collecting and interpreting qualitative materials*, 2nd edition (pp. 363–388). Thousand Oaks, CA: Sage.

Ramcharan, P. (2010). What is ethical research? In P. Liamputtong (ed.), *Research methods in health: Foundations for evidence-based practice* (pp. 27–41). Melbourne: Oxford University Press.

# 3
# FOCUS GROUP METHODOLOGY AND PRINCIPLES

## CHAPTER OBJECTIVES

In this chapter you will learn about:

- Focus group interaction
- Group composition
- How many participants and groups are enough?
- How long should a focus group take?
- What determines successful focus groups?

This chapter will introduce the principles of undertaking focus group research. As in other qualitative methods, focus groups require certain principles which would allow researchers to consider and plan carefully before they embark on doing the focus group interviews. There are several salient principles that I will include in the sections that follow and these include focus group interaction, focus group composition, number of research participants and groups required in focus group research, the length of time for conducting a focus group and the determination of successful focus groups.

## FOCUS GROUP INTERACTION

A focus group interview is not a group interview. It is a group of people gathered together to discuss a focused issue of concern. The emphasis is therefore on the interaction between participants in the group (Morgan 1997; Duggleby 2005). David Morgan (1997: 2) puts it clearly that 'the hallmark of focus groups is their explicit use of group interaction to produce data and insights that would be less accessible without the interaction found in a group'. Interaction creates a 'synergistic effect' (Stewart et al. 2007) because it allows the participants to respond and build on the reactions of other members in the group. Group interaction is able to 'reveal points of agreement, conflict, and uncertainty' (Pfeffer 2008: 2544). With this kind of interaction, focus groups enter the terrains which other research methods such as the in-depth interviewing method or questionnaire cannot do; that is, unpacking aspects of understanding which often 'remain untapped' by conventional methods (Kitzinger 1994a: 109).

According to Jenny Kitzinger (1994a: 107), there are two kinds of interaction in focus groups: complementary (sharing experiences, concerns and needs) and argumentative (questioning, disagreeing with and challenging each other). Complementary interaction allows the principles of 'the social world' which provide 'frameworks of understanding' for the participants to emerge (Bryman 2008: 486). But arguments in the group can also reveal people's underlying beliefs. Disagreement can offer the opportunity for the participants to review their perspectives or to consider the reasons for holding such perspectives. Within this group of interaction, the moderator will play a significant role in exploring differences of perspectives and working with the participants to uncover the factors which may lie underneath them (Kitzinger 1994a; Bryman 2008). In Deborah Warr's focus group research on intimacy among young people (2001; 2005), the participants expressed both agreement and disagreement. This permitted Warr to extract the tensions between individuals' private matters and wider public expectations and controversies. Having groups with a mixture of agreement and disagreement was crucial for Warr's research on intimacy since it helped the participants to resolve disagreements about what is and what is not appropriate when love and sex are concerned. Focusing on areas of agreement and disagreement in focus groups, Warr contends, is a valuable starting point for the analysis and interpretation of the derived data.

Interaction is an essence of focus groups because it unveils the reality of the group and provides an understanding about how group members think and express their viewpoints (Ivanoff & Hultberg 2006: 127). Interaction provides a good understanding of the world of the participants since it reveals the group's shared experiences of everyday life, language and culture. Interaction takes place because the participants are not only the products of their own environment, but also influenced by others around them (Krueger 1988). Focus group methodology posits that the researchers can gain understanding by listening to the participants' discussions, challenges and contradictions that take place in the group. Multiple understandings and meanings held by the participants can be unpacked and this provides the researchers with insights into different perspectives. Hence, the differences between what individuals say and what they do can be understood. Jenny Kitzinger (1994a: 113) refers to this as the 'importance of difference' in investigating interaction in her focus group study of constructions of AIDS. This 'importance of difference' offers the researcher an insight into how the participants understand and negotiate differences in meanings. For the participants themselves, they have an opportunity to take part in the process of clarifying their own perspectives and uncovering why there are differences in viewpoints on an issue. In Barbara Pini's study with rural women in Queensland (2002), one issue which was raised often in her focus groups and heatedly debated by participants in two different groups was the view that women are naturally difficult and bitchy. In one focus group, three participants were discussing that women have 'a natural proclivity for nastiness'. One woman said that 'women are the worst; they are the worst critics' (Pini 2002: 346); another woman intervened and argued that not all women have this tendency. The way some women act, or are able to act, depends on their own social status. This shows that interaction in focus groups allow alternative viewpoints to emerge (Pini 2002).

In Jude Robinson's work (2009: 267) with mothers of low socioeconomic status who smoke at home in England, she tells us about this interaction among the women: 'The women's contributions to the discussions were participative, with women typically ending comments with a question, inviting a further response from other members of the groups, which was usually taken up by the other group members.' The women tended to interrupt each other. This was not seen as being rude, but a way for them to express their agreement, common experiences and understanding. The women also talked over one another so that they could finish off another person's sentence. This was a way to show their understanding by anticipating what other persons were going to say as well as their own thoughts. What Robinson articulates can be seen in one of her focus groups:

P5-1:   They have smokers' tables or non-smoking areas as well, don't they?
JR:     Do you think that makes a difference?
P5-2:   No.
P5-1:   Not really no, because the smokes going round.
P5-3:   The smoke's in the same room, isn't it? So …
P5-4:   If it is a big place and there is just a small area where you can smoke then I suppose …
P5-3:   I suppose you could have the smokers outside on like a veranda.
P5-1:   Yes, in the middle of winter, raining!

(Laughing and talking over each other)

In this focus group, most women had met for the first time, but some of the women knew one another and some were friends. Yet their interaction in the group seems to suggest that they had formed a temporary bond within the groups. This is important in discussing a sensitive issue like smoking and motherhood as it is frowned upon by others in society.

Interaction between participants and the researchers helps to improve 'the quality of the data' (Wilkinson 1998: 117). In group work, as in a focus group, the participants' 'hierarchy of importance, their frameworks for understanding the world and their language and concepts' is given priority (Wilkinson 1998: 117). Listening to conversations between participants allows the researchers to learn about the preferred languages or terms used for speaking about the topic of focus and this will prevent the researchers from generating meanings prematurely (Kitzinger 1994a: 108). In a 'girls' group' of their focus group research on negotiating territories of gender, class and difference, Pat MacPherson and Michelle Fine (1995: 193) provide an example where Michelle became familiarised with the language used in the school context from three 17-year-old-girls, Janet, Shermika and Sophie:

Michelle: Now do you think guys [at your school] brag to each other about this stuff?
Janet: Yes [giggles]. Oh yeah, in a major way.
Shermika: (simultaneously) Girls brag, too.
Sophie: All they *talk* about is what they're getting.
Michelle: Is that their language, 'What they're getting'?

[All laugh while Pat and Michelle say, 'Wait a minute!']

Shermika: 'She *all* that!'... I *hate* that!
Sophie: 'All that and more.'
Janet: 'Fly' is, like, totally hot, she's the most gorgeous woman on the earth.

Interaction between the three participants and the researcher results in 'the production of high quality data' (Wilkinson 1998: 117) because the participants are able to question, disagree with and challenge each other. The interaction serves 'to elicit the elaboration of responses' (Merton 1987: 555).

## THE PARTICIPANTS: GROUP COMPOSITION

There are several important issues regarding the composition of participants in focus groups. As the emphasis is on group discussion, the composition of the group plays a major role in the interaction process. Conventionally, it is argued that participants should have something in common so that maximum interaction within the group can be achieved and individuals dominating or withdrawing can be avoided. But this may not work at all times. In general, there are three points of concern regarding this group composition, as follows.

### A Homogeneous Group or a Heterogeneous Group?

The participants in focus groups are often selected because they are homogeneous, like-minded people and have something in common which is of interest to the researchers (Ivanoff & Hultberg 2006). It is argued that if the participants share social and cultural backgrounds, they may feel more comfortable talking to each other and also are more likely to talk openly. Indeed, as David Morgan (1997: 35) suggests, it is this social and cultural homogeneity that allows for 'more free-flowing conversations' among the participants. Social and cultural backgrounds here include such factors as class, gender, ethnicity, religion, educational background, occupation, status within the community and sexual preference. It is crucial to note that homogeneity in focus group research refers to the background or personal characteristics of the participants, and not their views and attitudes (Morgan 1997; Peek & Fothergill 2009).

In general, focus group researchers tend to adopt homogeneous focus groups. It is crucial that the participants in a focus group share some of the social and cultural backgrounds or have similar lived experiences, or some combination of these. Homogeneous groups are appropriate when the researchers wish to generate insight into the thoughts or experience about a specific issue of the participants.

Homogeneous groups create comfort within the group and this enhances more fluid discussion among the group participants. This is essential in focus groups involving sensitive issues such as miscarriage, abortion, violence, depression, addiction, racism, body disturbance and sexuality.

Participants with different backgrounds can restrict the openness and sincerity of the discussion. For example, researchers interested in sexual practices in a project concerned with the prevention of HIV/AIDS should not conduct focus group sessions that mix younger and single women with older and married women. The reason for this is that young and single women may feel that they have to speak only about the 'acceptable' norms within the community, rather than their true experiences and behaviours, in front of older and married women. In Skeggs and others' study (1998–2000) of sexuality, safety and violence, they conducted focus groups with gay men, lesbians and heterosexuals separately. This was to ensure a supportive environment for discussion among group members because these topics are sensitive. They felt that in a homogeneous group, the participants would feel more open to discuss such sensitive information.

In a project on the geographies of home which David Conradson (2005) carried out using the focus group method in the UK, gender was an important issue as he was interested in the experiences among male and female students of going to university. He conducted four focus groups: two groups with women solely and two with only men. The homogeneity of the groups created an environment where each gender was able to speak about their experiences more freely. As David Morgan (1988: 61) argues, 'the sharing of ideas and experiences is at the heart of focus groups, and this requires a climate of mutual respect. At a minimum, the composition of each focus group should minimize suspicion and open disagreement.' Conradson (2005: 133) suggests that homogeneity does not mean that the researchers need to recruit individuals who think exactly the same. Instead, homogeneity requires 'bringing together people who have enough in common to allow the development of a productive conversational dynamic'.

However, some focus group researchers argue that heterogeneous group composition can sometimes work favourably (Litosseliti 2003; Hennink 2007; Smithson 2008), particularly if researchers want to 'maximize the possibility of exploring subjects from different perspectives' (Kitzinger 1995: 300). Heterogeneous groups are more suitable if the researchers look for a diverse range of responses (Hesse-Biber & Leavy 2010). Khan and colleagues (1991) point out that heterogeneity can be useful in assessing community attitudes and beliefs, and in maintaining the flow of the discussion in some cases. They give an example from their own research in India, in which younger women had difficulty discussing reproductive matters. The problem was resolved when a mother-in-law of one of the participants, who was present in the focus group session, started to talk. The younger women then joined in.

In Deevia Bhana's study (2009: 598) with children in South Africa, 26 focus group interviews were conducted with children in grade 2 (aged between seven and eight). The children were put in mixed-sex groups and relate to each other as girls and boys within the school context. In some groups there were more girls, in others more boys. The gendering of groups influenced what girls and boys could and could not say. Although girls and boys felt embarrassed to express specific things, especially those in relation to sex, Bhana (2009: 598) points out that 'the mixed sex groups allowed for the opportunities for boys and girls to come together, assert their positions and contest each other'. Rather than creating an artificial environment with single-sex groups, Bhana's study attempted to gain insight about how girls and boys relate to each other in real life. This, in turn, helped her to develop culturally sensitive AIDS prevention programmes which would reflect the children's actual lives as they opened up about the disease. The children in her study were comfortable with discussing sensitive issues which they might not be able to do with teachers and parents in the focus groups. Bhana (2009: 598) contends that using mixed-sex focus groups as a means of working with these girls and boys 'enables freedom of expression, gives them the confidence to ask questions and to refuse to talk and withdraw at their own volition'.

Having discussed the two group compositions in focus groups, readers may ask which one would be better. David Morgan (1997) suggests that researchers need to ask themselves which type of group – homogeneous or heterogeneous – might best serve the purposes of their research. Some research questions are more suited to one than the other. Morgan argues that careful consideration and common sense are vital in the selection of research participants.

## Shared Experiences?

Focus group participants should be homogeneous in terms of shared experience. People who have common attitudes towards certain issues or have similar lived experiences are more likely to talk openly with each other. The reason for this is simple: they feel that others in the group can understand them better because of the shared experience (Liamputtong 2009). For example, researchers interested in issues related to motherhood need to recruit, for their focus group sessions, women who have had children. If there is also an interest in the attitudes of those who have had no experience of motherhood, a separate group needs to be conducted for women who fall into this category. To combine the two groups in one focus group session might not be successful, as those who have no experience of motherhood may disagree in many ways with those who have.

Even if a group is heterogeneous, but has shared experience, the discussion can be very successful since the participants feel they have something in common. Hence, it is likely that meaningful discussions will take place because of shared experiences. This was clearly noticeable when I conducted focus group interviews on childhood immunisation with Chinese mothers in Beijing. Because all of the mothers had taken their children for immunisation, they had a shared experience about this health issue and its importance, and this made the group discussion really lively. Similarly, in a recent project on the use of Wii games to improve social connection between people, especially those who are socially isolated, we recruited older women to participate in a focus group following the Wii game (see Wollersheim et al. 2010). The Wii is a newly released interactive video console that requires both reasoning skills and gross physical movements. The focus group allowed us to investigate participants' group interaction. Because they shared their experience in using Wii and about growing old, this led to a lively discussion among the participants in the group.

In focus groups, the topics are discussed in a 'known context' because people who shared similar experiences are brought together (Ivanoff & Hultberg 2006: 127). Because of the shared experiences, focus groups highlight the collective view rather than the individual view, although the individual experiences are also clear in the discussions. In Jude Robinson's work (2009: 268), she tells us that discussions in the focus groups allowed the women to connect with other through the shared aspects of their lives. The shared experiences were not only about the topics under investigation, which involved motherhood and smoking, but also other shared lived situations including place of residence, living in social housing, being short of money and educational background. One woman said:

> Because everyone smokes, and we are all the same. None of us have got any airs or graces about it. We have got our kids here, they are getting looked after but at the end of the day we can sit and have a ciggie, have a chat and a cup of tea, and that's it and we are all one group. I know most of us do smoke a couple [in front of our children], don't we?

In this example, the woman referred to the social solidarity of the group by making a connection with their disadvantages due to social class and poverty before revealing the personal and sensitive issue that she smokes in front of the children. The woman also believed that everyone else in the room did so too. Furthermore, she made a strong link between class, poverty and place within the UK context and made reference to the fact that if the other mothers lived in the same area and smoked, they would have shared other aspects of their culture including home smoking. It was interesting that the other participants did not contest her claim. Instead, it provided a very useful starting point for further discussions in the group.

## Familiar Faces (Pre-existing Groups) or Strangers (Constructed Groups)?

Conventional texts about focus groups advocate having strangers in a focus group session. This practice is derived from focus groups employed in market research (Morgan 1993; 1998). Market focus group research texts have the tendency to insist that focus groups are undertaken with strangers so that both the 'polluting' and 'inhibiting' impact of existing relations between the participants can be avoided (Kitzinger 2005: 61). David Morgan (1993: 6) points out that 'this is an example of a useful rule of thumb that has become an overly rigid restriction on when to use focus groups'.

According to focus group researchers Julie Leask and colleagues (2001), there is ongoing discussion about the merits of pre-existing and constructed groups. Constructed groups, where participants are total strangers, are arguably useful when the group conformity which is brought about by pre-established group norms and patterns of leadership is to be minimised. The personal cost of group members will be less if they express different or challenging perspectives because they are unlikely to meet again. Hence, people may be more likely to express their views honestly (Peek & Fothergill 2009). Group members who are strangers are also less likely to attempt to set the discussion agenda, which can be particularly problematic for certain research questions. Lori Peek and Alice Fothergill (2009) say that researchers may prefer strangers participating in focus groups because of the possibility that participants in the group who know each other may 'hold back' in their sharing. There is also a concern about the disclosure or over-disclosure of private or confidential matters when pre-existing groups or friends are included in the same focus group (Brannen & Pattman 2005).

Often, however, social science researchers have to work with familiar faces or pre-existing groups because of the nature of their research interests. Pre-existing groups are essential when the aims of the research necessitate, or would be enhanced by, the presence of a group dynamic (Leask et al. 2001). This type of focus group is particularly useful for examining natural interactions among family, peer group or the dynamics in organisational settings (see Munday 2006). Pre-existing focus groups are used when the researchers aim to obtain conversations and interactions, which may appear in the normal environment where attitudes are negotiated and formed. They are also useful in focus group research involving specific groups or examining sensitive issues (see Chapters 6, 7 and 8 in this volume). There are also some practical and advantageous aspects of having pre-existing groups. For example, the recruitment of potential participants could be easier since the participants know each other, and little time is needed for the group to warm up. Lastly, they are able to prompt each other by referring to shared experiences and stories. These advantages, indeed, can counterbalance any difficulties that might occur in a focus group (Bloor et al. 2001; Munday 2006).

Also, there are many circumstances when having strangers in the focus groups is not permissible or practical because the group members are reluctant to talk with strangers (Leask et al. 2001). In these situations, familiarity rather than anonymity may be the key to free-flowing discussions. In their research regarding stressors, coping and social support with women in Papua New Guinea, Rachael Hinton and Jaya Earnest (2010: 227) tell us that, due to the localised setting of their research, all of the women knew each other in the focus group. As such, dialogue flowed freely and the women were willing and felt supported to disclose their personal perspectives regarding polygamy, contraception and violence against women among friends and family. The nature of the group permitted 'a sense of camaraderie in the group, shared empathy, and commonality in experiences'.

There are situations where women, for example, do not wish to talk openly in front of strangers but are willing to do so with their acquaintances. In rural areas or in small villages and slums in developing countries, where most people know or know about each other, strangers can be difficult to recruit. For example, in Fuller and colleagues' (1993) study on the effects of household crowding in slums in Bangkok, they say that it is difficult to recruit strangers in slums and low-income flats because people tend to know each other. They live in close proximity in such areas and gossip is very common. More importantly, in Thai culture, strangers are not trusted and hence people do not wish to talk about family matters with strangers. In the focus groups, the participants were therefore recruited from acquaintances. In the study with women in shelter that Lori Peek and Alice Fothergill (2009) carried out soon after Hurricane Katrina in 2005, the women had lived together under one roof during an extremely stressful time for over a month. Attempting to recruit a total stranger for the focus groups would not have been feasible.

However, according to Jenny Kitzinger (2005: 62), social science researchers tend to work with familiar faces or pre-existing groups, individuals who know each other through living, socialising or working together. Kitzinger refers to this as the 'naturally-occurring group'. It is in this context that opinions are constituted and decisions are obtained. By using familiar faces or pre-existing groups, the research-ers are able to observe 'fragments of interactions' which resemble data that occurs naturally. Also, friends and colleagues are able to connect what others say to the actual happenings in their shared daily lives. They can challenge each other on con-tradictions between what they say or believe and their actual behaviour. Robin Jarrett (1993) contends that focus groups conducted with acquaintances allow the participants not only to share their experiences, but also to disclose personal infor-mation. The more the participants interact, the deeper the levels of disclosure that can be obtained. Because of this self-disclosure, the participants are able to examine more intensely their own views and the views of others in the group. This enhances the richness of the information gathered. For example, in Pat MacPherson and Michelle Fine's study (1995), the participants themselves brought along their best friends, and this turned out to work well for the group: 'The best friend pairing ensured that each girl had a familiar audience and, as it turned out, a critical one; challenges came only from the friend at first, uncritical questions came from the other girls' (MacPherson & Fine 1995: 182). By knowing each other, the partici-pants may revoke shared experiences, bring out half-forgotten memories, or chal-lenge each other (Wilkinson 2004: 276). This can be seen in Kitzinger's study that I presented above.

In Deborah Warr's research regarding heterosexual health issues with socioeco-nomically disadvantaged young people in Melbourne (2001; 2004), the participants were asked to provide feedback on their experiences of participating in the focus group discussion. Most participants made comments along the lines of 'it was fun and I felt comfortable because I know these people even though we don't usually talk about these things' (Warr 2001: 121). Tellingly, Warr (2001: 122) suggests:

> feedback epitomises the ambiguous nature of the data that are collected from existing groups, and is at the intersection of naturalistic and contrived interaction. Both fea-tures are brought together in focus group interaction because people feel comfortable being with people whom they know, and the discussion draws on existing group dynamics and experiences.

However, a focus group which comprises familiar faces or a pre-existing group needs to be carried out slightly different from one consisting of strangers (Morgan 1993; Munday 2006). The established hierarchies and patterns of interaction between group members must be referred to, as this effect can be potentially detrimental to the results generated by the focus group method (Krueger & Casey 2009). However, in some research projects, this hierarchical nature is what is needed as part of an investigation.

I will now provide an interesting study undertaken by Julie Leask and colleagues (2001). The study aimed to develop communication strategies for parents who were ambivalent about childhood immunisation. Leask and colleagues carried out four focus groups with parents who were recruited via Early Childhood Health Centres (ECHCs) in the northern suburbs of Sydney, Australia, in 1999. Two groups involved pre-existing first-time mothers' groups and two were composed of mothers who were strangers to each other but who were recruited individually from the waiting room. Each focus group commenced with a general discussion about childhood immunisation. Two video prompts were then shown. One video was an extract from a controversial television documentary which reflected the anti-vaccination discourses and included footage of children who have been allegedly harmed by vaccines. The other video was a section from a tabloid current affairs programme about a pertussis outbreak which was generally pro-vaccination. It showed footage of babies who were hospitalised with the illness. The participants were telephoned the day after the focus groups were held in order to allow those who did not feel that they could contribute properly in the groups to articulate their experiences and clarify certain issues.

Leask and colleagues (2001: 153) found marked differences between the pre-existing and constructed groups. In the pre-existing groups, discussions appeared to be 'cold' (Krueger 1994: 17) since the participants talked less and seemed reluctant to take part. They were less enthusiastic and interested in the topic. The researcher had to prompt more in order to generate discussion. The participants tended to agree with each other more and hence the groups finished sooner. Additionally, they tended to conform to positive conventional ideas about vaccines. In the constructed groups, however, the participants were more eager to contribute, debated the topic more intensely and interrupted each other more often. However, the groups took longer and were more difficult to finish. Opinions about vaccination were more diverse in constructed groups. Telephoned interviews also supported the observations: 'Participants from the constructed groups described enjoying the opportunity to *discuss* the issue and meet other mothers, whereas participants form the natural groups described the session as *informative*, even though it was not intended, nor perceived by the researchers, to be' (p. 153, original emphasis).

Leask and colleagues (2001: 153) also found what they called a 'protective dynamic', where the participants voiced a need to protect others in the group from disturbing stories about vaccination that were generated through discussion or from the videos. This 'protective dynamic' emerged in both the pre-existing and constructed groups, but the effects were different. In the pre-existing groups, it served as 'more of a censor'. For example, a participant from a new mothers' group, who was also a health professional, said in a post-group interview that she was reluctant to discuss her own experience about caring for hospitalised children whom she claimed were vaccine damaged, which had led to her concerns about vaccinating her own child because this might upset one participant of the group who was particularly sensitive about the issue. Conversely, in the constructed groups, the protective dynamic was explicitly made during the group discussion. For instance, a woman with three children overtly expressed her concern about the impact of the anti-vaccination video on two first-time mothers in the group: 'I felt in a way disappointed, that especially (name) and (name) saw that, because I think it could sow a seed of doubt.' The women in the group then had the opportunity to respond to her concerns and also articulate their views about the videos.

In the constructed groups, participation among group members was more 'fresh'. The women who did not know each other were more enthusiastic about sharing their own personal stories with the group. For instance, one new mother asked the group if she could tell the others about her experience and went on to tell a powerful story about her baby being subject to a whooping cough scare in the maternity ward. Leask and colleagues (2001: 153) contended that, 'had she been part of an existing group, it is likely that this story would have already been told'.

Interestingly, Leask and colleagues (2001: 154) argued that the tendency of the pre-existing groups to agree with others quickly when discussing vaccination issues could be treated as a 'finding' instead of a flaw in research design. This is particularly so if the aim of the research is to understand more about how social processes influence the way mothers speak about vaccination. However, in their research, there was a greater need to examine a range of responses from the participants. Thus, they avoided having pre-existing groups but ensured that their participants were homogeneous in terms of socioeconomic status.

Whatever choices the researchers may make about the nature of their participants (familiar faces or strangers), we must remember that they generate different group dynamics. Think carefully about the nature and objectives of the research before making a decision about group composition of your focus groups. Lori Peek and Alice Fothergill (2009: 41) contend that the researchers should decide the composition of their focus groups based on the aims and context of their research project. In the case of Lori Peek's research with young Muslim Americans (Peek & Fothergill 2009), one of the most crucial aspects which contributed to the success of her data collection was the fact that the focus groups were carried out with friends and acquaintances in pre-existing groups. When Peek arrived in New York City, only weeks after September 11, a large number of Muslims, Arabs and South Asians living in the United States had already been questioned or detained by the federal authorities. Many students that she attempted to speak to were reluctant to discuss anything with an unfamiliar researcher, and certainly not in a group of complete strangers. It would have been much more difficult to get groups of strangers, regardless of whether they shared the common characteristic of being Muslim or not, to interact in the focus groups. In addition, Peek did not live in New York. Due to time and distance constraints, it would have been difficult to organise focus groups consisting of complete strangers.

## HOW MANY PARTICIPANTS AND GROUPS ARE ENOUGH?

There are two important issues which deserve great attention. These include how many people should be in a focus group and how many groups are needed in a research project.

## How Many People in a Focus Group?

Group size is crucial for the success of the focus group method. But there is variation in the idea of 'ideal size' for a focus group (Peek & Fothergill 2009). Generally, it is recommended that there should be six to ten participants in one focus group session, but some sessions may have up to twelve people. Susan Dawson and others (1993) point out that focus groups work well with four to twelve people. Jenny Kitzinger (2005) suggests that the ideal size of a group should be between four and eight.

In general, these numbers are based on the argument that if the number is less than six and if the participants have a low level of involvement with the issue, it may be difficult to generate interest and maintain an active discussion, hence one or two people may try to dominate the discussion. The information generated may not be adequate or rich enough since there are fewer people to interact. For a group that has a smaller number than four, it 'can lose some of the qualities of being a group' (Smithson 2008: 359). However, this may not be the case for some research with small numbers of participants in a focus group. Rona Rubin (2004), for example, explored attitudes to Viagra in a social context with men in New Zealand. Rubin conducted two focus groups with men aged between 45 and 65. The first group contained six members recruited from a sports club, but the second one had only three patients who attended a clinic for men with erectile dysfunction. Despite the small number of the second group, the data yielded was different from that of the larger group. In this group, a theme of sadness for not being able to 'confess' about their problem due to potential loss of masculine image was prominent. Masculine image was seen as more important to these men than their own health. Robyn Longhurst (1996) employed the focus group to examine the experience of public space among pregnant women in Hamilton, New Zealand. Three of these focus groups had only two women. Initially, Longhurst (1996) classified them as 'failed' focus groups, but later acknowledged that the groups were also useful for her data collection.

On the other hand, a group with more than eight people may be difficult to manage. Some participants may find it difficult to talk in a big group where everyone else is trying to talk. So, they may 'remain silent or speak very little' (Smithson 2008: 359). Others may have to wait a long time for their turn and hence may lose interest before their turn finally comes.

Often, smaller groups comprising of 4 to 6 individuals offer an environment where the participants can discuss actively in the group (Smithson 2008). Prominent focus group researchers Richard Krueger and Mary Anne Casey (2009) refer to this as 'mini-focus groups', and suggest that focus groups with four to six participants are becoming increasingly popular. Smaller groups provide more room for all participants to speak and to explore the discussed issues in greater detail and this often leads to more relevant and interesting data. In her research with poor Latina women, Esther Madriz (2003: 380) points out that she carried out 18 focus groups and the group involved between five and twelve participants. She remarks: 'I avoided using larger groups because of the difficulties they would pose for handling the discussion and keeping the conversation around the topic of research. Larger groups make it more difficult for all the participants to have their opinions heard.' Myfanwy Morgan and colleagues (2002), in their research exploring the experience of living with asthma with children aged 7–11 years in the UK, tell us that the size of their focus groups ranged from two to seven children. The very small groups were the result of the practicalities of recruitment and last-minute dropouts because of other family commitments. Their experiences with this research suggest that four or five participants are an ideal size of focus groups with children, particularly with younger children aged 7–8 years. A larger group size would make it difficult for moderators to encourage interactive discussion among the children. It would also mean that the focus group session is not too noisy, which can make the transcription task more difficult to do (see also Chapter 4 in this volume).

It is important that the size of the group needs to be shaped to suit the needs of the project. When employed in the right contexts, small focus groups can be more efficient than large ones (Munday 2006). In Jennie Munday's WI focus group research (2006), the group was successful with a small number of participants. Since the questions posed centred around issues which were important and familiar to the women, there were many things that all of them wished to speak about. Additionally, the project required an in-depth discussion from the group. Hence, a larger group with more participants would not have given the women the opportunity to articulate their views fully.

In Peter Hopkins' focus group research with young Muslim men in Scotland (2007), the groups comprised between three and twelve participants. The focus groups with smaller numbers of young men went smoothly and all participants had an opportunity to express their views on important matters which were significant to them. Often, with the larger groups, the tape-recordings were inaudible as many of the participants spoke on top of each other because of their frustration and anger with the inequalities they experienced. Hopkins contends that instead of focusing on how many participants should be included in a focus group, perhaps the researchers should consider other possible influences on the dynamic of the group. From his experience of using focus groups, 'the number of participants is important, but only alongside a range of other issues, such as the age and composition of the participants, the location of the focus group meeting and the sensitivity of the topic being discussed' (Hopkins 2007: 531; see also the theoretical sampling model discussed in a later section).

Jean Toner's (2009) recent writing also discusses the very small size of the focus groups with women of colour in her research regarding substance-abusing behaviour in a rural area of the southwestern United States. She examined the lived experience of women within a raced, gendered and classed society. She had planned to have six to eight women in each group. She managed to recruit seven women in the white women's group, but was able to have only two Native American women and two Latina women participating in each respective group. However, in these small focus groups, there was more intimate interaction among the women than in the white women's group. A small group setting made the women feel safe enough not only to disclose their profound and traumatic experiences, but also to make jokes about their own cultures, themselves and their families. Such intimate interaction did not occur in the larger white women's focus group.

Although an ideal focus group should have between four and ten participants, sometimes the researchers may have to work with fewer or more participants

(Conradson 2005). In practice, the size of the group is determined by the preferences of the research design (such as the nature of the social groups which are essential for the research questions) and the practical constraints of doing research (such as who is accessible and willing to participate) (Conradson 2005: 133–134). Generally, it is advised to over-recruit participants since those who have agreed to participate may not turn up on the day. This may be due to some unforeseen events which prevent people's involvement. Some participants may not attend as they assume that others will be participating. However, the researchers must also ensure that the arranged venue can cater for a larger group, in case all of the invited individuals attend (Smithson 2008).

In her study with poor Latina women, Esther Madriz (2003: 379) tells us that many Latina women of low socioeconomic status have many responsibilities to fulfil (such as being mothers, caretakers, cooks and keepers of the family). This makes it difficult for some of them to participate in activities outside their homes. Often, these women would have other unforeseen demands on their time too, and hence are not able to keep their schedules. As a result, Latinas may arrive late or not show up at all. In Madriz's own experience, out of the 12 or 15 who confirmed that they would participate, only a few women would attend. Madriz suggests that the provision of transportation for participants, such as picking them up by arranging drivers to bring them to the focus group meeting, or offering reimbursement for transportation costs, would certainly improve their attendance. However, it is best to organise a focus group meeting at the most convenient location, for example the church, schools with English as a second language, or soup kitchens where they attend (see also Chapters 4 and 8 in this volume).

## How Many Groups are Needed?

An important question that most researchers often ask is how many focus groups are needed to ensure adequate coverage in one research project? David Morgan (1997) suggests that, as a rule of thumb, three to five sessions may be enough for each variable of investigation. However, this could become unmanageable if the researchers wish to examine a number of variables, such as age, gender, class, religion, education, ethnicity, language, sexual orientation, rural or urban residence and marital status (Kitzinger 2005). If the rule of thumb is followed (three to five sessions for each variable), the researchers may end up with 30–50 focus groups. If each focus group contains about 10 participants, the researcher has to analyse transcripts from 300–500 participants. Given time and cost constraints, this could be difficult to manage.

The final number of focus groups to be undertaken should reflect the research plan (Bloor et al. 2001; Peek & Fothergill 2009). If the groups are segmented, for instance by class, race, gender, age or sexuality, then more groups will be required (Morgan 1995). In Lori Peek's Muslim American student study, she conducted 23 focus groups: 11 all-female groups, 3 all-male focus groups and 9 mixed-gender focus groups. Due to the need to be sensitive to gender issues, Peek carried out more than the recommended 'ideal number' of focus groups. Also, as Peek planned to conduct more in-depth interviews with the Muslim American students, she wanted to ensure that she would have the number of individual students with whom she could make contact later on. In their Hurricane Katrina research, Peek and Fothergill conducted seven focus groups: four with children, one with parents and two with teachers. In each focus group, new insights emerged. Hence, they felt that the additional groups were needed. More importantly, they felt that focus groups were important for the participants because the groups functioned as a means for them to connect with others and to see their situation in a larger framework. Thus, they would organise more focus groups if people indicated that they were interested in participating.

Saturation theory can be applied in most situations. Saturation occurs when additional information no longer generates new understanding (Liamputtong 2009; 2010b). At this point, it is time to wrap up the research (Morgan 1997; Kitzinger 2005). This may happen after only three sessions have been conducted with one group, or it may occur in the fifth or sixth session with another group. Morgan (1997: 43–44) argues that the number of focus group sessions needed for saturation to occur will depend on the variability of the research participants, both within and across groups. Within groups, research projects that comprise more heterogeneous participants will require more groups in total. This is because the diversity in the group makes it more difficult to identify 'coherent sets of opinions'. Across groups, 'projects that compare several distinct populations segments' will need more total groups in order to 'achieve saturation within each segment'.

Another rule of thumb is that a researcher should conduct as many sessions as is required to provide a reliable answer to the research question. However, one needs to take into account limitations of time, budget and personnel. Susan Dawson and colleagues (1993) warn us not to make the selection process too complicated. For example, in their research examining reasons for attending or not attending mammogram screening among Swedish women, Lagerlund and colleagues (2001) tell us that 321 letters were sent out but only 31 women agreed to take part in three focus groups. It is too easy to dive into great detail about group composition. In the end, one may not have enough time, resources or energy to complete all tasks. Lettenmaier and colleagues (1994: 96), for instance, provide an example from their study in Burkina Faso, in sub-Saharan Africa, where they over-recruited participants. The researchers point out that those extra focus group sessions were not necessary since they did not 'enrich the results, but merely prolonged the collection and analysis of the data'.

I argue that perhaps the best thing that focus group researchers should do is to adopt the theoretical sampling technique. This requires that the researchers continue to collect data until each theme or category developed from the data has reached saturation (see above) (Kitzinger 2005; Charmaz 2006; Liamputtong 2009; Skeat 2010). Most focus groups in the social sciences adopt this theory in determining the number of participants and groups (Kitzinger 2005). What is important is that the participants should be selected to reflect a range of the whole study population or to test particular theories. For example, if the research aims to examine individual's views on AIDS, the researchers would need to include people who have tested HIV positive and those who have tested HIV negative. Likewise, if the researchers wish to investigate the experience of prostate cancer, they might want to conduct focus groups with men at different stages of their treatment, and include a group of women whose partners have prostate cancer.

Following theoretical sampling theory, 'imaginative sampling is crucial' (Kitzinger 2005: 63). For example, in her research exploring the notion of 'habitus' theorised by Pierre Bourdieu (1977), Gill Callaghan (2005: 1) undertook three focus groups to resemble three different socioeconomic statuses as identified by cluster analysis of census data. She wanted to explore the impact of changes brought about by restructuring and globalisation on people's experiences, in work, their family life and their relation to their neighbourhoods and communities. Hence, in this research, three groups were selected from three different areas (affluent, intermediate and poor) to highlight differences which might appear in relation to class and to neighbourhood.

## HOW LONG SHOULD A FOCUS GROUP TAKE?

As a rule of thumb, a focus group should not last longer than two hours. Most focus groups are conducted within one and a half hours. However, depending on the participants, they can sometimes go on for three hours. Sometimes the participants find the discussion really interesting and have many views to contribute, and this makes the discussion difficult to stop. But this is rare. There are a number of reasons why a session should not take too long:

- The participants may find the discussion tiring. To concentrate on a particular issue for two hours is exhausting for anyone. If the session continues for too long, people's attention will drop and this will markedly change the dynamic of the group.
- Some participants may run out of ideas to contribute and hence find the discussion boring.
- The participants may have other important matters to attend to, such as childcare, cooking or returning to work.

It is important to have a balance between allowing enough time for a group to warm up and commencing the discussion about the issue (Conradson 2005). It is a good idea to have some tentative ideas about how long the focus group would last. The participants should also be informed about the timeframe before the group is started. However, the researchers must also leave some opportunities for an extended discussion if interesting issues emerge. Often, the precise duration of focus groups will depend on the flow of conversation and dynamic of the group. Less time may be needed if the examined issues have been effectively covered. Generally, it is of little value in continuing the group if the researchers sense that the discussion has reached saturation (the same perspectives begin to repeat themselves). In a situation like this, the focus group should be concluded. In other circumstances, however, the group may have a lot more to discuss; although the researchers may wish to stop at, say, 90 minutes, it may be more productive if the session lasts a bit longer, say two hours for example.

Sharon Vaughn and colleagues (1996) suggest that focus groups with children under 10 years of age should not last longer than 45 minutes, and for children between 10 and 14 years old, a group should be limited to one hour. Myfanwy Morgan and colleagues (2002) recommend that for children between 7 and 11 years of age, a focus group should be separated into two sessions of about 20 minutes by a break for refreshments – a good strategy to keep their interest in the discussion. But these timeframes should serve only as a guide. In practice, the researchers need to consider the dynamic of the group. They should be prepared to finish the group discussion early if children seem tired or bored, but may lengthen the session if children are eager to contribute and engage in the discussion (Hennessy & Heary 2005).

## WHAT DETERMINES SUCCESSFUL FOCUS GROUPS?

Successful focus groups occur when their use is consistent with the purposes and aims of the research (Stewart et al. 2007). There are at least four criteria by which success or good quality can be determined (Merton et al. 1990):

- *Specificity:* focus groups should provide information that is as specific to the participants' experiences and perspectives as possible.
- *Range:* successful focus groups should cover a maximum range of relevant issues, not only providing important issues relevant to the research questions, but also revealing some unexpected or unanticipated issues.
- *Depth:* focus groups should foster interaction, which enhances the exploration of the participants' perspectives in some depth.
- *Personal context:* focus groups need to take into account the personal context in the generation of participant responses. In other words, what is it about the person that makes them respond in a particular way? Thus, information gathered may make sense to the researcher in both the data collection and analysis processes.

Richard Krueger (1994) points out several factors that can be used to determine the quality of focus groups (see also Krueger & Casey 2009):

- *Clarity of purpose:* the purpose of focus groups must be clear and focus groups should not stretch beyond their limits.
- *Appropriate environment:* this includes both physical and sociopolitical environments.
- *A proper physical environment,* such as the location of focus groups, needs to be provided for maximum group interaction. In addition, they need to be organised to be free of intimidation and possible conflicts between the participants and the sponsors and/or the researcher.
- *Sufficient resources:* when resources such as time and budget are not realistic, this can affect the quality of focus groups. Remember that all research takes longer than originally planned, and focus groups are no exception. The researchers conducting focus groups may, however, need to be more cautious about this since working with groups is more complicated than working with an individual.
- *Appropriate participants:* it is essential to select the right people for focus group sessions. Participants therefore need to be carefully recruited to answer the research question.
- *Skilful moderator:* moderating a quality focus group interview requires group interaction skills. Without these skills, the quality of information collected can be affected greatly.
- *Effective questions:* quality focus groups depend on the questions asked. If there are too many questions, if they are not asked specifically, and if there is no follow-up for clarification, these factors can affect the quality of information gathered.

- *Honouring the participant:* the quality of focus groups can be affected when the participants are not respected or their needs are not taken seriously. If the participants can sense this, they will not willingly provide their experiences and perspectives. Hence, the information collected will be adversely affected.

## CONCLUSION

By the time you reach this conclusion, you may agree with Richard Krueger and Mary Anne Casey (2009: 2) who argue that 'a focus group isn't just getting a bunch of people together to talk. A focus group is a special type of group in terms of purpose, size, composition and procedures.' Often, people think that focus group research is a group interview, where people are brought in to speak about their needs and concerns. However, the focus group method entails many crucial principles which make it distinctive from a group interview. In this chapter, I have provided readers with the principles of the focus group method. In particular, I first introduce a focus group interaction which is the distinctive feature of the focus group method. Issues relevant to group composition have been discussed and these include: whether a group should be a homogeneous group or a heterogeneous group; whether the participants should have shared experiences; and whether a group is composed of familiar faces (pre-existing groups) or strangers (constructed groups). I have provided suggestions about the number of participants and groups which is needed in a focus group project. The question of how long a focus group should take has also been provided. Lastly, I pointed to factors which would determine successful focus groups. These principles are crucial when conducting focus group research as they can determine not only the quality of the data that you have collected, but also the success of your research project.

## TUTORIAL ACTIVITIES

1  You are a research assistant in a research project concerning gender issues and you have been asked to plan and undertake focus group research to explore how gender relations impact on the lived experience of women and men who are from younger and older generations and from different social–cultural backgrounds.

- What are the important issues that you need to consider in planning this project?
- How would you actually recruit your research participants and estimate the length of your project?

2  You are planning to carry out your focus group research on people's experiences of unemployment in your local area.

- How will you know if your focus group project will be successful or not? Discuss.

## FURTHER READING

Barbour, R. (2007). *Doing focus groups.* London: Sage.

Barbour, R., & Kitzinger, J. (eds.) (1999). *Developing focus group research: Politics, research and practice.* London: Sage.

Bloor, M., Frankland, J., Thomas, M., & Robson, K. (2001). *Focus groups in social research.* London: Sage.

Krueger, R.A., & Casey, M.A. (2009). *Focus groups: A practical guide for applied research*, 3rd edition. Thousand Oaks, CA: Sage.

Leask, J., Hawe, P., & Chapman, S. (2001). Focus group composition: A comparison between natural and constructed groups. *Australian and New Zealand Journal of Public Health* 25(2), 152–154.

Morgan, D.L. (1997). *Focus groups as qualitative research*, 2nd edition. Newbury Park, CA: Sage.

Peek, L., & Fothergill, A. (2009). Using focus groups: Lessons from studying daycare centers, 9/11, and Hurricane Katrina. *Qualitative Research* 9(1), 31–59.

Stewart, D.W., Shamdasani, P.N., & Rook, D.W. (2007). *Focus groups: Theory and practice*, 2nd edition. Thousand Oaks, CA: Sage.

Toner, J. (2009). Small is not too small: Reflections concerning the validity of very small focus groups (VSFGs). *Qualitative Social Work* 8(2), 179–192.

# 4

# FOCUS GROUP METHODOLOGY AND PRACTICAL CONSIDERATIONS

## CHAPTER OBJECTIVES

In this chapter you will learn about:

- Recruitment and gaining access to research participants
- Compensation or incentives
- Location, venue and timing
- Essential research staff
- Use of stimulus materials and activities in focus groups
- Humour in focus group research

This chapter will focus on practical issues relating to the conduct of focus group research. There are several considerations that researchers should take into account if a more successful focus group project is to be achieved. Salient practical considerations that I will discuss in the chapter include: how to recruit and gain access to potential participants; whether the participants should be provided with compensation or incentives; the importance of focus group location and timing; and who should be involved in focus group research. I also provide suggestions on the use of stimulus materials and activities and humour in focus group research. These two aspects have not been given much attention in focus group texts, but they have become more important for many focus group research.

## RECRUITMENT AND GAINING ACCESS

In focus group research, as in other qualitative methods, a purposive sampling method is normally adopted. Put simply, the participants need to be selected to suit the investigated issue. They are chosen because the researchers believe they will provide the best information. Focus group researchers Jeffery Borkan and colleagues (1995: 978) argue that the purposive sampling method 'adds power' to focus group research because it 'selects "information-rich cases" which can best generate the desired data' (see also Patton 2002).

A random sampling method is seldom used in focus group research (Morgan 1997). Random sampling can, in fact, be a real disadvantage in focus groups (Dawson et al. 1993). For example, if a researcher wants to find out why women do not breastfeed, it would be more appropriate to recruit women who have young infants and children than their family members. Similarly, if the issue of concern is the lived experience of homelessness, it would be more useful to recruit women and men who have been homeless. There are two reasons to explain why random sampling is rarely used in focus groups. First, a small sample is not adequate to represent the whole population. And, more importantly, a random sample cannot guarantee that a shared perspective on the issue of investigation will occur, and hence the participants may not interact well to generate meaningful discussions (Morgan 1997; see also Chapter 3 in this volume).

There are multiple ways that researchers can follow to access their potential research participants. Without proper consideration, gaining access can be problematic. The snowball sampling method has been extensively adopted in focus group research, particularly when it is related to vulnerable or marginalised participants who often are difficult to reach (Bernard 2006; Liamputtong 2007; 2010a). Esther Madriz (1998) and Adriana Umaña-Taylor and Mayra Bámaca (2004: 267) refer to this approach as the 'word-of-mouth' technique in their study with Latinos in the United States. They assert that this approach is extremely useful in research with ethnic minorities, as the potential participants are more likely to take part if someone they know is also participating.

In Lori Peek's focus group study of Muslim Americans after September 11 (Peek & Fothergill 2009), she communicated with her first contact soon after the attacks, a university student in New York City who was willing to gather other members of his university's Muslim Student Association (MSA) so that Peek could 'talk to a bunch of people all at once'. Soon afterwards, Peek was able to establish contacts via telephone and email with a number of student leaders at MSAs. Peek worked with these contacts to organise the focus group interviews in her research. These students would post fliers which Peek created for them to advertise the focus groups and also send email messages to their group lists, soliciting members to participate. But most importantly, the students often convinced their friends and fellow MSA members to participate in Peek's focus group sessions. In order to persuade others to participate, they would say things like: 'Come on, she came all the way from Colorado just to interview us!' Peek and Fothergill (2009) contend that the support from these contacts was essential for Peek because she lived far from her research site and had no previous relationships with the students before the commencement of her research. More importantly, it was crucial because she was an outsider to the Muslim community.

Some focus group researchers have used a personal touch or network as a means to recruit potential participants who are difficult to access and who do not trust researchers who are strangers to them (Madriz 2003; Liamputtong 2010a). Esther

Madriz (2003: 377–378), in her research with low-socioeconomic Latina and African American women on fear of crime, made use of personal networks in recruiting the women. As a Latina researcher, Madriz thinks that impersonal recruiting strategies, which often are preferred by positivistic researchers, would not work with lower-socioeconomic-status women of colour, particularly with undocumented women. Madriz employed her personal networks such as friends, community leaders, students and friends of friends who worked in non-profit community organisations to assist her with the recruitment. For some potential recruiters whom she did not know personally, she asked her friends and students to help make the contact. She says that her personal networks would often inform the potential recruiters that she was a professor who was doing her research on social justice and social change. Madriz (2003: 378) tells us that: 'This personalistic approach was extremely useful given the reluctance many people of color, and particularly undocumented women, feel about participating in research.' Similarly, Robin Jarrett (1993) argues that impersonal recruiting strategies are not suitable for research with low-income minority popula-tions. In her study of low-income African American women, in order to gain their participation she travelled to many Head Start programmes in poor neighbourhoods throughout Chicago and spoke to women directly about her study. This strategy has been adopted frequently in research concerning sensitive topics and with marginalised participants.

Advertising can be used to recruit participants. This can be done by placing an advertisement in specific areas (such as shopping malls, hair studios, health centres and hospitals), or through specific means (such as radio, bulletin boards, the Internet, ethnic newspapers). In their focus group research concerning oral health and disable-ment in Canada, Mario Brondani and colleagues (2008) conducted six focus groups with 42 older men and women who were purposefully selected through advertise-ments posted in community centres and retirement homes. The recruitment for Talya Salant and Sarah Gehlert's research on breast cancer risk in Chicago (2008) was car-ried out through advertisements in local newspapers, and posters and fliers which were distributed within neighbourhoods, for example at bus stops, on streets and in parking areas. In Alice Fothergill's daycare study in Ohio (Peek & Fothergill 2009), she recruited the parents by putting fliers in the children's mailboxes. These are the places where parents would normally pick up classroom reports, their children's art-work, and any other school matters such as reminders for cake stalls.

Most human ethics committees (see also Chapter 2) prefer advertising for people to volunteer as it is less likely that potential participants will be coerced to participate (Padgett 2008). However, some groups of participants, such as those from ethnic minorities or indigenous people, will not respond to advertised recruitment (Liamputtong 2007; 2010a). Advertising may only reach certain groups of potential participants. For example, placing an advertisement in local health centres will be unlikely to reach those who do not attend these centres.

Very often, researchers gain access to their potential participants through rela-tionships with stakeholders and community organisations. Stakeholders may include formal and informal group leaders, service providers, business people and residents who have an interest in the particular community. These stakeholders help research-ers to develop important links with the community and to identify and respond to important issues and situations within the community. To recruit women to participate in their focus group research in the United Arab Emirates, Wendy Winslow and colleagues (2002) approached the Abu Dhabi Women's Association, an organisation that provides the education and domestic skills to care for a family to Emirati women who left school early. The Association was a place where these women congregated for their educational and social activities. It was an ideal place for focus groups, as it reduced problems with transportation for the participating women. In their research on perceptions of African American men's health, Joseph Ravenell and colleagues' (2006) recruitments were assisted by community organisations, including an HIV halfway house, youth organizations, men's shelters and churches. In Peter Hopkins' research with young Muslim men (2007), gaining access to all of the 11 focus groups he conducted was done through several adult gatekeepers including a teacher, youth worker, office worker and religious leader. Adriana Umaña-Taylor and Mayra Bámaca (2004) emphasise the importance of working with local community organisations. In their research, they even made use of a somewhat unusual strategy by visiting consulates to recruit Latino women from Colombia, Guatemala, Mexico and Puerto Rico living in the Unites States. When they visited the Guatemalan and Colombian Consulates, they were informed about Guatemalan and Colombian picnics and evening cultural events. They attended those functions and were subsequently able to recruit some participants from both cultural groups.

Community leaders or stakeholders can play a 'gatekeeping role' in focus group research (Willis et al. 2009: 133). They can help the researchers to organise a meeting so that the nature of the research and its potential value can be explained to the group. This will also allow the researchers to develop a rapport with group members. Community leaders or stakeholders provide many advantages for focus group researchers. For example, the researchers may learn about tensions and dynamics within a community and some unforeseen circumstances which may require rescheduling of a focus group session. Community leaders and stakeholders can provide assistance with logistical matters such as potential focus group venues and finding childcare staff or interpreters who are acceptable to community members. In some circumstances, it is important that the location of the venue needs to be properly organised so that 'inadvertent disclosure' of the participation can be avoided and confidentiality of the participants outside the focus group setting can be protected (Willis et al. 2009: 133). Interestingly too, Inger Jonsson and colleagues (2002), in their research examining the experiences and perceptions of food of Somalian women living in Sweden, not only worked with gatekeepers to help with their recruitment, but also had them as their focus group participants.

Potential focus group participants can also be recruited through opportunistic sampling strategies. An opportunistic sampling strategy occurs when there is an opportunity to sample during the course of data collection (Patton 2002; Carpenter & Suto 2008). Opportunistic sampling is also known as emergent sampling (Liamputtong 2009). In carrying out research, new opportunities may present themselves and the researchers need to make on-the-spot decisions to include them in the research. This sampling technique 'takes advantage of whatever unfolds as it unfolds' (Patton 2002: 240).

This strategy is what Lori Peek and Alice Fothergill (2009: 36) call 'spontaneous recruitment'. This type of recruitment is somewhat unplanned. The focus groups occur naturally because a number of individuals volunteer to take part. It is more likely to happen in locations where people move in and out of public spaces where the focus group interviews are being conducted. In their focus group, undertaken at the Baton Rouge Baptist Church evacuee shelter, it commenced with three women. In the middle of the focus group session, a fourth woman walked past, and the initial three women persuaded her to join in, saying: 'Come join us, we're talking about our kids!' The woman did participate in that focus group. Additionally, when the researchers were visiting one family at their home, the mother suggested that her children and neighbour's children could meet with them as a group (without parents) to speak about their experiences and the impact of Hurricane Katrina.

More often, researchers employ a combination of methods in gaining access to research participants. Andrea Shelton and Nahid Rianon (2004) provide an interesting recruitment strategy in their focus group research on spousal abuse among Bangladeshi immigrants living in Houston. Shelton and Rianon conducted three stages of preparation, contacting and following up in their attempt to recruit Bangladeshi women to take part in their study. Shelton and Rianon contend that a moderation of the recruitment strategies suggested by MacDougall and Fudge (2001) offer useful means for 'the recognition of cultural diversity, intercultural differences, and social differentiation with the Bangladeshi community'. Initially, the researchers were not able to obtain any participation from the women despite attempts that were made to meet their needs and despite the fact that Rianon is a Bangladeshi woman who speaks the same language and shares the cultural background of the women. But through the outreach efforts of the first two stages, they decided that recruitment had to be done at a large social gathering where the whole family would attend. They suggested that the interviews conducted in this setting were about immigrant experiences, the quality of life, physical and mental distress, and suffering. After these, information about spousal abuse might be volunteered. Most women suggested that:

> there would be less attention given to them individually and that they would feel less intimidated at a social outing with their husbands and peers in the midst of a large group of people engaged in the same activities (eating, watching a band, listing to music).

In the end, 29 women were recruited during three cultural events held in January and February 2000 with the approval of the Bangladeshi Association. More women were invited to take part in the study, but most declined as their husbands did not approve. It took Shelton and Rianon a year of repeated efforts to engage the women in their research.

Essentially, it must be noted that gaining access to a community and recruiting participants does not guarantee that they will attend focus group sessions. There are other circumstances that may prevent attendance, for example emergencies, illness (their own or that of family members), or transport problems. The researchers need to prepare for such an eventuality before the focus group sessions begin. The best way is to over-recruit slightly for each session. Inviting two more participants is better than having to cancel the session because there are not enough participants (Umaña-Taylor & Bámaca 2004; Hennink 2007; Colucci 2008; see also Chapter 3 in this volume).

The key to successful recruiting is to understand the working and living patterns of the participants. It may be necessary to make attendance at sessions easier and, perhaps, to provide incentives (see the later section on this). For example, doctors may be more easily recruited if the focus groups are conducted in a hospital where they usually spend their working time; mothers with young infants may be more likely to attend if the session is organised in a maternal and child health centre where they normally take their infants for a routine check-up; and poor people in a slum may turn up if the session is set in close proximity to their area and a meal is provided. Focus group researchers David Stewart and colleagues (2007: 59) argue that this understanding is essential in the planning of focus groups, since 'it provides a basis for developing a recruitment plan that includes a location that optimizes participation, the identification of ways to eliminate barriers, and provides incentives for participation in a focus group'.

Although gaining access to certain groups of people may pose some difficulties, with careful preparation and sensitivity it is possible to do so. Robin Jarrett (1993) provides an example from her focus group research with low-income minority women in the United States. Jarrett made a special attempt to recruit this hard-to-reach group through personal means, by visiting them before the interviews and spending time with them in order to establish a relationship with them. She made it clear to them that she 'was genuinely interested in hearing about their lives on their own terms … Unlike the usual helping professionals who entered their lives, [she] was there to listen, not to advise' (p. 199). Accordingly, she successfully conducted 10 focus groups with 82 low-income African American women to discuss their contemporary patterns of family life in the United States.

## COMPENSATION AND INCENTIVES

In focus groups in marketing research, participants are paid for their time and participation. In health and social research, however, compensation or payment for participating in a research project is a controversial issue. Some researchers argue that payment is necessary if the researcher needs to recruit those who are hard to find because of their busy schedules, such as high-level administrators, medical practitioners and some bureaucrats (Morgan 1997; Krueger & Casey 2009). Such participants are paid in the range of $100 to over $500 per session in compensation for their time (Krueger & Casey 2009).

Some researchers argue that payment in research is not appropriate. Payment can also be seen as 'coercion' if researchers work with extremely poor people, the homeless, or drug users who need money to buy drugs (Holloway & Jefferson 2000). Nancy Crigger and others (2001) point out that potential participants from poor countries are indeed vulnerable to coercion. The income level (if there is any) is very low compared with Western standards: US$10 may be equivalent to a week's income for a worker in Jamaica or Indonesia. Hence, these vulnerable poor people may try to be included in research and this is seen as coercion (forcing potential participants to take part in research for money). But other researchers argue that payment should be made to poor people who may need the money for their survival (Liamputtong 2007). Researchers need to 'value the contribution, knowledge and skills' of the participants and payments should be provided to them, particularly if they have no or little money (Umaña-Taylor & Bámaca 2004).

However, compensation for the time that the participants give the researchers is crucial (Krueger & Casey 2009). Compensation is essential because of the efforts that the participants have to make in their participation in focus groups. Unlike in other types of qualitative methods, focus group participants are required to travel to a venue and this incurs financial and other expenses such as transportation costs, child-care or taking time off from work or family matters (Krueger & Casey 2009). For Wendy Holloway and Tony Jefferson (2000: 84), payments for participants' time should be seen as 'equalising the relationship (our money for their time) or as having the material power that the financial relation afforded us'. In Jude Robinson's focus groups with poor women regarding smoking at home in England (2009), she offered a payment of £25 plus £10 babysitting money to each of the women as a means of acknowledging the time they had to give up to participate in her research.

I argue that compensation is also a symbol of the researchers' respect for the participation of these people. This stance is applicable to researching marginalised and vulnerable people, as most of these groups, such as ethnic women, homeless persons and the mentally ill, tend to be poor and money may assist them with their daily living. Some feminist researchers have also argued that money given to research participants should be perceived as compensation for being research partners in the research project (Landrine et al. 1995; Paradis 2000).

Incentives or compensation may not need to be in cash. Adriana Umaña-Taylor and Mayra Bámaca (2004) suggest that if personal information is needed for compensation, researchers may provide other means of incentives such as gift vouchers. They supplied their participants with $20 gift vouchers from a local general store. In Andrea Shelton and Nahid Rianon's study about spousal abuse within the Bangladeshi community in Houston (2004), the participants were given a gift bag that included sample products and coupon vouchers donated by local shops. In their study, Deborah Bender and colleagues (2001) gave a gender- and language-neutral baby toy to Latina immigrant women as a way of thanking them for their participation. Richard Krueger and Mary Anne Casey (2009: 80) provide some examples of effective focus group incentives including a 50 pound (23 kg) bag of rice for Southeast Asian Americans in a cancer research project, a manicure during the focus group for female sex workers in New Orleans, and a bucket of fried chicken to take home for the families of low-income parents.

Incentives can include free products (for example, condoms or other contraceptives), free transport and free accommodation (Stewart et al. 2007; Krueger & Casey 2009). For some people, the focus group itself is an incentive since it offers some enjoyment in talking with others and the chance to talk about something that they may not have the opportunity to discuss outside the focus group. Many people too feel honoured when they are invited to take part in focus groups in research projects as they believe that their views will be valued (Krueger & Casey 2009). In my focus groups discussing communicable diseases with elderly Chinese in Beijing, the participants were given a pen as a gift. Although the incentive was minimal, the elderly people said that they enjoyed meeting others and felt good about having a chance to discuss health issues, which they did not have in their local areas.

It is also recommended that snacks or light refreshments be provided at the end of a session, regardless of the form of incentive to be employed. People tend to feel more relaxed if they have the chance to eat and drink together, and this may also allow the researcher an opportunity to clarify some issues in further discussions (Umaña-Taylor & Bámaca 2004).

In online focus groups, payment or incentives may be done differently. Ted Gaiser (2008: 304) provides an interesting suggestion. Because the participants are drawn from physically diverse locations and may involve international settings, there may be some constraints with the provision of payments or other compensation to online participants. It has become a popular trend among virtual focus group researchers to offer potential participants a chance to receive compensation which tends to be larger than what is typically adopted. For instance, rather than offering a $50 incentive, the researchers might arrange an opportunity for anyone who participates to win an iPod or a $250 gift certificate. Gaiser contends that the participants will have more incentive to take part in the project and the researchers themselves will be 'freed of the administrative burden of making a number of small payments to a large number of participants'.

Nevertheless, as researchers, we need to be sensitive to the sacrifice that participants make for our research. The incentives they receive mean little compared with the effort they have to make to meet our requirements (Stewart et al. 2007). This has to be remembered when planning focus groups. Stewart and others (2007: 60) put it bluntly: 'Researcher arrogance may be the single most important factor in the failure of a focus group: participants are doing the researcher, and his or her sponsors, a favor, regardless of the compensation and other incentives provided.'

## FOCUS GROUP LOCATION, VENUE AND TIMING

Consideration of the location and venue of a focus group is a crucial aspect in the planning of focus group research. A productive group discussion is enhanced by both the physical location and the internal environment of the venue. Essentially, the group location and venue should 'set a positive tone for the group discussion, and provide a comfortable, relaxed and informal environment which is conducive to a productive discussion' (Hennink 2007: 152). An ideal location for a focus group should be a neutral venue which is private, quite, comfortable, spacious and free from distractions (Halcomb et al. 2007; Hennink 2007). But this ideal location and venue may not be realistic in some research contexts, such as focus groups conducted in resource-poor countries, which often are held in outdoor locations (see also Chapter 8 in this volume). And in some cases, focus groups may be carried out in a moving vehicle (see Propst et al. 2008 for example).

Successful focus groups can be held in various locations and venues. It is possible to conduct focus groups successfully in locations and venues such as cafés, shopping malls, parks, student bars, home living rooms, hotel rooms, classrooms, school halls and workplaces (Conradson 2005). Of course, permission will be needed for some of these venues. Depending on the context of the research, the venue used for focus group discussions may vary. For focus group research carried out in cross-cultural settings, focus groups are often conducted in a range of community venues, for example school rooms, church buildings, community health centres or meeting rooms. Group discussions may be held in private venues such as the home of a community leader or a participant (Hennink 2007). Often, too, focus groups are conducted outdoors (see also Chapter 8 in this volume). It is important that a venue which is regularly used by the participants should be considered, as it provides them with a familiar and comfortable discussion environment. For example, focus groups with school children should be carried out at the school, or group discussions with new mothers in an antenatal care setting.

However, in preparing the locations and venues, it is important to ensure that there is nothing obvious about it which will prohibit discussion (Conradson 2005). Also, some compromises may have to be made when selecting a suitable location for a particular project, especially when group discussions are being carried out in outdoor locations (Hennink 2007). Very often, the choice of locations and venues is restricted by the availability or cost of appropriate venues. An important issue that researchers must consider is whether and how these compromises may have an impact on the group discussion and the quality of the data which will be generated (Barbour 2007; Hennink 2007). As focus group researchers Michael Bloor and colleagues (2001) point out, there is no such thing as a neutral and universal setting which will be suitable and acceptable to the participants and other people involved. Hence, in order to maximise participation, focus group researchers should be flexible with the locations and venues of their focus groups.

I should like to point out here one interesting debate about the location and venue of focus group research. Alan Jones and colleague (2000) reported in the *British Medical Journal* that focus groups discussing guided self-management plans for asthma were conducted at a number of convenient locations, including schools, surgeries, the local community hospital and pubs in the UK. Their paper brought about some debate in the letters pages of the same journal in the following year. In particular, Jennifer Cleland and Mandy Moffat (2001: 1122) criticised the research venue, saying that 'holding group discussions on guided self management plans for asthma with asthma patients, nurses, or doctors in a public house seems dubious'. Michael Bloor and colleagues (2001: 38–39) contend that holding a focus group with participants who have alcohol problems in a pub might be inappropriate. However, for focus group research which makes use of a creative range of locations, the participants would have been offered some choice over the location and venue.

It is essential to ensure that the size of the room is appropriate for the number of participants in the focus group. A big room does not provide an intimate discussion environment, which can hamper the quality of discussion. And if the room is too small, it can create a confined environment and lead to uncomfortable feelings. This makes the participants want to finish off quickly (Hennink 2007). The room should also have appropriate conditions to allow productive discussion in the group. If a room is noisy, too hot or cold, or has many distractions, it can create an uncomfortable environment and lead to stress among the participants (Fern 2001). All these conditions may make the participants less motivated towards the group discussion, less able to remember, and less tolerant of the opinions of other members in the group (Hennink 2007).

Some researchers have also suggested that a focus group should ideally be organised in a neutral location with which the participants do not have any link (Hennink 2007). For example, despite how they actually feel, a focus group discussing the quality of health services which is conducted at a health centre may make the participants reluctant to speak about negative aspects of or their dissatisfaction with that particular health service. The quality of the group discussion, and hence data that is generated, will be affected by this condition (Hennink 2007). In order to allow the participants to express their true opinions, researchers must take great care to ensure that the group is located in a venue with as few associations as possible so that the quality of the data collected can be improved (Hennink 2007).

One practical aspect of the location and venue of a focus group that the researchers must seriously consider too is accessibility to the participants. As the participants are usually required to travel to a central venue, the researchers need to plan this carefully in order to enhance their participation. Physically, the location and venue should be easy to find and travel time should be minimal (Hennink 2007). There should also be compensation for travel, for example parking fees or tickets for public transportation. It is likely that in focus groups conducted in rural villages or in densely populated urban settlements, the participants will walk to the venue. Hence, the location of the focus groups should be in close proximity to their homes. The focus groups need to be organised at a time of day when it is safe for them to walk outside. And if the groups are held in the evening, the venue must be in a safe and well-lit neighbourhood. Usually, transport to and from the venue should be provided for the participants. Characteristically and socially, if the participants are older persons, distance to the venue and any physical layout which may prevent access to the room must be seriously considered. Similarly, if the participants are children or are from some sociocultural groups, it is crucial to provide transportation and accompaniment by a familiar person to the focus group venue (Hennink 2007).

Apart from the broader geographical setting of the focus group discussion, the particular timing of focus groups in terms of local, national and global events and circumstances is also an important issue that researchers must take into consideration (Hopkins 2007). It can, and often does, have a marked effect on the interaction and discussion of focus groups. In particular, the range and intensity of discussions is influenced by the particular timing of focus groups. This may simply be the time of day or week when a focus group is carried out. But more importantly, it is the timing that links with particular geopolitical events or other circumstances (Hopkins 2007). In Peter Hopkins' research with young Muslim men in Scotland, all focus groups were carried out in the period following the events of 11 September 2001 in New York. During his research with these men, British and American troops waged the first attacks in Iraq on the evening of 19 March 2003 and this continued for some time. The final focus group discussion of his research was held the day before the Scottish Parliamentary elections on 1 May 2003, when many Muslims planned to vote tactically so that the repeated success of the Labour Party which had sanctioned the UK's participation in the war could be prevented. Hopkins contends that this geopolitical timing had huge influences on the nature and intensity of the discussion in his focus groups.

## ESSENTIAL RESEARCH STAFF

Regarding the research team, there are at least two members who are crucial for the running of a focus group: the moderator and the note-taker.

### The Moderator

One of the key players in a focus group, who has a significant influence on the collection of rich and valid information, is the moderator (sometimes called a facilitator). Often, in market research, moderators are specifically employed and trained to facilitate focus groups, but in the health and social sciences, the researchers tend to moderate the group themselves (Smithson 2008).

The task of the moderator is to stimulate the participants to engage actively in the discussion of the topic. The moderator also needs to be flexible enough to manage the group to proceed in the direction that the focus group should take. Hence, the main task of the moderator is not only as a leader but also as a navigator. I think the description that Bob Gates and Mary Waight (2007: 113) have provided sums up nicely the role of the moderator: 'To use an analogy of exploration, the facilitator is not so much the expedition leader; rather, a combination of navigator and cartographer, ensuring that the group heads in the right direction but happy to investigate new paths if relevant to the purpose of the expedition.'

Moderating a focus group discussion is a demanding task. Anyone can be a moderator, but not everyone can be a good one. It is argued that inexperienced moderators may have an impact on the quality of data collected. Moderators have a great impact on the flow of the discussion. This, in turn, influences the dynamic of the group (Hesse-Biber & Leavy 2010). Particular aspects which the moderators are expected to deal with include making sure that all participants are included in the discussion, dealing with disagreement and conflicts in the groups, noticing when the participants are uneasy with a discussion and ensuring that this is dealt with appropriately, and making sure that crucial issues are covered in the available time (Smithson 2008). But more importantly, moderators must attempt to ensure that discussion occurs between participants instead of between them and the moderator.

There are a number of characteristics of a good moderator. A good moderator needs to:

- be sensitive to the needs of the participants;
- be non-judgemental about the responses from the participants;
- respect the participants;
- be open-minded;
- have adequate knowledge about the project;

- have good listening skills;
- have good leadership skills;
- have good observation skills;
- have patience and flexibility.

Here, I would like to raise several salient issues regarding moderators and their role in focus group research. Ideally and in theory, a moderator should be 'a neutral person' who is able to stimulate the discussion and elicit the responses and stories of the participants (Smithson 2008: 362). In practice, however, a moderator cannot be a neutral spectator. Rather, moderators should be reflexive and aware of the way their social positions and behaviour can impact on the interaction of the group (see Wilkinson & Kitzinger 1996; Stokoe & Smithson 2002). It is also possible for moderators to use their own experience as a means to encourage discussion in the group. For instance, a moderator who has experienced unemployment may refer to this experience to commence the group discussion or to stimulate the participants to discuss issues relating to unemployment. This is what has been referred to as self-disclosure (Liamputtong 2007). According to feminist researchers Shulamit Reinharz and Susan Chase (2002: 227), researchers' self-disclosure occurs when the researcher 'shares ideas, attitudes, and/or experiences concerning matters that might relate to the interview topic in order to encourage respondents to be more forthcoming'. Although it is seen as 'contamination' in conventional research (Dunbar et al. 2002: 286), it encourages the participants to elaborate on their subjective experiences. Researchers need to be more open to their participants; that is, they need to be willing to share their experiences with the participants. In undertaking a study of sexual abuse or domestic violence, for example, the researchers might disclose their own experiences of having been sexually or physically abused. This self-disclosure may put the participants at ease, and hence help them to be more articulate with their stories.

As in other qualitative research methods, the positioning of the focus group moderator contributes greatly to the dynamic of the group and the data generated (Allen 2005; Barbour 2007; Smithson 2008). This positionality includes gender, class, ethnicity, age and other socially constructed identities (Manderson et al. 2006; Liamputtong 2007; 2010a). Gender differences between the researcher and the researched play an important role in conducting research (Järviluoma et al. 2003; Allen 2005). The gender of the researchers may influence the perceptions of the participants and how they place the researchers in the research process (Pini 2002; Allen 2005). For example, female researchers are likely to generate lively discussion about sexual conduct among female participants than among male respondents and vice versa. There are other social structures that have an impact on the research process. For instance, despite gender similarity, barriers to understanding in the research process can be created because of social class differences between the researcher and the participants (Madriz 1998; 2003). In her focus group research with Latino women in New York, Esther Madriz (1998) was extremely cautious about the class differences between herself as a researcher and the women of low status. Due to her middle-class background and her position as a professor in a university, she stood in stark contrast to the women who worked mainly as cleaners, street vendors and nannies. Most of the women were just stay-at-home mothers. However, Madriz (1998) tried to reduce this difference by carefully dressing in the manner of most Latino women who are cautious about the way they dress. She also referred to the women and herself by first names and used informal Spanish pronouns. And by sharing the language with the women, the gap between herself and the women was markedly minimised.

Another salient aspect relevant to the role of a moderator is the issue of control (Munday 2006). One of the main limitations of the focus group method is that the moderator may lose control of the group (Bryman 2008). There are various suggestions about how a moderator can regain control of a group if it becomes problematic. The moderators do have some degree of control over the groups (Munday 2006). For example, the moderators can select which issues to cover and which questions to ask. They will make sure that all participants have an opportunity to speak and be ready to intervene if the discussion goes off track. However, focus groups do not need to be run in such a controlling way. As I have suggested in Chapter 2, the methodology offers a non-hierarchical way of doing research (see also Wilkinson 1999; 2004). Very often, in Jannie Munday's research (2006), the participants themselves took control of the research process and yet the group did not 'descend into chaos'. In fact, she admitted that there were times when she felt that the group needed to be redirected back to the topic, and she exerted too much control over the group by intervening too quickly. Munday regretted this as the participants should have been given more control of the discussion so that they could explore the issue as they liked. This could have brought out some issues that had not previously emerged.

The reduction in the control or influence of moderators in focus groups should be seen as an advantage rather than a limitation (Wilkinson 2004). David Morgan (1988) too suggests that an interaction among the participants themselves replaces their interaction with the moderators. This leads to more focus on their own perspectives. The following example is taken from the study of Hannah Frith regarding the refusal of sexual relations among young women (1997, cited in Wilkinson 2004: 282). The interchanges among three participants shift the control of the moderator to greater dialogues among the women when they were instigated with examples of excuses they might use to avoid sex:

| | |
|---|---|
| Cath: | Do you mean like really naff excuses? |
| Researcher: | Well, anything that you would use. |
| Lara: | But I mean … |
| Cath: | But it depends how far you've got because that can go completely. |
| Helen: | No, but … no, but that just gives you a few days respite doesn't it? – And then I think that after a few days you'd just feel so shitty that you had to rely on that. |
| Lara: | That's horrible, why should you have to lie on an issue that is just perfectly right and you feel strongly about, why do you have to come up with excuses? |
| Cath: | That's right. |

| Lara: | I mean, I would much rather, it would be so nice just to be able to say no, for no particular reason. I don't really know, I haven't felt the need to think about it, I just don't particularly fancy it. |
| Helen: | I just don't feel like it at the moment. |
| Lara: | Wouldn't that be nice! |

This example shows the shift in thinking about the fact that women need to find excuses in avoiding sex, and this notion only comes from taking control of their expressions from the moderator in the focus group. Because the balance of power and control in focus groups is shifted towards the participants, it allows them to voice their own agendas and explore their own interpretations (Wilkinson 2004). For the moderators, the reduction in their power permits them to consider the views and concerns of the participants more. As a result, they are able to elicit better understanding about the issues under investigation and the people involved. See also Chapter 5 in this volume regarding direction provided by a moderator in focus groups.

## The Note-taker and Assistant Moderator

A note-taker is also essential in focus group interviews. The moderator is not able to take notes because of the demanding nature of the task of running focus group sessions. The note-taker records the key issues emerging in the session and other factors that may be important in the analysis and interpretation of the results. Also, if there are group activities or movements during the session (see a later section), a tape-recording cannot capture all the information, and hence needs to be supplemented by extensive field notes and memos (Willis et al. 2009).

The note-taker will assist the moderator by checking if any key issues have been overlooked (Hennink 2007). A note can be passed to the moderator before the end of the session. More commonly, however, towards the end of the interview, the moderator will ask the note-taker if there are any issues which have not been discussed or if there are any extra questions to be discussed. The most successful focus group team is when the moderator works closely with the note-taker. The moderator can focus on conducting the discussion whereas the note-taker takes extensive notes on the discussion content and handles any interruptions that may occur (Hennink 2007).

Usually, the note-taker would sit outside the discussion circle to take notes unobtrusively. Note-takers do not participate in the group discussion and ideally should not make any eye contact with the participants in order not to disturb the dynamics of the group. Sitting outside the discussion circle allows the note-taker to deal with any disturbances and latecomers and to control the condition of the room, such as lighting, heating and cooling. The note-taker also operates the tape-recorder and changes the cassettes in order to allow the moderator to continue the discussion without any interruption (Hennink 2007).

Practically, the note-taker is essential when participants or the group do not consent to the recording of their discussion. This often occurs in focus group research involving some ethnic minorities or in a cross-cultural context (Makhoul & Nakkash 2007; Liamputtong 2009; 2010a). The notes taken by the note-taker will be the only data that the moderator could generate from such groups. In the focus group research with South Asian immigrant women in Toronto that was carried out by Farah Ahmad and colleagues to examine experiences of partner abuse (2009), for example, the women in one of the focus groups did not consent to have their discussions audiotaped. Hence, extensive notes were taken by a bicultural note-taker during the session. Jihad Makhoul and Rima Nakkash (2007) also came across this problem in their research regarding young people and health issues in Beirut. In addition, in some situations the recording equipment may not work, or the recording has a poor quality, such as inaudible or lost sections. Hence, it is recommended that in all focus groups, the note-taker should always be present (Hennink 2007).

Often, too, some focus group projects would have another helper in the running of the focus groups. This helper can assist in many practical ways in order to allow the moderator and the note-taker to concentrate on their tasks. Sometimes this person is referred to as 'an assistant moderator' (Napolitano et al. 2002; Barbour 2007; Krueger & Casey 2009). In their research with migrant farmworkers in Oregon, Marie Napolitano and colleagues (2002: 181) contend that:

> The role of an assistant moderator behind the scene was to take notes regarding moderator and participants' behavior, listen for dropped points to be revisited, and to clarify and expand any information provided. This person proved to be valuable in pulling together the loose pieces of information obtained during the session and asking any questions that may have been lost.

## USE OF STIMULUS MATERIALS AND ACTIVITIES IN FOCUS GROUPS

Increasingly, focus group researchers have incorporated some stimulus materials and activities as part of their group discussion. These stimulus materials and activities may include cartoons, prompts, games, exercises and vignettes (Punch 2002; Kitzinger 2005; Barbour 2007; Bailey 2008). Stimulus materials and activities can be used as both a 'common external reference point' and a 'party game' to 'warm up' the participants (Kitzinger 1994a: 107; Hesse-Biber & Patricia Leavy 2010). They also allow the participants to feel more relaxed and comfortable in the group. The stimulus materials can also simply be a flip chart and pens, some newspapers headlines, or taking along an object. Kitzinger (2005: 64) tells us that Lai-fong Chiu and Deborah Knight, for example, brought a speculum along to their focus groups regarding cervical smears. They invited the women to pass it around and comment on it. In another focus group, a breast prosthesis was passed around the group. This too generated fascinating information from the women. Michele Crossley (2002) brought health promotion leaflets to her focus groups in order to explore resistance to professional advice.

Stimulus materials taken from published sources such as cartoons, newspaper headlines or clippings and sections from books work well in focus group discussions.

Gerald Zaltman (2003) develops an elicitation technique which encourages the participants to pinpoint pictures in magazines which would represent their opinions and feelings. Additional questions are then asked in order to uncover reasons for particular responses to their picture identification tasks. Cartoons are effective stimulus materials, Rosaline Barbour (2007: 84) points out, because 'they often tap into and express succinctly in an amusing way, difficult and keenly felt dilemmas, but take the sting out of thinking about these'. Hence, cartoons 'simultaneously break the ice and give permission to raise difficult issues' among the participants in focus groups. Raymond Macdonald and Graeme Wilson (2005: 416), in their focus group research concerning the perceptions of jazz music and lifestyle with Scottish jazz professionals, read out the following quote, from an interview with the conductor Michael Tilson Thomas which was published in the *Guardian* newspaper, to commence the group discussion: 'Composing takes more than simply enjoying the feel of the notes and the fingers that gifted improvisers share with us.' Similarly, newspaper clippings offer access to topical issues. The use of newspaper clippings in focus groups resembles discussion among people in their everyday conversations (Barbour 2007). In her work exploring the challenges of work involving both mental health problems and child protection issues, Rosaline Barbour (2007: 85) used a newspaper clipping which was published around the time the research was being conducted. The newspaper clipping portrayed an incident where a woman, without a definite psychiatric diagnosis, who had had her baby returned to her care, threw her baby from a bridge only a few days later. The article questioned the lack of a diagnosis by quoting a psychiatrist who, after the incident, diagnosed the woman with personality disorder. The newspaper clipping stimulated forceful discussion among the participants.

A television programme and movie have also been used to stimulate discussion in focus group research. In their Sexual Terminology Project (STP), which aimed to examine the problems of discourse in sexual behaviour and understanding of specific terms and their social meanings of sexual expression among young people, Kaye Wellings and colleagues (2000) commenced the discussion with a short excerpt from a film about two students on a date. The participants were then asked about their opinions of the dating strategies employed by the main characters in the film. In her research with general practitioners in the UK, Rosaline Barbour (2007: 84) used a photograph from a television soap, *Peak Practice*, which depicted the unfolding events in a fictional primary care group practice. The moderator showed the photograph and asked: 'This is one general practice that you're probably all familiar with. How does your own GP practice compare with this?' Barbour suggests that this photograph is not only used as a stimulus material but also as an icebreaker question.

In Deborah Warr's research with socioeconomically disadvantaged young people in Melbourne (2001), the focus group method was used to elicit information regarding (hetero)sex-related health issues. Warr used 'icebreaker questions' to commence the focus group discussion. The first such questions referred to the Hollywood movie *Titanic*, which was very popular at the time of her study. Warr selected this movie:

because the plot involved issues of both class and romance and its box office appeal ensured that it was widely viewed. This approach was effective in getting people comfortable with the format of a group discussion. In one group discussion this question quickly led to an insightful and provocative discussion of the social differences between 'yuppies' and 'normal people like us'. (2001: 120–121)

The second icebreaker question was asking the participants about famous people whom they admired. This was also a useful means to commence the discussion in the group. Warr suggests that feedback from the participants showed that nearly all of them enjoyed the discussion. They described it as 'fun' or 'interesting'. See also the work of Julie Leask and colleagues (2001), Samantha Punch (2002) and Louisa Allen (2005) for interesting examples of using published materials and the media as a way to stimulate discussion in focus group research.

The use of vignettes (short stories) to stimulate discussions in focus groups has also been carried out. According to Haluk Soydan (1996: 121), vignettes are 'short stories about hypothetical characters in specified circumstances, to whose situation the interviewee is invited to respond'. Vignettes are composed of stimuli which represent tangible and detailed descriptions of social circumstances and situations. They present real-life contexts which allow the participants to see that 'meanings are social and situational'. Hence, the participants are more likely to express their beliefs and values in concrete contexts rather than the abstract ones (Alexander & Becker 1978: 94). This is important for focus group research as it would allow the participants to express their concerns and interact with other group members more effectively.

Ajay Bailey (2008), for example, used vignettes in focus groups in his research on HIV/AIDS risk assessment in Goa, India. Bailey and the research team introduced vignettes in the focus group discussion; they were derived from in-depth interviews which were real experiences of migrant and mobile men. The vignettes were made localised by including names such as Lingappa – a common name for rural migrant men from north Karnataka – and by situating Lingappa in a migrant area in Goa. This projective technique yielded lively discussions about Lingappa. Bailey found that men were more vocal when they had to talk about these fictitious persons. Men also shared other stories of people living with HIV/AIDS or about incidents relating to HIV/AIDS. Bailey contends that the use of the fictional people and the manner in which he and the research team culturally adapted the vignettes show that men could both identify with the characters and find other anecdotes to make sense of the situations.

Michele Easter and colleagues (2007: 43–44), in their focus group research exploring stress and health with Latina women in eastern North Carolina, adopted the vignette method because it allowed the participants in a group to speak about sensitive issues regarding stress, anger and interpersonal conflict without having to disclose their personal information. The beginning of the vignette portrayed a fictitious working mother named Isabel and her family:

Isabel is 34 years old. She has four children: two teenagers in Mexico (Francisco is 17, Mari is 15), and two children here (Carmen is 6 and Tito is 2). Isabel is married to Rafael, who is 37 years old and works at a chicken-processing plant, where she also works. He makes $7.50 per hour as a packer and she makes $6.50 per hour as a line-worker. 12 years ago Rafael moved from Michoacán to Florida to work on a farm, and 5 years ago he moved to North Carolina. Isabel moved here from Michoacán 3 years ago with Carmen when Carmen was only 2 years old. Isabel and Rafael have a car and drive together to the chicken-processing plant. Isabel does not speak very much English. (p. 44)

Two subsequent vignettes concentrated on Isabel's arrival home after her workday, and her sister Juana's plans to move to the United States. The participants were asked questions about the vignettes' characters and their opinions about stress at home and work. Easter and colleagues (2007) contend that the vignette focus group method worked well for the Latina women. It allowed them to have access to the participants' own ideas in rich detail. The participants also enjoyed and responded well to the vignette-based focus group method. This may be due to the fact that the format provided an opportunity for them to speak without being threatened or needing to discuss their personal information because they could refer to what someone else would do (Easter et al. 2007). See also the interesting work of Mario Brondani and colleagues (2008) on vignettes in their focus group research concerning oral health and disablement in Canada.

Nevertheless, stimulus materials and activities may not always work in an intended way or provide a desirable outcome (Barbour 2007). The underlying meanings which the materials and activities may have for participants can never be certain. Hence, the researchers need to monitor carefully the effect of stimulus materials and activities and be prepared to change or terminate their use if they result in unintended consequences (Barbour 2007). Michele Burman and colleagues (2001) abandoned the use of vignettes and role-playing activities in their study of teenage girls and violence because it led to a fist fight and a girl was hurt in one situation. In her own research, Rosaline Barbour (2007: 88) tells us that the outcome of the stimulus material was not as she had intended. When she conducted a focus group workshop on the challenges of parenting, she used a newspaper clipping from a UK-based tabloid newspaper (*Scottish Daily Mail*, Monday 14 January 2002: leading item), which described Prince Harry as having been exposed to abusing drugs and alcohol. The headline of the piece quoted Prince Harry saying: 'I'm sorry, father.' Barbour thought that the example of problems which also occurred in the royal family would provide participants with an opportunity to speak about their own concerns and challenges about being parents. Instead, the material stimulated 'animated discussion about the Royal Family and relationships within it – other than parent and child ones. Indeed, these relationships appeared to hold less interest than did the opportunity to speculate on whether Prince Charles would marry Camilla Parker-Bowles.' See Chapter 7 for the use of stimulus materials and activities in focus group research with children and young people, and the use of participatory activities in cross-cultural focus groups in Chapter 8 in this volume.

## HUMOUR IN FOCUS GROUPS

Recently, researchers have discussed the role of humour in focus groups (see Wellings et al. 2000; Allen 2005; Bhana 2009; Robinson 2009). Jude Robinson

(2009: 264) contends that humour acts as 'a symbolic resource, deliberately employed by people to help them cope with, and possibly resolve potentially "difficult" social situations, with shared laughter as an act of "social solidarity"' (see also Sanders 2004; Billig 2005). Humour is usually shared. Hence, it helps to develop and 'smooth' social relationships among individuals (Norrick 1993). It is also suggested that individuals enjoy sharing humour about sensitive issues and taboo subjects because it 'can often evade censorship and restriction by its temporality' (Robinson 2009: 264). This is what Jenny Kitzinger and Clare Farquhar (1999) refer to as 'sensitive moments'.

In her own research on women, poverty and smoking, Jude Robinson (2009: 265) suggests that mothers who smoke near their children find themselves increasingly stigmatised by non-smoking people. Her study examined when and why women smoke in their homes in front of their young children. In all focus groups, humour and laughter were manifested and happened throughout the course of the group discussions. Robinson (2009: 267) tells us: 'Through laughter, the women defined their common ground and shared experiences, and connected with one another by creating intimacy. Laughter and humor appeared to enable women to talk about "dark secrets" within the group context, which may not otherwise have occurred.'

In the following interaction in one focus group, the participants were exaggerating their behaviour in order to raise laughter (Robinson 2009: 267):

P4-1:   The only cinema, which is the one in Woolton and you, can still smoke in there.
P4-2:   See how we all knew that!
Jude:   But you wouldn't take your children there?
P4-2:   No.
P4-1:   You'd go there with your partner.
P4-3:   But you would go there of a night time.
P4-2:   Grab a ciggie, one in each hand!

[*Laughing*]

P4-4:   You wouldn't be able to see the film! You're eyes would be like that!
P4-3:   Everyone would be going there!
P4-1:   'Cos everything else is smoke free.

The excerpt illustrates that the women were stressing their real desire to smoke and well aware that others would disapprove of their attitudes and behaviours. But they were constructing their smoking stories to provoke laughter among the group members, instead of pity, silence or censure. In this instance, the women deliberately resisted any attempt to be understood, pitied or patronised by the moderator. They attempted to show that they were knowledgeable about the realities of being a smoking mother, and it was bad to smoke in front of their children. The women 'subverted the negative image by laughing at themselves, and so retaining a degree of control (agency) over the stereotyped image of themselves that they (re)produced'.

## CONCLUSION

In this chapter, I have provided readers with several salient practical considerations in conducting focus groups and these include: how to recruit and gain access to potential participants; whether the participants should be provided with compensation or incentives; the importance of focus group location and timing; who should be involved in focus group research; and the use of stimulus materials and activities and humour in focus group research. Most of the issues I have discussed are arguably crucial in ensuring that focus group research can be carried out more successfully. But more than that, I have also offered some interesting means for conducting your research. The use of stimulus materials and activities, for example, allows participants to engage better with the topic and this would lead to more interesting data. Humour in focus group research allows researchers to gain a deeper understanding about certain aspect of the lives of their participants. This too would lead to more accurate interpretations of the research findings.

## TUTORIAL ACTIVITIES

You have been planning your focus group research to examine the lived experiences and needs of low-socioeconomic households for your local council. You have thought about the theoretical aspects of your focus groups but you know that you also need to consider other practical issues which would ensure the success of your project. You have read the chapter in this volume and you need to incorporate the issues into your research proposal.

1   How will you recruit and gain access to your participants?
2   Will you provide some compensation for them?
3   Where will you carry out your focus groups?
4   Do you have to consider the timing of your project?
5   What will help you to stimulate more interesting discussion in the groups?
6   If there is a presence of humour and laughter in the group, how will you treat this?

### FURTHER READING

Bhana, D. (2009). 'AIDS is rape!' Gender and sexuality in children's responses to HIV and AIDS. *Social Science and Medicine* 69(4), 596–603.
Bloor, M., Frankland, J., Thomas, M., & Robson, K. (2001). *Focus groups in social research*. London: Sage.
Easter, M.M., Linnan, L.A., Bentley, M.E., DeVellis, B.M., Meier, A., Frasier, P.Y., Kelsey, K.S., & Campbell, M.K. (2007). 'Una mujer trabaja

*(Continued)*

*(Continued)*

doble aquí': Vignette-based focus groups on stress and work for Latina blue-collar women in eastern North Carolina. *Health Promotion Practice* 8(1), 41–49.

Krueger, R.A., & Casey, M.A. (2009). *Focus groups: A practical guide for applied research*, 4th edn. Thousand Oaks, CA: Sage.

Munday, J. (2006). Identity in focus: The use of focus groups to study the construction of collective identity. *Sociology* 40(1), 89–105.

Peek, L., & Fothergill, A. (2009). Using focus groups: Lessons from studying daycare centers, 9/11, and Hurricane Katrina. *Qualitative Research* 9(1), 31–59.

Propst, D.B., McDonough, M.H., Vogt, C.A., & Pynnonen, D.M. (2008). Roving focus groups: Collecting perceptual landscape data in situ. *International Journal of Qualitative Methods* 7(3), 1–14. Retrieved on 12 February 2010, from http://ejournals.library.ualberta.ca/index.php/IJQM/issue/view/352

Robinson, J. (2009). Laughter and forgetting: Using focus groups to discuss smoking and motherhood in low-income areas in the UK. *International Journal of Qualitative Studies in Education* 22(3), 263–278.

Umaña-Taylor, A.J., & Bámaca, M.Y. (2004). Conducting focus groups with Latino populations: Lessons from the field. *Family Relations* 53(3), 261–272.

# 5
# CONDUCTING FOCUS GROUPS AND PRACTICALITIES

## CHAPTER OBJECTIVES

In this chapter you will learn about:

- Practical issues in conducting a focus group
- Question guides in focus groups
- Probe and prompt questions
- Direction and the moderating styles
- How to manage difficult situations in focus groups
- How to record focus group data

This chapter will focus on the practicalities of conducting focus group sessions. In particular, I will provide practical stages in running a focus group, from preparation to the ending stage. I will also provide discussions regarding the use of a question guide and the types of probe and prompt questions which moderators can use to elicit information in focus groups. Issues relevant to the direction and moderating styles and how to manage difficult situations in focus groups are included. Lastly, I provide some discussion regarding the recording of a focus group session.

## RUNNING A FOCUS GROUP: PRACTICAL STAGES

It is assumed that by the time researchers have reached this stage of their research, they have recruited the participants and organised the date on which the focus groups will be held. There are several practical stages when conducting focus groups. These are discussed below.

## Preparation

It is essential that the location and setting of the focus groups (as discussed in Chapter 4) must be prepared in advance. The research team should also visit the site before the day scheduled for the session to check if it is accessible for the participants. All equipment including a tape-recorder and microphone is checked (see later section in this chapter) (Barbour 2007; Hennink 2007: Liamputtong 2009).

It is recommended that the table and chairs are arranged in a circle in order to facilitate interaction. A circular seating arrangement allows all the participants to face each other. It is more likely that individuals would interact with those who are seated directly across from them (Vaughn et al. 1996). A circular seating style will also enable all group members to have equal access to each other and hence discussion can be fostered. This is essential for the development of the interactive dynamics in a group, which is the essence of a focus group discussion (Hennink 2007). In addition, if the participants cannot see each other, naturally they will orientate their comments and questions towards the moderator, rather than respond directly to the comments of other participants in the group (Hennink 2007). Furthermore, according to Monique Hennink (2007: 162), round tables should be used in focus groups because with rectangular tables there are 'dominant seating positions at the table ends'. See also Chapter 8 for seating in cross-cultural focus groups.

Although a circular seating arrangement can be organised with or without a table in the middle (see Hennink 2007), most focus group participants would feel more comfortable sitting around a table (Stewart et al. 2007). Numerous reasons can be given for this. A table provides a protective barrier between the participants which gives those who feel insecure, or who are a bit more reserved, some sense of security. It also offers a sense of personal space which may make the participants feel more comfortable in a group. In focus groups comprising both men and women, a table can act as a shield for the legs which could eliminate distraction. For practicality, if refreshments are served during the session, participants can rest their arms and hands on the table and it would be easy for them to handle plates and cups (Stewart et al. 2007).

## On Arrival and Pre-discussion Stage

The researchers must be at the location early so that they can greet the participants when they arrive. Hot or cold drinks should be prepared so that the participants can settle before the session is commenced. Researchers including the moderator, a note-taker and an assistant moderator should also engage in 'small talk' to make the participants feel welcome and comfortable (Barbour 2007; Daly 2007; Hennink 2007; Stewart et al. 2007). The researchers may be able to set up the equipment while the coffee or tea is being prepared. Some administrative tasks such as gaining informed consent from the participants and payment of incentives can also be done during this stage. It is also practical to get the participants to complete their sociodemographic questionnaires during this introductory time (Hennink 2007).

It is good to provide all participants with a name tag during this stage (Stewart et al. 2007). Only first names should be used in order to ensure some protection of the privacy of the participants. Using first names provides a basis for the group members and the moderator to build rapport. Referring to each other by first names helps to create a greater sense of group identity and cohesiveness. It also allows the moderator to direct questions to a particular group member, which can result in immediate responses from the person. The participants' names can then be removed during the transcription period to preserve their confidentiality and anonymity.

The researchers can use this pre-discussion stage to assess the characteristics of participants, particularly to determine if there may be any particularly quiet or talkative persons. This will allow the research team to situate them strategically in the discussion circle so that the moderator can manage the group dynamics better. The seating of these individuals can be done by placing name cards around the table. For example, a shy and quite participant should ideally be sat directly opposite the moderator in order to allow full eye contact, which would encourage the person to speak (see the later section on managing difficult situations in focus groups) (Hennink 2007).

## Introductory Stage

The moderator should commence the session by introducing him- or herself and should also introduce the note-taker and the assistant moderator. All participants must be invited to introduce and say a little about themselves, such as their work, families or interests and perhaps the reason for them joining the focus group. This is a useful way to build rapport and a sense of group cohesion (Conradson 2005; Kitzinger 2005; Stewart et al. 2007). An invitation to the participants to introduce themselves can be used to ensure that all participants have contributed something from the beginning of the discussion. This assists the participants in feeling confident to contribute to the discussion. It also helps the transcribers to differentiate between the voices in the discussion (Kitzinger 2005; Hennink 2007).

Then the moderator briefly introduces the focus group session, the research topics and the aim of the group discussion. During this stage, reassurances of the value of all members' views, regardless of how different or unusual they are, empathy for all participants, and confidentiality are crucial (Stewart et al. 2007; see also Chapter 2 in this volume). Also, permission to record the interview should be requested at this stage.

The moderator must explain to the group members that the aim of focus groups is to encourage individuals to speak to each other instead of addressing themselves to the moderator (Kitzinger 2005). It is also crucial for the participants to be informed that there are no right or wrong answers to the questions and their views are valued (Madriz 2003). Also, the participants need to be told that it is acceptable for them to disagree on issues. Disagreements among the participants will allow the researchers to elicit the range of perspectives on a topic (Madriz 2003; see also Chapter 3 in this volume).

I wish to provide an example that Raymond Macdonald and Graeme Wilson (2005: 415–416) used to brief participants during the commencement of the focus groups in their research concerning the perceptions of jazz improvisers with two groups of professional practitioners in Scotland:

Initial study into how a range of practising jazz musicians view themselves as improvisers, and how they explain to other people what they do. Not much been done on this before, and there should, since it's a unique form of music.

Looked for professional jazz improvisers as best placed to understand the process; and a range of different instrumentalists. Obviously all play other forms of music. But you're all fairly busy as jazz musicians – have all spent a lot of time improvising in that genre with other musicians.

This is a focus group; ideally, we'd just like you all to talk to each other about being jazz improvisers, and how you improvise. To try and get your views of what's important and not ours, we want to take as little part in this as possible; should also emphasize that we're not testing you, to see if you give 'right' or 'wrong' answers. We have some broad questions we can ask to get the ball rolling or steer things back on course if the discussion goes too far off track. You can say as much or as little as you want; we might try and come in on the conversation if it seems that someone isn't getting a chance to chip in. Other than that, leave you to it for about an hour; though if some or all of you want to run on a bit, that's fine.

The conversation's being tape-recorded for us to transcribe and look at later. One of us will be taking notes; this is just to make it easier to know who's talking when we're listening back. However, it's only us that will ever hear the tape, and nobody will be named on the transcript.

We'll be writing up what we find to be published as an article/presented at a conference; again, nobody would be named in that. Will let you know what comes out if you like. Also try and go on to more work on the basis of what you tell us.

Do you have any questions? You can always get back to us later.

See also Davidson and colleagues (2010) for some introductory statements that focus group researchers can use. Also, it is during this stage that stimulus materials and participatory activities are useful for initiating discussion (Conradson 2005; Kitzinger 2005; see Chapters 4 and 8 in this volume).

## Questioning Stage

This is the time when the moderator commences the questions relevant to the issues under investigation. Initially, the moderator needs to establish 'a nonthreatening and nonevaluative environment' (Stewart et al. 2007: 89) which allows the participants to feel free to speak about their issues and concerns openly and without having to think whether their perspectives would be agreed upon by other members of the group (as I have mentioned in the introductory stage). Once this environment has been created, the moderator needs to ensure that the discussion is on track, manage the time properly and make sure that all members of the group actively participate in the discussion (Stewart et al. 2007).

The question guide which will have been prepared beforehand is used to elicit discussion from the participants. Prompts and probes are used to make people discuss and interact more (see the later section on question guide and prompts). Stimulus materials and participatory activities can be used to encourage the participants to speak (see Chapters 4 and 8 in this volume). The discussion is continued until all questions are covered in great depth. During this stage, it is important that the moderator should continually consider whether the information obtained from the discussion is sufficient to answer the research questions. It may be that the moderator will have to redirect or refocus the discussion towards the key issues if the group does not go as planned (Hennink 2007). Although this cannot be anticipated beforehand, good preparation of the question guide may help to make the group focus on the key areas of investigation.

## Ending the Interview Stage

After the focus group discussion, the moderator must debrief the participants. Often, the moderator would ask the participants if they have anything else to add. The moderator may also ask the participants about their experiences of the session. This is a good way to debrief a focus group session.

The moderator may finish the focus group by summarising some of the main points that the participants have given during the session. The moderator may say to the participants, for example: 'I have no more questions to ask but is there anything else you all would like to bring up, or ask about, before we finish this session?' This sometimes gives the participants an opportunity to talk about some important issues that they have been thinking or worrying about during the focus group session. Additionally, it is important to finish off the session by thanking the participants for their valuable contribution (Hennink 2007).

## After the Session

Snacks or refreshments should be provided at the end of the session. People feel more relaxed if they have the chance to eat and drink together, and this may allow an opportunity to clarify some issues in further discussions. See also Chapter 8 for the importance of providing food in cross-cultural focus group research.

## A QUESTION GUIDE IN FOCUS GROUPS

Typically, focus group researchers would prepare a question guide or topic guide in order to help them to direct the discussion and cover key issues that they wish to examine in a session. The question/interview guide is one of the critical components which would determine the success of a focus group. The question guide contains the main issues and, usually, the wording of questions that the moderators will be using in a session. However, good questions, which are designed to obtain the kind of data that the researchers are looking for, are crucial to the success of focus groups (Davidson et al. 2010; Hesse–Biber & Leavy 2010).

Focus group researchers Patricia Davidson and colleagues (2010: 65) suggest that the question guide allows the moderators to navigate through the different parts of the discussion in a focus group session. Using a heart attack as an example, Davidson and colleagues provide a template for planning the question guide which they have adopted from their previous writing (see Halcomb et al. 2007). Readers may replace the heart attack with any other health and social issue for their focus group question guide.

---

**BOX 5.1 EXAMPLE OF A FOCUS GROUP QUESTION GUIDE**

| INTRODUCTORY QUESTION | Can you please tell us about your experience of having a heart attack? |
|---|---|
| TRANSITION QUESTION | Can you tell us briefly about what helped your recovery from a heart attack? |
| TRANSITION QUESTION | Do you know of any help or support services that are available for people who have had a heart attack? |
| FOCUS QUESTIONS (These should be based on research questions) | What are the greatest needs faced by people after a heart attack? What can health professionals do to help people recover from a heart attack? |
| SUMMARISING QUESTION | As you know, we are going to be implementing a programme to assist those who have recently experienced a heart attack. Think back on your experiences and our discussions today and tell us what we can do to improve the care people receive. |
| CONCLUDING QUESTION | Is there anything else that anyone feels that we should have talked about but didn't? |

---

The aim of this question guide is to initiate the discussion with a simple introductory question which would encourage more interaction among the group members (Halcomb et al. 2007). The introductory question allows the moderator to generate some knowledge about the participants' perspectives regarding the issues under investigation. The transition questions follows gradually from the introductory question. This would help the moderator to narrow down the focus of the discussion and eventually lead to the key questions, which are the core of the research interest. However, some researchers may follow the format that in-depth interviewers tend to adopt in their research. These researchers would argue that in carrying out the focus group interview, the moderators should not strictly follow the guide. Instead, they should make up the questions during the session, and often have to rephrase the questions and change the order of the questions. Depending on the answers of the participants, it is usual for the moderators also to ask additional questions which are not listed in the interview guide (Kvale 2007; Liamputtong 2009; see the later section on questioning and direction provided by the moderators).

Additionally, although the researchers may have prepared some question guide for their focus groups as presented above, it is crucial that probes and prompts are needed in order to follow the points raised by the participants so that more in-depth explanations and meanings can be obtained (Conradson 2005; Davidson et al. 2010). In failing to follow up the points in greater depth, the data generated may be superficial and hence may not suffice to address the research questions properly (Davidson et al. 2010).

## PROBE AND PROMPT QUESTIONS

Similar to the questions adopted in in-depth interviews, there are different types of probe and prompt questions that focus group researchers can use. Below I list several types of these questions which I believe are useful.

### Probing Questions

The moderators prompt the participants to discuss the issue further so that they have a clear understanding of the topic being examined. Some examples include: 'Can you say more about what you have just told me?' and 'Can you give me a bit more example of this issue?' There are many general probes that researchers may find useful and these include: 'What happened?', 'When did it happen?', 'How did it happen?', 'Where did it happen?', 'How did you get involved in it?' and 'What was that like for you?' (Esterberg 2002: 104; Stewart et al. 2007; Hennink 2007).

### Follow-up Questions

This type of question is to encourage the participants to say more about the answer they have just given (Bryman 2008). Through a curious, persistent and critical attitude of the moderators, the participants' answers can be elaborated more. Following up what has been said can be done through direct questioning. Examples may include: 'Do you mean you had a negative experience with your last employment?', 'What is happening afterwards?' and 'You said earlier that you prefer not to have a child; could you tell me more about this?'

## Specifying Questions

Follow-up questions can be done by asking more specific questions, such as: 'What did you actually do when you lost your job?' and 'How did you react to what people in the community said about you?' A more precise question can also be asked so that a more specific response can be obtained, for example: 'Have you actually experienced this yourself?'

## Direct Questions

The moderators may also ask some direct questions to clarify the issues or some ambiguity during the discussion. However, such direct questions should be left until the later parts of the discussion, particularly after the participants have provided their own explanations and when it is clearer to the moderators about the issue of importance. Examples are: 'When you mention the way the doctor treats you, do you mean a positive or negative treatment?', 'Have you ever experienced discrimination from others in your community?' and 'What stops you from looking after your ill father as you would like to do?'

## Indirect Questions

There are several indirect questions that the moderators may adopt. Projective questions, such as 'How do you think other men would react to domestic violence?', may be used. This question may lead to responses about the attitudes of others, but it may also suggest the participants' own attitudes, which they do not indicate directly. However, with this type of question, further careful questioning is essential in order to interpret accurately the responses of the participants. For example, the moderators may ask: 'What do most people in your local area think of the ways that older people are treated by their carers?' In order to gain the participant's own perspective, the moderators should follow it with a question such as: 'Is that your experience too?' Rosaline Barbour (2007: 119) calls these 'contextualizing questions', which include questions such as: 'Do you think that other people in your situation would have the same experience as you?' If the answer is negative, perhaps the moderators can ask: 'What do you think may make your experience different from others?'

## Structuring Questions

This type of question assists the participants to move on to the next line of questions. The moderators should indicate to the participants when a theme of the former question has been done. For example, the moderators may briefly summarise their understanding of the answer provided by the participants and then say 'I would like to introduce another issue now', or 'We have been talking about the way you take care of your new baby, now I would like to talk about the way mothers feed their babies. Can you please tell me how you feed your baby?' This type of question can also be used when the participants provide a long discussion of issues which may not be relevant to the research. When the participants pause for a moment, the moderators may introduce the next line of questions as a way to bring the participant back to the research topic.

## Interpreting Questions

From time to time, the moderators may need to ask questions which will assist them to interpret what the participants have suggested. The moderators may simply rephrase the answer, and then say something like: 'You mean that this is how you are treated by your doctor?' The interpreting question can be used to clarify the participants' responses, like: 'Is it correct that you feel that you are being discriminated against?', 'Does the expression of your father cover what you have just said?' and 'Is it correct that your main worry about your baby's illness is the same as what your husband has?'

## DIRECTION AND THE MODERATING STYLES

The degree of structure and direction that is provided by the moderator has a great impact on the quality and types of data generated from the focus groups (Stewart et al. 2007). This degree is determined by the research agenda on which the focus group is based. This includes the specificity of the information which is required by the particular project and the way in which the data will be utilised. More structured focus groups will be highly controlled by the moderator. The agenda and structure of the group are determined by the moderator and tend to reflect the interest of the researchers or funding agencies more than that of the participants. Less structured focus groups are adopted to pursue issues which have more relevance, importance and interest to the research participants. They tend to be used if the aim of the research is to understand things which are most important to the group members.

Focus group researchers Phil Macnaghten and Greg Myers (2004: 71) differentiate focus group moderators into different groups. These include those who are more interventionist or flexible, those who may be more or less empathetic towards their participants, those who may contribute more or less of their own personal perspective in the group discussion, and those who are identified by the participants as being one of the group. Phil Macnaghten sees himself as an interventionist moderator. In running his focus groups, he would adhere to the questions guide. He would bring up the issues directly, point out some participants and block others, interrupt any discussion which seems unproductive, and challenge vagueness or contradictions. However, Greg Myers is a more flexible moderator. Hence, he would allow the participants to continue speaking despite the fact that they may drift away from the question guide, as he sees this as important for the participants. Myers seems to adopt the practice of the feminist focus group, which posits that the moderator should not act as a control person, but rather allow the participants to take their own course in a group session (see Chapters 2 and 4 in this volume).

Moderators should try to balance the control and flow of the focus group in order to match particular research purposes so that the best outcomes can be produced (Hesse-Biber & Leavy 2010). The moderators need to ask whether the research project requires some form of standardisation or not, and at what level. The moderators will administer a high level of control in focus group research which requires high standardisation. Less control and a more flexible style of moderation will be appropriate for more evolving design research (Hesse-Biber & Leavy 2010).

Nevertheless, as I have suggested in Chapter 1, focus group research in the health and social sciences has the tendency to adopt the less control moderating style (see Morgan 1996). More flexible moderation is seen as more synchronised with the nature of the qualitative approach since it provides the participants with 'a voice in shaping the topic and conversation' (Hesse-Biber & Leavy 2010: 184). Flexible moderation allows the participants to 'do most of the talking, thus providing rich descriptions of social life and in-depth explanations of social processes' (Hesse-Biber & Leavy 2010: 184). When the moderators do not adhere to a strict and structured interview guide and permit the participants to speak as they wish, the interaction may move in directions which the moderators might not have expected. Flexible focus group moderation allows the participants to put more emphasis on the areas which are meaningful and important to them. This provides great opportunities for the moderators to follow the group interaction in novel and exciting directions. The data generated from flexible moderation is situated within the experiences of the participants as they see them. As a result, the moderators will be able to acquire in-depth knowledge about things which are of importance to the group members. Furthermore, if the moderators wish to investigate the group dynamic itself as part of the study aims, the group interaction must be permitted to take its course freely. This is essential in research which, for example, attempts to examine how members of minority social groups and of dominant social groups interact in a group setting so that the moderators can see 'who speaks freely, who dominates, who is silenced' (Hesse-Biber & Leavy 2010: 184). See also Chapter 4 in this volume on the role of the moderators and their control in focus groups.

## MANAGING DIFFICULT SITUATIONS IN FOCUS GROUPS

The focus group method presents one difficulty which may not easily occur in other qualitative approaches: that is, the difficulty of having certain types of people in a group. According to focus group researchers Richard Krueger and Mary Anne Casey (2009: 100–101), there are several groups of people whose nature can make the running of a session more challenging. These include dominant talkers, shy participants and those who proclaim themselves as experts. Often, the moderators need to find ways which can reduce difficulties in having these individuals in a group (see also Gates & Waight 2007; Stewart et al. 2007).

Dominant talkers see themselves as experts on the topic, but often they do not know how they are seen by others in the group. Dominant talkers can be spotted easily during the greeting session when people engage in small talk. In a group, it is wise to seat the dominant talkers next to the moderator so that the use of body language can be applied to control these individuals (see also Hennink 2007; Stewart et al. 2007). If this strategy fails, the more direct means of 'verbally shifting attention' is needed. The moderator may say, for example, 'Thank you, John. Are there others who wish to comment on the question?' or 'Does anyone feel differently?' or 'That's one point of view. Let's hear what others have to say' (Krueger & Casey 2009: 100). However, the moderator must be cautious about shifting attention as harsh comments to the dominant talkers can also stop all participants from speaking (Krueger & Casey 2009).

In contrast to the dominant talkers, shy individuals are likely to speak little. They tend to think carefully before they talk. Often, these individuals have a good understanding of the issues but they have to make some effort to elaborate their ideas. It is crucial to seat shy participants directly opposite the moderator so as to maximise eye contact. Very often, eye contact is sufficient to encourage the shy participants to speak. If this does not work, the moderator may call them by name: for example, 'Tom, I don't want to leave you out of the conversation. What do you think? Megan, you haven't had a chance. How do you feel about this?' (Krueger & Casey 2009: 100).

However, Rosaline Barbour (2007) contends that instead of seeing these individuals as problematic, the moderators should take this into account in moderating focus groups. Individuals who have been silent for a while are likely to be aware of their non-participating role and will attempt to find something important to say. And if they cannot find anything to say, the more silent they will become. Hence, a gentle invitation from the moderator, such as to express their views about what others have said, can be 'a relief for the uncomfortable quiet group member' (Barbour 2007: 82). Often, people are not silent totally. They may use some non-verbal expressions such as smiling, nodding and shaking their head, to signify their agreement or disagreement. The moderator may encourage their participation by picking up these non-verbal behaviours and inviting the participants to say something. This would stop shy participants from being silent in a group session.

Individuals who may present particular challenges and make focus groups problematic are those who proclaim themselves to be 'experts' (Krueger & Casey 2009). Some individuals see themselves as experts because they have extensive knowledge or experience about the issue and/or had prior experiences with focus group sessions. Others consider themselves as experts since they have influential positions in the local area. What these 'self-appointed experts' say and how they say it can have great impact on the others in the group (see also Stewart et al. 2007). Some participants may hold back their views when there are others whom they see as having more experience or knowledge about the issue in the group. They may also be intimidated by the self-appointed experts. The most

effective way to deal with self-appointed experts is to emphasise that all participants are experts and they all have important knowledge and understanding which
need to be spoken about. The moderator may apply more assertive techniques, for
example avoiding eye contact, interrupting in the middle of talk, and not paying
attention to the person when he or she tries to speak. Some non-verbal cues, including appearing bored or tired, can be used to stop the experts talking. Showing a lack
of interest and changing the subject after they speak can also be a useful means for
controlling these people (Stewart et al. 2007: 99).

According to Richard Krueger and Mary Anne Casey (2009: 101), in the introduction stage, the moderators may need to include a statement which underscores
the importance of having everyone speak, as follows:

> From past experience in groups like this we know that some people talk a lot, and
> some people don't say much. We really want to hear from all of you because you have
> had different experiences. So if you are talking a lot, I may interrupt you and if you
> aren't saying much I may call on you. If I do, please don't be offended. We have a lot
> to cover here tonight, and it's just my way of making sure we get through all the ques-
> tions and that everyone has a chance to talk.

This may prevent some of the challenges that the dominant talkers, shy participants
and self-appointed experts may pose in focus groups.

Occasionally too there may be clearly hostile individuals who turn up for a focus
group session (Stewart et al. 2007). It may be that the topic for discussion is not what
they have anticipated or they have a hostile personality. The presence of these people
in the group would make other participants feel uncomfortable and it can inhibit
group discussion. If these people are spotted before commencement of the session,
it is wise to ask them politely to leave. If the hostility appears during the discussion,
the moderator should have a short break and ask these individuals to leave. If they
do not wish to leave, a lack of eye contact and attention to these individuals may
allow others to participate more freely (Stewart et al. 2007).

## RECORDING FOCUS GROUP DATA

Focus group discussions are generally recorded in two ways. First, the note-taker or
assistant moderator records the information in written notes (see also Chapter 4).
The note-taker writes down the participants' responses as well as observing and
recording non-verbal responses which may assist in understanding how participants feel about particular issues (Dawson et al. 1993; Barbour 2007; Liamputtong
2009). Non-verbal responses include facial expressions, body postures and silences,
which may convey some feelings (such as approval, interest, boredom, impatience,
resentment or anger). In their research on perceptions of African American men's
health, Joseph Ravenell and colleagues (2006) had their note-taker take notes on
non-verbal communication and interpersonal dynamics among the participants
which could not be captured by audio-recording. An example of note-taking during focus group sessions on smoking (taken from my own field observations in
1995) is given below.

---

**AN EXAMPLE OF NOTE-TAKING**

Moderator asks question about what makes people smoke. Man 1 says, 'I find it relaxing'. Man 2 says, 'I smoke because it helps me to deal with stress better. I tend to forget things if I smoke.' [Several men nod their heads – do they agree? One smiles after hearing that remark – why does he smile?] Man 3 says, 'Some women smoke because they work in a bar or nightclub. The work they do makes them smoke.' Man 4 quickly says, 'Only some women, not all of them' [Gender issue seems to be an issue here; this needs to be followed up by the moderator.]

---

Patricia Davidson and colleagues (2010: 69) develop a template that a note-taker can use in a focus group session as presented below. I think this is a good format that readers may wish to adopt in their focus group research.

---

**BOX 5.2   EXAMPLE OF A FOCUS GROUP DATA COLLECTION TEMPLATE**

**Date:**
**Start time:**
**Stop time:**
**Moderator:**
**Observer (s):**
**Venue:**
**Participants:**

| Focus question | Responses | Key issues |
|---|---|---|
| What would be the greatest needs or most important issues confronted by people suffering from a heart attack? | | |
| What do you think would be the barriers and facilitators to recovery from a heart attack? | | |
| What can health professionals do to promote recovery from a heart attack? | | |
| **Summary and reflections** | | |

---

Second, the discussions are recorded by a tape-recorder. This method is invaluable and generally recommended for all focus groups. The moderators have to pay close attention to what the participants say and to follow up the conversation, to probe and to clarify in the focus group session. The tape-recording will assist the moderators with the recording of the discussion. They can then focus on the topic and the dynamics of the discussion. Typically, the note-taker will not be able to record everything that is discussed, but this can be overcome with the tape-recorder. More importantly, the recording of group discussion is crucial for the detailed analysis which is essentially required in focus group research. This is to ensure that the participants' responses are captured in their own words. Some researchers may adopt videotape to record the data and group interactions (Gates & Waight 2007; Hennink 2007). This poses more ethical and practical problems than an audiotape record. Tim Rapley (2007: 39) asks: '*Do you really need the additional information video data offer?*' So, ask yourself if this is really needed. If not, it is wise to stick to the audio recording. This is the stance I take in running my own focus groups.

Alan Bryman (2008) offers the following points for the need to record the focus group interviews. First, as I have discussed in Chapters 1 and 2, the focus group method provides a possibility for the researchers to examine the processes by which the participants collectively construct their meanings in a group session. It is essential to keep track of who expresses what and this would not be easy to do by taking notes. According to Bryman (2008: 476), 'if this element is lost, the dynamics of the focus group session would also be lost, and a major rationale for doing focus group interviews ... would be undermined'. Second, focus group researchers are interested not only in what the participants say, but also the way they say it. The particular language they use and the way they express it is very important for focus group research. It is likely that the subtle meanings of language will be lost if the researchers have to rely solely on notes taken during the sessions.

The participants need to be fully aware of the presence of the tape-recorder and to understand that its purpose is to capture their comments as accurately as possible. The moderators also need to obtain permission from the participants. This must be organised before the focus group starts.

When recording, the researchers should ensure that the room does not have too much background noise, as it may be difficult to hear the discussion on the tape when transcribing it. The inaudible sounds on the recorded interviews have been a problem for many researchers, both novice and experienced. If the interview is carried out in a room or in a quiet building, this may not be a problem. But sometimes the discussion must be done in an open space or in a pub where noise can be a problem. So, the researchers must prepare for this. However, digital tape-recorders (see below) appear to be able to deal with background noises better than the old-style recorders.

It is crucial that the researchers have a good-quality tape-recorder and microphone. Many researchers (including myself) have been left with bad transcripts or nothing at all because of poor recording or bad recording machines (Bryman 2008). In the past, researchers had to rely on the cassette tape-recorders. Nowadays, digital audio-recorders are available. They provide a high sound quality and can record the interviews for many hours without interruption. The digital tapes can also screen out background noise, so that the recording is still audible even if the focus group interviews are carried out where there is a noisy background (Rapley 2007; Bryman 2008).

Recently, some discussions about 'real-time' recording of transcriptions have emerged (see Scott et al. 2009). This refers to the use of court reporters to record the focus group data. According to Shannon Scott and colleagues (2009), this unconventional way can provide more accurate data and transcription than the traditional tape-recording one. The court reporters can record the discussion verbatim using specialised equipment.

Although most participants will allow the researchers to tape-record the group discussions, in some situations this may not be so. People from some cultural groups may not wish their discussions to be tape-recorded (Liamputtong 2010a; see Chapter 8 in this volume). In other situations, the researchers themselves may decide that tape-recording the group discussion is too intrusive for their participants, hence note-taking would be adopted. In their research concerning the reproductive health needs of migrant women in Canada, Luciana Ruppenthal and colleagues (2005) decided to take extensive notes rather than tape-record the group sessions. They wished to reduce the feeling of discomfort that the participants might have from sharing personal or confidential information, especially in relation to asylum applications, with others and the researchers. Two moderators worked together in their focus groups and took turns as designated note-taker during each session. The designated moderator also wrote down key points throughout the group session in order to verify the notes taken by the note-taker. At the end of each focus group session, the participants were invited to summarise their main concerns and make further suggestions.

## CONCLUSION

The practicalities of running focus groups form an important part of any focus group research. Rosaline Barbour (2007: 74) says this clearly: 'It would be a pity to scrupulously develop your research design and sampling strategy only to be let down by failing to take account of the practicalities involved.' Often, people who have not had any experience in running focus groups assume that it would be easy and simple to do so. As readers may have realised by now, this is not always so. Although many things have been prepared well in advance (as I have discussed in previous chapters), the time when the focus group is actually run can become problematic. In this chapter, I have provided practical stages for running a focus group, from preparation to the final stage. I have also provided discussions regarding the use of a question guide and the types of probe and prompt questions which can be adopted to elicit more information in focus groups. Some discussions regarding the direction and moderating styles and how to manage difficult situations in focus groups are also included. Finally, how to record focus group sessions are provided. I hope that these points will assist researchers to run their focus groups more successfully.

## TUTORIAL ACTIVITIES

You are working on your focus group research project in which you wish to learn about disability and chronic illness in your local area.

1  How will you prepare your focus groups?
2  How will you run your focus groups?
3  What questions will you use to elicit information from the participants?
4  How will you ensure that you obtain in-depth information?
5  How will you record your focus groups?

Write down your plans and your question guide so that others can duplicate your work in other local areas.

## FURTHER READING

Barbour, R. (2007). *Doing focus groups*. London: Sage.

Bedford, T., & Burgess, J. (2001). The focus group experience. In M. Limb & C. Dwyer (eds.), *Qualitative methodologies for geographers: Issues and debates* (pp. 121–135). New York: Arnold.

Conradson, D. (2005). Focus groups. In R. Flowerdew & D. Martin (eds.), *Methods in human geography: A guide for students doing a research project* (pp. 128–143). Harlow: Pearson Prentice Hall.

Dawson, S., Manderson, L., & Tallo, V.L. (1993). *A manual for the use of focus groups*. Boston, MA: International Nutrition Foundation for Developing Countries (INFDC).

Hennink, M.M. (2007). *International focus group research: A handbook for the health and social sciences*. Cambridge: Cambridge University Press.

Krueger, R.A., & Casey, M.A. (2009). *Focus groups: A practical guide for applied research*, 4th edition. Thousand Oaks, CA: Sage.

Macdonald, R., & Wilson, G. (2005). Musical identities of professional jazz musicians: A focus group investigation. *Psychology of Music* 33(4), 395–417.

Macnaghten, P., & Myers, G. (2004). Focus groups. In C. Seal, G. Gobo, J.F. Gubrium, & D. Silverman (eds.), *Qualitative research practice* (pp. 65–79). London: Sage.

Stewart, D.W., Shamdasani, P.N., & Rook, D.W. (2007). *Focus groups: Theory and practice*, 2nd edition. Thousand Oaks, CA: Sage.

# 6

# THE USE OF FOCUS GROUP METHODOLOGY IN THE HEALTH AND SOCIAL SCIENCES

## CHAPTER OBJECTIVES

In this chapter you will learn about:

- The specific application of the skills acquired in Chapters 3–5
- Focus groups as a self-contained method
- Focus groups as a supplementary source of data and in mixed-method studies
- Focus groups in multi-method studies
- Focus group and needs assessment
- Focus groups and community-based participatory research (CBPR)
- Focus groups and the photovoice method

Focus groups can be used in multiple ways. However, there is a mistaken tendency to see them as only a preliminary or exploratory method of data collection, to be backed up by other methods, particularly quantitative ones. David Morgan (1997: 18) contends that focus group researchers, like other qualitative researchers, are more interested in 'understanding the particular than the general' and in 'issues of meaning than in precise numerical descriptions'. Therefore, focus groups can be employed to answer diverse research questions as their use is not restricted to preliminary or exploratory research, as has been perceived.

This chapter will refer to the different ways that focus groups can be used in health and social science research. These include using focus group as a stand-alone method, the use of focus group as supplementary and mixed-method research and its use in multi-method studies and needs assessment. I will also point to the relationship between the focus group method and other qualitative methods such as community-based participatory research and the photovoice method. These issues will be discussed in great detail in this chapter with examples from research in the health and social sciences.

## FOCUS GROUPS AS A SELF-CONTAINED METHOD

Commonly, focus groups are used as a self-contained method for a single research project. They can be used to examine research questions from the perspectives of the participants as well as to explore new research areas. The basic argument for using focus groups as a self-contained approach, as opposed to individual interviews, is that they reveal the participants' experiences and perspectives that may not be accessible without group interaction (Warr 2001; 2005; see also Chapters 1 and 3 in this volume).

Focus groups are particularly valuable for research when little is known about the phenomenon of interest (Stewart et al. 2009). For example, Kristina Holmgren and Synneve Dahlin Ivanoff (2004) used focus groups in the exploratory stages of a research project that examined the experiences of women who were on sick leave as a result of work-related injury in Sweden. They explored how the women perceived and explained their possibilities for and obstacles to returning to work. This research provides distinctive insight into the complex circumstance of being on sick leave. It points to the importance of recognising the situation of the person and the interplay between the individual woman and her environment. Holmgren and Ivanoff contended that this knowledge can be used as a basis for a rehabilitation programme for helping women return to work.

In the UK, Jenny Kitzinger (1994a) used focus groups in the AIDS Media Research Project, a three-pronged study of the production, content and effect of media messages about AIDS. Kitzinger pointed out that focus groups were employed to examine 'the "effect" element in this equation – to explore how media messages are processed by audiences and how understandings of AIDS are constructed' (p. 104). She was interested not only in 'what people thought but in how they thought and why they thought as they did'. In addition, she attempted to examine 'how diverse identities and social networks might impact upon research participants' perceptions of AIDS and their reactions to the media coverage'. Therefore, Kitzinger argued, her research objectives 'necessitated the use of in-depth work'. A group approach was, however, chosen because of her 'interest in the social context of public understanding'. In her study, 52 focus group sessions were undertaken, with a total number of 351 participants. Each focus group had an average of six participants. The participants were drawn from 'general population' groups, including women whose children attended the same playgroup, members of a retirement club and civil engineers who worked at the same place, as well as some specific groups who might have particular views on AIDS, such as prison officers, male prostitutes, IV drug users and lesbians. The focus group discussions lasted about two hours and were tape-recorded.

This study is rather unusual in terms of the number of sessions because Kitzinger made more extensive use of focus groups than most such research. The main reason was that the participants covered a wide range of different groups of people in England, Scotland and Wales. More importantly, the groups were chosen to explore diversity rather than to establish any kind of 'representativeness'. An interesting aspect of this study is that Kitzinger chose to work with pre-existing groups (see Chapter 4), including people who knew each other through living, working or socialising together. The reason for this was to find out how people talk about AIDS within the 'various and overlapping groupings within which they actually operate' (1994a: 105; see also Chapter 3 in this volume).

Gabrielle McClelland and Robert Newell (2008) explored the experiences of mothers involved in street-based prostitution and substance abuse in the north of England. The research aimed to enable the women to articulate their personal experiences of motherhood in the context of problematic substance use and street-based prostitution and the impact on the separation from their children. Twenty women who were mothers involved in prostitution were recruited to the study from a women-only clinic at a drug agency. Six focus groups were conducted. The women were provided with a list of dates and times of each focus group and they were invited to select one of the focus group that they would like to take part in. This was done to allow each woman to participate in a focus group with women with whom they felt comfortable. Gabrielle McClelland and Robert Newell acknowledged that existing relationships might have influenced the interactions, but it seemed to promote communication and encouraged discussion among the women. The maximum number of women in a group was five, but one group had only two women because two participants did not turn up on the day. Despite this low number, the researchers decided to go ahead with it.

In McClelland and Newell's (2008) study, all the focus groups were conducted at the drug agency at weekly intervals and were audio-recorded. In order to maximise opportunities for the women to interact with each other, the dialogue from the moderator was very minimal. McClelland and Newell found that being involved in street-based prostitution was extremely risky for both the women and their children. The women had high levels of stress as a result of parental responsibilities and lifestyle, and typically this was compromised by problematic substance use. When timely and appropriate support was unavailable for them, risks were increased for both the mothers and the children. From what they found, McClelland and Newell recommended that in order to help these women and their children to deal better with the problems, proactive identification and implementation of positive supportive strategies should be emphasised.

As a self-contained focus group study, this can provide generalisation of the theoretical concept generated from the study (Willis et al. 2009). In her research regarding disadvantaged young people and love and intimacy (2001), Deborah Warr situated her study within a contemporary theoretical framework which connected personal and interpersonal experiences with broader social and economic changes. This led Warr to explore how these young people experienced broad social patterns of change in sexual behaviour. This was also the reason that led her to select focus groups as a method of her study instead of individual in–depth interviews. The participants in her focus groups were recruited from pre-existing groups of young people who had been disadvantaged by long-term unemployment, with different class backgrounds, and from both urban and rural areas. In her analysis, she thoroughly presented the interaction about love and intimacy between the participants. The dynamics within groups as well as differences between groups of same-gender, mixed-gender, blue-collar, friendship-based and newly formed group participants are also theorised thoroughly. The comprehensive presentation of the analysis of the dialogue and the interaction that Warr has done in her study provide a confidence in the sociological insights that her study offers. In connecting personal experiences to wider public issues such as social conditions, Warr provided strong research evidence which public health policy and practice can use to address the needs of disadvantaged young people and provide better health services for them (see also Warr 2004; 2005).

## FOCUS GROUPS AS A SUPPLEMENTARY SOURCE OF DATA AND IN MIXED-METHOD STUDIES

Focus groups can be used as a supplementary source of data. For example, information from them can be used as a source of preliminary data in quantitative research. Most often, focus groups are used to generate survey questionnaires. These may be used for developing a programme or intervention. Focus groups can also be used to validate the findings of quantitative research methods such as surveys when the results of the survey method cannot provide a deeper understanding of the participants' perspective.

Focus groups, as David Stewart and colleagues (2009: 592) contend, are especially valuable for preliminary research which explores 'broad, "grand tour" questions about "why", "how", "when", "where", and "what kind"'. This is seen as a distinctive advantage of the method since it allows the researchers to generate responses which are related to quantitative questions efficiently, for example 'how many', 'how much' and 'how often' – without first knowing, for example, 'what kinds to quantify'. As such, qualitative data generated from the focus group method complements data from quantitative methods: 'The former helps identify important dimensions and aspects of phenomena, while the latter provides a means of assessing the frequency and/or magnitude of the types of phenomena discovered.'

However, a common way that researchers use focus groups is to use the method as the preliminary method for developing surveys (Hesse-Biber & Leavy 2010). Focus groups are used to guide the development of questions in quantitative surveys. This is particularly useful in exploratory research when the key issues and terminology are not known since the participants can discuss their perceptions and experiences, select what they wish to stress, and generate categorisations. Focus group data is valuable when constructing survey questions which are more applicable to the lives and needs of the participants. Jenny Kitzinger (2005: 59) too contends that focus groups 'can also provide fertile ground for eliciting anecdotal material and are therefore ideal "seed beds" for "germinating" vignettes for use in questionnaires'.

Focus group research can provide results which allow the researchers to learn more accurately about terms used by the participants and this will allow them to develop more accurate questionnaires (Wilkinson 1998: 117). Sue Wilkinson (1998: 117) contends that knowing about the language used and the relevant concepts of the research participants is 'a prerequisite for sensitive understanding of their lives'. Often, the problem with questionnaires, tests and scales is the 'lack of (sub)cultural sensitivity to people's own vocabularies'. Philip Schlesinger and colleagues (1992: 138) used both questionnaires and focus groups in researching women's responses to violence on television. The focus group interaction presented below shows how the researchers learned from the group data about a problem with the wording of one of the questionnaire items, which asked the participants to denote the extent to which they found a video clip 'entertaining':

Speaker 1:    Even though I said–what I meant by 'not entertaining', I just think it's the wrong word … I enjoyed it in a way, but entertainment's not the right word for it.

Speaker 2:    Gripping?

Speaker 1:    No.

Speaker 3:    Enthralling?

Speaker 4:    Riveting – something like that?

Speaker 3:    Because entertaining sometimes is something that's humorous, amusing, jovial.

Speaker 1:    Yes … that just grabbed you.

Sylvia Nassar-McMillan and DiAnne Borders (2002) tell us about the 'highly effective' use of qualitative focus groups to generate items for their actual questionnaire and to refine existing questions for the Volunteer Work Behavior Questionnaire. Focus groups were employed to allow them to find the language and terminology which would be more suitable to the population: people who were educationally diverse but shared the experience of being 'direct service volunteers'. Through focus group interviews, substantial modifications of the survey questions were made to the extent that Nassar-McMillan and Borders referred to the method as the 'quality control measure'.

Often, focus groups have also been very useful in the latter part of quantitative research, particularly in the analysis of large-scale quantitative methods such as surveys. According to Jenny Kitzinger (2005: 59), focus groups can help to 'tease out the reasons for surprising or anomalous findings and to explain the occurrence of "outliers" identified – but not explained – by quantitative approaches'. Although focus groups cannot generate quantitative data like quantitative methods can, they may in fact challenge how such data is interpreted. Focus groups not only can help to facilitate the interpretation of quantitative data, but also provide more depth to the results obtained from the more structured survey. Focus groups can also be employed as a 'confirmatory method' which can be used for testing hypotheses (Stewart et al. 2009: 590). This application is crucial when the researchers wish to confirm their hypotheses, as disconfirmation by even a small group of people can result in rejection of the hypothesis.

In the following paragraphs, I will provide an example of the use of focus groups as a supplementary method or in mixed-method studies in more detail.

Jihad Makhoul and Rima Nakkash (2007: 128) examined the health beliefs of young people using the focus group method to verify quantitative community indicators. They found that, more recently, in planning for community health promotion interventions, researchers have adopted qualitative methods as a means of understanding community settings and to provide insight into the behaviours of individuals within these communities because these methods are more 'sensitive to contextual meanings of health determinants' than quantitative approaches. The use of both approaches has consequently resulted in the development of better interventions for local communities since it contributes to 'the completeness of the phenomena of interest' and provides 'additional pieces of the puzzle'. Although qualitative methods have been employed to enhance the quality of survey questions and data, they are seldom adopted to verify results of quantitative approaches.

An urban health study in three communities of Beirut, namely Borj Barajneh Palestinian Refugee Camp, Hay el Sullum and Nabaa, was conducted by the Faculty of Health Sciences (FHS) at the American University of Beirut (AUB). The study aimed to examine the economic, social and environmental conditions which had affected various aspects of health at the three study sites. A household survey was carried out on a sample of 3300 households in spring 2002. An additional survey was undertaken with young people, aged 13–19 years, in 2003. All the youths in all the selected households were interviewed individually using questionnaires conducted by trained interviewers from the community after consent was secured from their parents or guardians and the young people themselves. A total sample size of 1294 adolescents was yielded. The questionnaire was developed from the review of published materials by a multidisciplinary research team whose background was in psychology, health behaviour and health policy to measure the health and risk behaviour of these youths and was translated into Arabic. It was pilot tested with 41 youths, aged 13–19 years, from the study communities. The final survey instrument comprised 228 items related to the adolescents themselves, their families and their communities, and included questions about behaviours perceived to be risky to young people's health, such as smoking cigarettes and argileh (water pipe) smoking, weight control for obesity and exercises.

The research team in Makhoul and Nakkash's (2007) study conducted six focus group discussions in the Borj Barajneh refugee camp with 41 adolescents to gain a better insight into the results generated from the survey so that an appropriate community-based intervention with Palestinian youth could be planned. The adolescents were placed into the following groups: girls 13 to 19, boys 13 to 19, girls and boys 13 to 15 and 16 to 19, and one group of boys and one of girls who were not attending school. Makhoul and Nakkash (2007: 130) stated that the reason they selected the focus group method was mainly due to its ability to generate timely data on topics of particular interest from a number of research participants so that their perceptions can be uncovered. They contended that an advantage of the focus group method is its ability to permit marginalised individuals to talk about their views, because it allows the group members to support each other mutually in articulating feelings which are common to them but would otherwise be unexpressed in another environment. Focus groups would also permit them to become familiarised with group norms and those which deviated from these norms.

Both Makhoul and Nakkash facilitated three groups each with the assistance of note-takers. Each group discussion lasted from 90 to 120 minutes. It commenced with an icebreaking activity which was led by volunteer members of the community. The funnelling questions process, which is a technique that is based on commencing the discussions with general questions and moving on to specific ones, was adopted. A general topic such as how young people spend time in the camp directed the discussion to sports and leisure activities in which they had participated. This unconfined discussion allowed them to verify the relevant indicator they had gained from the survey. For instance, the opinion of the univariate indicator 'percentage of adolescents who engage in sports activities' of the youths was asked by the following question: 'What percentage do you think answered that they engage in sports activities?' After their answer, the quantitative indicator that had been obtained was shown to them. This resulted in further dialogue on that topic and the indicator as well as on other topics which were of importance to them but were not included in the survey.

Makhoul and Nakkash (2007: 131) contended that the qualitative data generated from focus group discussions with the youths in the Borj el Barajneh Palestinian refugee camp 'substantiated and contextualized the quantitative findings of an earlier survey' which was conducted with Palestinian youth. Due to the flexible and open nature of the focus group method, it decreased the social distance between the youths and the moderator and this encouraged the young people to talk about issues which were of importance to them. This was not possible with the questionnaire. Data analysis was directed by emerging themes and patterns inherent in the data itself, and gender differences became more transparent in the data obtained through the focus group discussions. In the survey, these differences would have been brought up by an analysis only if the researchers were interested in gender differences rather than the general categories and designed the questionnaire accordingly.

Subsequent focus group discussions with several young people not only revealed differences between the indicators and the lived realities of the youth, but also provided interpretations of the issues raised. They also brought up other issues of importance to the adolescents themselves. This has marked ramifications about the adopted research approach and the type of information collected. Makhoul and Nakkash (2007: 134) contended that if they did not go back to the adolescents to verify the data collected, their intervention planning might have missed important issues which require attention.

## FOCUS GROUPS IN MULTI-METHOD STUDIES

Focus groups have been popularly employed in multi-method studies, where a combination of several qualitative methods is used to generate data. For example, they can be used in conjunction with in-depth interviews, participant observation, art-based research or the photovoice method. David Morgan (1997: 3) argues that the combined uses of qualitative methods will contribute 'something unique to the researcher's understanding of the phenomenon under study'. The main purpose of using multi-methods in studies is the 'mutual enhancement' that complements each method that is used. This is known as 'triangulation' (Patton 2002; Cho & Trant 2006; Lambert & Loiselle 2008; Padgett 2008; Liamputtong 2009).

The most common multi-method research is the use of focus groups with in-depth interviews (Lambert & Loiselle 2008; Hesse-Biber & Leavy 2010). The combination of these two major qualitative methods yields great benefits to researchers.

Currently, there are two main design strategies: focus groups are employed as a follow-up to in-depth interviews and individual interviews are utilised as a follow-up to group interviews. Often, the two methods are used because the research questions necessitate both depth and breadth (Morgan 1996; Lambert & Loiselle 2008). In-depth interviews offer more depth from individual participants whereas focus groups provide the researchers with a more extensive range of data in a shorter timeframe (Hesse-Biber & Leavy 2010). Focus group interviews may be used as a follow-up for in-depth inter-views in order to corroborate data from individual interviews, explore how responses from individual participants differ in a group environment, expose individual partici-pants to the group dynamics as a way of empowerment or education, and to have a larger number of participants which may not have been possible for in-depth inter-views (see Mmari et al. 2009).

However, what we tend to see commonly is that the researchers would employ focus groups as the principal research method and then use in-depth interviews with some or all of the focus group participants as a follow-up method. It permits the researchers to generate initial data from the group which provides a group dialogue in general, and then they can explore more data on particular aspects of the dialogue. This strategy provides the opportunity for the participants to be able to share their perspectives in the group environment and then have a particular time to speak about their personal perceptions, beliefs and experiences as well as the impact of the focus group in greater depth. In addition, it is likely that in the process of group discussion, many other issues which are not included in the original questions will emerge. Being able to follow up with in-depth interviews, the researchers are able to obtain more data where necessary so that their research questions can be answered as well as possible (Lambert & Loiselle 2008; Hinton & Earnest 2010). In their research regarding stressors, coping and social support with women in Papua New Guinea, Rachael Hinton and Jaya Earnest (2010) tell us that often the women would ask for an individual interview to discuss their point of view about sensitive issues, such as being a second wife or domestic violence, which was difficult to speak about during group discussions.

Hannah Bradby and colleagues (2007), in their research concerning the use of Child and Adolescent Mental Health Services (CAMHS) among families of South Asian origin who are underrepresented as service users in an area of a Scottish city, employed focus groups and in-depth interviews as tools for data collection. They carried out six community focus groups and individual interviews with families who had used CAMHS and with CAMHS professionals who had been involved in the cases of those families. They also held focus groups with parents of children who had problems usually referred to CAMHS but who had not used the service.

They divided the study into two phases. Phase 1 was concerned with community focus groups. Six focus groups were conducted with a total of 35 participants. The groups were all conducted by one author who is multilingual (Hindi, Punjabi and English). Hannah Bradby assisted in one focus group. The participants had childcare responsibilities and never had any contact with CAMHS. They were recruited by a community education worker, a member of the Hindu Temple and a bilingual NHS worker. Different recruiting strategies were adopted to ensure that no single network would be overrepresented. The recruitment of their study was also done following the themes which recurred in the group discussions. For example, when 'grannies and aunties' were consistently identified as influential people, a group of older women was then convened. The purposively sampled groups included Hindus, Sikhs and Muslims, women and men, older and younger adults and were carried out by making contact with friends of friends and neighbours.

Each focus group was presented with three vignettes which portrayed common problems that would be referred to CAMHS, including a 12-year-old depressed girl; a 9-year-old boy with behavioural problems; and a 16-year-old boy with psychotic symptoms. The participants were then asked 'what advice they would offer such children's parents and whether health and social services would be helpful to those with similar problems'. Bradby and colleagues pointed out that focus groups are a good approach for initiating group norms, cultural values and expectations. These were then examined further in individual interviews in phase 2.

In phase 2, Bradby and colleagues carried out individual interviews with family and professionals. They interviewed seven families who had a child currently using the services or who had recently used the services, whom they referred to as the 'service users'. The families were recruited through a community CAMHS team in the study location. They also interviewed five families who had children with diffi- culties, but who had not been referred to CAMHS. These families were recruited through a range of community professionals, including general practitioners, health visitors, general-practice-based nurses, school and a classroom support worker. These families were referred to as 'potential service users'. All interviews were semi-structured, following a topic guide which was developed from the results and issues emerging from focus groups and their previous research.

Evidence from the two qualitative methods carried out in phases 1 and 2 suggested that due to the stigma of mental illness and the fear of gossip, many families did not wish to use CAMHS. For those families who had sought help from CAMHS, they attempted to decrease the stigma they suffered by declaring that mental illness was not madness and could be healed. Families whose children had complex emotional and behavioural difficulties expressed that their child's difficulties were exacerbated by discrimination from health, education and social care professionals. Culturally inap- propriate services were experienced by families of children with severe and enduring mental illness. Additionally, fear of gossip about their children's 'madness' was a major obstacle to the use of the services. Bradby and colleagues suggested that because of the widespread concern over the stigma of children's mental illness, culturally com- petent services for children's mental health should be developed.

Some researchers may use a series of focus groups and in-depth interviews in their research. For example, Bronwyn Lichtenstein (2005), in her research regarding domestic violence, sexual ownership and HIV risk in women in the deep south of the United States, employed a series of focus groups and in-depth individual inter- views to obtain information on domestic violence and HIV risk. Lichtenstein (2005: 704) contended that 'a triangulated approach to qualitative data-gathering was taken to generate insights into domestic violence as well as to obtain knowledge and understanding of dominant cultural values'. Two focus groups, comprising eight women in each group, were conducted in order to establish a working definition of domestic violence. This was followed by individual interviews carried out with

50 women in order to examine the interactions between domestic violence and HIV risk. In accordance with the feminist research framework, a final focus group of eight women was chosen to provide feedback about the results and to cross-validate the findings.

Often, focus groups are used as part of ethnographic research which requires researchers to carry out extensive fieldwork in their research sites. According to Jenny Kitzinger (2005: 59), the combination of in-depth interviews and participant observation with focus groups allows the researchers to 'gain access to different aspects of people's experience'. In their study concerning female tourists, casual sex and HIV risk in Costa Rica (2008), Nancy Romero-Daza and Andrea Freidus employed focus groups as part of their ethnographic research. They examined how young female tourists who visit rural Costa Rica were involved with gringueros, local men who vigorously pursue sexual relationships with foreign women and perceive this as their outlets for sexual adventure. They also considered the implications of these relations for sexual behaviours which could accommodate the spread of HIV/AIDS. Their findings revealed the necessity to use tourism-related locales to implement HIV/AIDS awareness strategies targeted at women tourists, gringueros and other local young people.

Their research was carried out in Monteverde, a rural area in the Tilarán mountain range in the Puntarenas province of Costa Rica which has become one of the main tourist attractions in the country. Annually, there are about 250,000 tourists visiting Monteverde. However, a newer attraction that attracts more young tourists is adventure tourism. This provides tourists with adventures such as trekking, spelunking, white-water rafting, mountain climbing and ropes courses. Often, due to the nature of the adventures, it facilitates relationships between local guides and tourists that often include sexual liaisons.

Data of this ethnographic research was collected through six focus groups, 25 in-depth individual interviews and extensive participant observation in several locations where locals and tourists interact. Recruitment of participants was undertaken through convenience and snowball sampling (see Chapter 4). Extensive participant observation was carried out prior to the collection of focus groups and individual interviews. This permitted the researchers to build rapport with the locals and assisted them in developing personal networks which led to word-of-mouth referrals for further participants.

The six focus groups were conducted by Andrea Freidus (an American woman in her mid-twenties) and a field research assistant in either Spanish or English. On average, each one took about one and a half hours. Three focus groups were held with adult local residents and three were conducted with foreign women. The focus groups with locals included two with females (seven in each group) and one with males (four men). The three focus groups with foreigners comprised: one with twelve American women who were quite new to the area; one with nine participants (five women and four men) from the United States who were undergraduate students attending a field school and had been in the area for about four weeks; and one with a group of seven American women who had made decision to live permanently in Monteverde or to stay indefinitely, and, at the time of the fieldwork, all of the women were in a relationship with a local male.

Seventeen in-depth individual interviews were carried out with foreign visitors. All of the interviews took about one hour and were undertaken in English in private settings by Andrea Freidus. Additionally, eight individual interviews were held with local residents. Seven of these were carried out with men who worked in tourism or were involved with female tourists. They included a rainforest guide, a taxi driver, a bartender, a waiter, two Internet café workers and a representative from the Tourism Commission. One in-depth interview was conducted with a local woman who had been working as a tourist guide for about 12 years. All of the interviews with locals were carried out in Spanish and took about one hour.

Extensive participant observation was carried out in restaurants, Internet cafés, discos, bars and other locations where locals and tourists socialised. Data obtained from participant observation was used to corroborate the findings from in-depth interviews and focus groups. For six months with an average of four nights a week, Andrea Freidus visited the bars where tourists and locals tended to congregate. She also worked as a waitress in one of the local restaurants which hosted live music and was a frequent attraction for both tourists and locals a few nights per week. Additionally, she acted as the coach of the local women's soccer team. This provided her with the opportunity to build relationships with local people.

According to Romero-Daza and Freidus (2008: 184), their findings suggested that 'women tourists who initiate relations with local men are driven by stereotypes of the Latin lover as romantic and attentive. Thus, for both tourists and locals, stereotypes of the exotic "other" appear to be the main motivating factor.' Data from focus groups, interviews and participant observation revealed that these stereotypes are fortified by the behaviours of both foreign women and locals, hence confirming the ideas each group has about the other. The data shows that relations between female tourists and local men were often in the form of casual sex, group sex and, most importantly, unprotected sex. This posed a risk to tourists, gringueros and their local female partners. The situation was further complicated by the limited availability of condoms outside clinic settings. The findings point to the urgent need for specially designed HIV prevention campaigns for young female tourists who are involved in sexual relations with local men.

This study is an example of a good study which makes use of multi-methods such as focus groups, in-depth interviews and participant observations to triangulate the findings.

## FOCUS GROUP AND NEEDS ASSESSMENT

In needs assessment, focus groups are invaluable. Focus groups are often employed in health education and promotion, particularly as part of the process of programme planning (see Goldman & Schmalz 2001; Kegler et al. 2001; Crowe 2003; Liamputtong & Jirojwong 2009). As in any piece of research, in needs assessment, a focus group interview is a useful research tool when the researcher does not have deep knowledge about the participants or local community (Liamputtong & Jirojwong 2009; Ardalan et al. 2010).

A needs assessment is a process which is employed to identify the needs expressed by an individual or a group. For individuals, they may carry out needs assessment to express their personal needs. Their needs, importance and practicality are reviewed, and steps to address them are taken. The reported needs from this representative group can then be adopted for planning purposes (Gilmore & Campbell 2005).

Needs assessment permits a logical starting point for individual action and programme development. It also provides a continuing process for keeping activities on track (Gilmore & Campbell 2005). A needs assessment process helps health and social welfare professionals in several ways. For instance, reported needs can be used to develop health and social programmes and target groups can take part in more meaningful and appropriate activities. Furthermore, needs assessment can be more closely profiled, and health and social welfare professionals can assess changes and trends over a period of time.

Needs assessment also enables health and social welfare professionals to examine a number of factors that affect the health and social issues of the target groups and their ability to influence them positively (Hodges & Videto 2005). It is a crucial aspect of programme planning, implementing and functioning as the starting point of programme evaluation. Needs assessment can be used to identify the health and social problems in a target group and gaps in the levels of the group's wellness can be pinpointed (Hodges & Videto 2005). Once health and social welfare professionals have identified these, they can prioritise the problems and make decisions about which health and social needs should be developed to provide direction to programme developers. Through this process, programming can be developed, implemented and presented efficiently, and it will be more likely to be effective in reaching the goals and objectives of the groups (Hodges & Videto 2005). Most importantly, needs assessment permits not only a method of measuring and enhancing equity in the provision and use of health and social welfare services, but also health and social inequalities to be addressed in the target groups.

In needs assessment, Hodges and Videto (2005) suggest, it is wise to undertake a number of focus groups which consist of representatives of different subgroups in the local community. As part of a needs assessment for planning a Queensland Rural Chronic Disease Initiative, Sansnee Jirojwong and the research team (2005) carried out focus group interviews with several interest groups including senior citizens and male farmers of four rural Queensland communities. This way, information gathered is likely to be sufficient for making decisions in health promotion programmes developed for the community.

Teresa Crowe (2003) documented needs assessment research sponsored by the Department of Health and the HIV/AIDS Administration in Washington, DC, in collaboration with Deaf-REACH, a community service centre for deaf and hard of hearing (HOH) individuals in Washington, DC. The main aim of this qualitative research study was to develop HIV and AIDS prevention materials specifically catered for the deaf and HOH community. The literature has pointed to the barriers that deaf and HOH persons experience. Also, there is a strong consensus among researchers, educators and practitioners that the deaf and HOH community has special needs which must be addressed properly (Crowe 2003). Recognising this need, one of the main objectives of this qualitative study was to address the following question: 'What are the needs of the deaf and HOH community in terms of being educated about HIV-related issues?' (p. 5).

Two needs assessment focus groups were held with 14 participants, grassroots members and those with a mental illness who used community services from Deaf-REACH. The focus groups were organised at a rented local coffee house. The participants were provided with refreshments as well as breakfast for the morning group and lunch for the afternoon group. They were informed that the purpose of the focus group was to gain an understanding of their knowledge, beliefs and practices related to HIV, to obtain an understanding of the need for culturally specific HIV prevention materials, and to generate an understanding of accessibility issues in terms of service acquisition and prevention materials.

Data was recorded by two certified interpreters who pronounced their translation onto an audiotape and two deaf note-takers who took notes of general themes and discussion on pre-typed note sheets. The notes were completed during and at the end of the focus group sessions. Debriefing sessions with interpreters and note-takers were undertaken soon after the group sessions so that any ambiguous issues and clarification of any unfamiliar signs, such as name signs, gestural signs and so on, could be discussed.

Teresa Crowe contended that the results of this study suggested crucial issues to be taken into account when developing HIV prevention materials for the deaf community. The most important issue is the need to recognise that there are distinctive cultural and linguistic needs for deaf people who use sign language as their primary means of communication. They are likely to be at risk for potential HIV infection primarily due to inaccessibility of services, lack of available interpreters and lack of culturally sensitive prevention materials. Crowe (2003: 305) suggested that it is misleading to assume that deaf people are able to access and understand prevention materials which are designed mainly for English-speaking and hearing individuals. In fact, the results of this study led to the conclusion that 'some deaf people may not grasp the importance of prevention material that is mismatched for their culture and linguistic needs'. Hence, in designing HIV prevention materials for the deaf community, simplicity of language, an emphasis on visual images, and using ASL-structured word phrases should be among the most important aspects to consider.

The results of this project confirmed many issues found in previous research. The participants in the needs assessment focus groups articulated their desire and motivation to know more about HIV. Often, social barriers such as difficulty obtaining interpreters and inaccessibility of services and materials prevented them from becoming knowledgeable persons. They also expressed difficulties in learning about HIV through traditional written materials such as brochures and pamphlets. They said that the language used in these written materials is often too difficult to understand and easily misunderstood. Additionally, many participants had partial information or misinformation about HIV. Crowe argued that if people do not know or are unclear about HIV, prevention efforts can be unsuccessful. Therefore, efforts at decreasing social barriers for deaf individuals may be useful in accommodating prevention activities. See also the recent study conducted by Ali Ardalan and colleagues

(2010) on the self-perceived needs of older people in the aftermath of the Bam earthquake in Iran.

## FOCUS GROUPS AND COMMUNITY-BASED PARTICIPATORY RESEARCH

Focus groups have also increasingly been employed in the context of community-based participatory research (CBPR), where community members become 'agents of change by telling their stories and suggesting strategies for collective action' (Kieffer et al. 2005: 147). CBPR is an emerging research approach which equally involves the community, such as community members, agency representatives and organisations, and the researchers in all facets of the research process (Israel et al. 2005; Mosavel et al. 2005). CBPR empowers different groups to collaborate in research in order to appreciate and address the complex social, cultural, political and structural factors impacting on the lives of individuals and their communities. It has been referred to as employing 'the social sciences to advance the "democratic process"' (Mosavel et al. 2005: 2578). Through CBPR, the relevance, interpretation and use of the research data can be enhanced, and appropriate dissemination of research findings can be ensured (Israel et al. 2005; Mosavel et al. 2005; Rhodes et al. 2008). In the health area, there has been an increasing use of this partnership approach in cross-cultural research which especially focuses on eliminating health disparities and improving health outcomes of local people (see Mosavel et al. 2005; Maiter et al. 2008; Minkler & Wallerstein 2008).

Sora Tanjasiri and colleagues (2002) presented a case study of a project (the PATH Project) to reduce health disparities in breast and cervical cancer among seven Southeast Asian and Pacific Islander communities in Southern California. Their work is interesting as they applied the CBPR framework presented above to the process of needs assessment and programme planning in order to understand and address the complex circumstances which contributed to poor rates of breast and cervical cancer screening in these communities. The PATH Project aimed to achieve the Healthy People 2010 goals for breast and cervical cancer screening. This aim set the primary guidance for the development of the needs assessment attempt.

In monthly planning meetings of the project, the communities emphasised the necessity of conducting a needs assessment process. This process was seen as having several values. It would identify not only the needs of women in their communities, but also men, community leaders and health care providers, who were perceived to be crucial to addressing breast and cervical cancer problems. This process would therefore result in forms of enquiry which would be acceptable and appropriate to community members, and which would allow trust to be built with the communities. The process would also ensure that all needs assessment results would be shared with the members of each community so that the findings could be validated and ownership of the project by community members could be maximised.

The university partners planned a two-way needs assessment approach: focus groups with community members and leaders; and individual interviews using a survey with a convenient sample of women. The focus group guides and survey instruments were developed, discussed and modified until the PATH community partners were satisfied that the instruments were culturally sensitive and appropriate for their communities. The focus groups examined five forms of health promotion and cancer control. These included general health needs and concerns in the community, knowledge of health promotion, knowledge and performance of breast and cervical cancer screening examinations, community needs regarding improving breast and cervical cancer screening and control, and barriers to basic health services.

The focus group guides were translated into the appropriate Southeast Asian or Pacific Islander language after they had been approved by community members. Bilingual, bicultural focus group moderators were then appointed to run the focus groups in their communities. Both men and women moderators were recruited since it was important for men to carry out the male group and women to hold the female group in several communities. A half-day planning workshop was held for the bilingual, bicultural focus group moderators for training in the focus group method.

Each focus group took about two hours and was usually carried out in the evenings or at weekends. Food was always provided as a means to create a comfortable social environment for the participants. For each focus group, the community partners recruited about 10 to 12 participants. Each participant was provided with $20 at the conclusion of the group to 'thank' them for their time and participation.

In addition to focus groups, the PATH Project also conducted individual interviews with the women in order to examine their levels of knowledge, beliefs and behaviours concerning breast and cervical cancer screening. These interviews were done after the initiation of the focus groups and hence included culturally specific issues and concerns which were identified through focus groups. Once the initial draft of the survey was approved by the PATH community partners, it was translated into each language and pilot tested with five women from each community. These pilot tests allowed the community partners to modify the instruments. A total of 30 women per community were recruited via friendship circles and other convenience sampling techniques. They were invited to participate in the 45-minute survey after providing verbal consent. Each woman was also given $20 at the conclusion of the survey.

At the conclusion of the needs assessment activities, the PATH community and university partners participated in a three-month process of exhibiting and prioritising possible intervention strategies for each community. During the partner planning meetings, PATH community partners who acted as facilitators and interviewers shared their ideas about emerging issues which were important for their communities and recommendations for actions of their particular communities. The emerging ideas and actions were collected and analysed into major themes and categories by the university partners. They were then brought back to share with the PATH community partners for discussion and further refinement. The resulting documents were labelled as 'the Community Action Plans (CAP)' for each community.

Sora Tanjasiri and colleagues (2002: 152) contended that, through the process of CBPR and needs assessment, it became clear that restraining and decreasing breast and cervical cancer disability and mortality requires 'a multipronged approach that includes not only early detection but support services for women and their families throughout the process of cancer screening, treatment, and survival'. However, it was the community partners who took steps and cultivated their existing resources to manage the problems. For example, a mini-grant programme was created, to provide other organisations with some grants to develop and support their own cancer screening and support activities. The community partners also fulfilled the communities' requests to assist them in negotiating the complex medical care system and developed a plan to train community volunteers as 'navigators' who could travel with the women to their medical appointments. These navigators would also provide education, which would allow the women in their communities to 'become their own best advocates for care' (p. 152).

## FOCUS GROUPS AND THE PHOTOVOICE METHOD

Within CBPR, the method of photovoice has emerged as an innovative means of working with marginalised people and in cross-cultural research (Jurkowski et al. 2009; Valera et al. 2009; Liamputtong 2010a; Wilkin & Liamputtong 2010). Photovoice is a research method which is based on the principles of critical consciousness theory developed by Paulo Freire (1970) and feminist theory developed by Caroline Wang and Mary Ann Burris (1997) (Valera et al. 2009; see also Chapter 2 in this volume). The photovoice method rejects traditional paradigms of power and the production of knowledge within the research relationship (McIntyre 2008). The researchers are concerned about developing critical consciousness and empowerment among their research participants. Hence, the photovoice method tends to be used in collaborative and participatory research.

Essentially, photovoice methodology allows people to record and reflect the concerns and needs of their community via taking photographs. It also promotes critical discussion about important issues through a dialogue about the photographs they have taken. Their concerns may reach policy-makers through public forums and the display of their photographs. By using a camera to record their concerns, it permits individuals who rarely have contact with those who make decisions over their lives to make their voices heard.

Methodologically, photovoice requires the participants to take photographs which represent their understanding and meanings of life. The photographs are then used as the basis for discussions in later interviews, which often occur in group settings. The discussion of the photographs permits the participants to articulate the understanding and interpretations of the images they have taken. Elizabeth Carlson and colleagues (2006) posit that the aims of the photovoice method include:

- encouraging discussion around a topic of concern to the participants;
- creating a safe environment for discussion and reflection among the participants and the researchers;
- encouraging the participants to recognise a need for action in certain areas of their life or community;
- permitting their ideas to be disseminated to a wider community in order to facilitate changes.

As readers can see, the aims of the photovoice method are very similar to what the focus group methodology offers.

Previous photovoice projects have suggested that the participants benefit personally and collectively. This is another similarity to the aim of the focus group methodology (see Chapters 1 and 8 in this volume). Collective relationships often develop through working on the photographs together with others and through the group sessions that follow. Caroline Wang (2003: 190) tells us that in her research with homeless people, the participants, by taking part in the research, had the opportunity to know and build up ties and relationships with others. They were able to 'bond as a peer support group for problem solving and teamwork'. Photovoice allowed the homeless people 'to speak from their experience and talk about what mattered to them so that they could help one another survive'.

Pamela Valera and colleagues (2009) conducted a photovoice project, what they called 'Trying to Eat Healthy', with ethnic and racially minority mothers living in New York City. SisterLink is a programme of Community Action for Prenatal Care which is funded by the New York State Department of Health AIDS Institute. It is situated at the Northern Manhattan Prenatal Partnership in New York City. The nine participants in their study were recruited from SisterLink and were mostly ethnic and racially minority mothers with ages ranging between 20 and 45 years. Four were African American, three Afro-Caribbean, one Caucasian and one Asian American. Most of them came from low-income backgrounds; their annual incomes were less than $10,000. Six women received public assistance, and three were living in homeless family shelters.

The photovoice project was part of a CBPR project conducted between September 2007 and December 2007. Three focus group discussions, ranging from one to three hours, were held in a private and comfortable training room. During the first group meeting, the women were provided with an overview of the photovoice method. Consent from all participants was obtained. They were also informed that they would need to be involved in three additional sessions and that they would be given a disposable camera and $10 compensation for their participation. The women were informed about the importance of reflecting on their environments and of using photographs to share their lived experiences and perceptions about the social problems that they faced in their community. They were invited to take photographs which portrayed their experiences with access to healthy food in Central Harlem.

In the first focus group session, the participants discussed their concerns which had affected their families and they agreed to focus on particular questions. They were encouraged to take photographs which would reflect the research questions. They were also told to bring their disposable cameras for processing to the SisterLink office prior to the next meeting.

In the second focus group session, the women were invited to review their photographs. Each woman was instructed to select four to six photographs for discussion in the group. A focus group facilitators' guide, referred to as the objective, reflective, interpretive and decisional (ORID) questions, was used to facilitate their thought process. In the third session, the participants and researchers discussed the strengths and challenges of the photovoice project. The researchers acknowledged the accomplishments of each woman and presented the findings to the group. Possible solutions for the social issues were also discussed in this last session.

The ORID focus group discussions contained four sequent stages. First, the objective questions invited the participants to talk about the aim of taking the photographs including 'How many pictures did you take?', 'What did you observe?' and 'How long did it take you to complete your research assignment?' Second, reflective questions were used to allow the women to speak about how they felt about their photographs, for example 'How did you feel when you took that picture?', 'What was the most challenging part of taking these pictures?' and 'How did you decide to take this picture?' Third, using interpretive questions enabled the participants to describe the meaning of their photographs; these include 'What would you say about this picture to someone who is not from your neighbourhood?' and 'What did you achieve by taking this picture?' Finally, decisional questions were used to prompt the women to respond to the problems of food insecurity and limited access to healthy foods. Examples of the questions are 'What possible solutions do you have to address food insecurity?', 'What needs to change?' and 'Who should be involved in changing these issues?' (Valera et al. 2009: 303)

Pamela Valera and colleagues (2009) contended that their research was the first study to reveal the usefulness of photovoice as a method to identify the challenges to eating healthy foods in New York City. Photovoice allowed the women critically to examine their community through their lived experiences. They suggested that through focus group discussions and using photographs as evidence of the women's plight, the participants were able to document their own stories about the challenges in accessing healthy foods. What made this project different from other traditional focus group research is that the photovoice method allowed the participants to be involved in the whole process of research, including the dissemination of their research findings. With the photovoice method, the researchers could use focus group discussions to allow the participants to reflect on the pictorial data that they had collected. As such, both the researchers and the women ended their group discussions with rich data and their desire for social change.

According to Valera and colleagues (2009), the photovoice method provides a distinctive tool for understanding a social problem from the perspectives of research participants, which could lead to culturally appropriate solutions since the participants are engaged in the data collection, interpretation and dissemination of the research findings. In their research, the women suggested that food insecurities could decrease by providing better food stamp benefits to include more cash so that they could pay for organic and healthier foods. The provision of food vouchers to use at farmers' markets would also help them to afford healthier food and provide better access to fresh fruit and vegetables. They also suggested that the restricted food stamp programme, the poor food supplies, the dirty corner stores, and inadequate shelter accommodation could not be ignored. This study resulted in the implementation of two important action plans. First, the women wrote letters to their local assembly members to disseminate their research findings to policy-makers. Second, the participants also presented their photovoice project at the Second Annual Conference on Health Disparities at Teachers College, Columbia University. In their conclusion, Valera and colleagues (2009: 313) wrote:

> This photovoice project built on the assets, strengths, and resources of the community. A collaborative partnership was established, and the knowledge of the researchers and participants was integrated for the mutual benefit of both. The project was one way to shed light on the topic of food insecurity in a city that is filled with healthy foods, wealth, and abundance.

See also a recent article by Cooper and Yarbrough (2010) about the combined use of focus group and photovoice methods to obtain understanding of health issues in rural Guatemala.

## CONCLUSION

There are several different ways that researchers can use the focus group method in the health and social sciences. As David Morgan and Joan Bottorff (2010: 579, original emphasis) write, '*There is no single right way to do focus groups*. Instead, there are many different options, and for each research project investigators need to select a way of using focus groups that matches the goals of the project' (see also Barbour 2007). In this chapter, I have discussed the different ways that focus groups can be used as a self-contained method, as supplementary and mixed-method research, and in multi-method studies. I have also pointed to its use in needs assessment, community-based participatory research and the photovoice method. The application of the focus group method is indeed diverse. And this is one of the beauties of the focus group methodology.

## TUTORIAL ACTIVITIES

1  You are embarking on your PhD studies and you are interested in using the focus group methodology to explore the life and work of sex workers in your city. What kind of focus group method would be suitable for your research? What is the main reason that makes you decide on the use of such focus group? Discuss.
2  As part of your work in the local government, you need to design a research project which must be sensitive to the needs of older people in your local community regarding home care, and which eventually will lead to the implementation of an appropriate service for them. How will you use the focus group methodology in this study? Discuss this in great detail.

## FURTHER READING

Ardalan, A., Mazaheri, M., Naieni, K.H., Rezaie, M., Teimoori, F., & Pourmalek, F. (2010). Examining older people's needs following major disasters: A qualitative study of Iranian elders' experiences of the Bam earthquake. *Ageing & Society* 30(1), 11–23.

Bisol, C.A., Sperb, T.M., & Moreno-Black, G. (2008). Focus groups with deaf and hearing youths in Brazil: Improving a questionnaire on sexual behaviour and HIV/AIDS. *Qualitative Health Research* 18(4), 565–578.

*(Continued)*

*(Continued)*

Borghi, J., Shrestha, D.L., Shrestha, D., & Jan, S. (2007). Using focus groups to develop contingent valuation scenarios – A case study of women's group in rural Nepal. *Social Science and Medicine* 64(3), 531–542.

Bradby, H., Varyani, M., Oglethorpe, R., Rainec, W., White, I., & Helen, M. (2007). British Asian families and the use of child and adolescent mental health services: A qualitative study of a hard to reach group. *Social Science and Medicine* 65(12), 2413–2424.

Carlson, E.D., Engegretson, J., & Chamberlain, R.M. (2006). Photovoice as a social process of critical consciousness. *Qualitative Health Research* 16(6), 836–852.

Crowe, T.V. (2003). Using focus groups to create culturally appropriate HIV prevention material for the deaf community. *Qualitative Social Work* 2, 289–308.

Lambert, S.D., & Loiselle, C.G. (2008). Combining individual interviews and focus groups to enhance data richness. *Journal of Advanced Nursing* 62(2), 228–237.

Makhoul, J., & Nakkash, R. (2009). Understanding youth: Using qualitative methods to verify quantitative community indicators. *Health Promotion Practice* 10(1), 128–135.

Minkler, M., & Wallestein, N. (2008b). *Community-based participatory research for health: From process to outcomes*, 2nd edition. San Francisco: Jossey-Bass.

Mosavel, M., Simon, C., van Stade, D., & Buchbinder, M. (2005). Community-based participatory research (CBPR) in South Africa: Engaging multiple constituents to shape the research questions. *Social Science and Medicine* 61(12), 2577–2587.

Romero-Daza, N., & Freidus, A. (2008). Female tourists, casual sex, and HIV risk in Costa Rica. *Qualitative Sociology* 31, 169–187.

Valera, P., Gallin, J., Schuk, D., & Davis, N. (2009). 'Trying to Eat Healthy': A photovoice study about women's access to healthy food in New York City. *Affilia: Journal of Women and Social Work* 24(3), 300–314.

Warr, D. (2001). *The practical logic of intimacy: An analysis of a class context for (hetero)sex-related health issues*. PhD thesis, LaTrobe University.

# 7
# FOCUS GROUP METHODOLOGY AND SENSITIVE TOPICS AND VULNERABLE GROUPS

## CHAPTER OBJECTIVES

In this chapter you will learn about:

- Sensitive topics and vulnerable people
- The use of focus group methodology in sensitive topics and with vulnerable people
- Focus groups and sensitive topic research
- Focus groups and vulnerable people

Many researchers have adopted the focus group methodology in their research involving sensitive issues and working with vulnerable people. As I have suggested in Chapter 1, focus groups are a crucial research method for eliciting information from members of groups who are normally hard to reach, including the disadvantaged or disenfranchised. Focus groups allow peer group support and reassurance. As such, their structure empowers group members to share their views and experiences. This is especially crucial when the area of examination may be perceived as sensitive or uncomfortable for the respondents. The focus group method is suitable for examining sensitive issues and for research involving vulnerable and marginalised populations because people may feel more relaxed about talking about these issues when they see that others have similar experiences or views.

This chapter will focus on the way researchers can apply the focus group methodology in examining sensitive topics and with vulnerable people in the health and social sciences. In particular, I will discuss the use of the methodology in research concerning sensitive topics and these include sex research and mental health issues.

I also provide a discussion about the use of the focus group methodology with different social groups including children, people with disabilities and older persons. It must be acknowledged here that I am unable to include all sensitive topics and vulnerable people in one chapter. My intention is to provide some discussions about the application in certain areas as a means to provoke further discussion on this issue.

## SENSITIVE TOPICS AND VULNERABLE PEOPLE

Research is conceptualised as sensitive if the disclosure of opinions, attitudes or behaviours that would normally be kept private is necessitated. This disclosure may 'result in offence or lead to social censure or disapproval, and/or which might cause the respondent discomfort to express' (Wellings et al. 2000: 256). Sociologists Claire Renzetti and Raymond Lee (1993: ix) suggest that sensitive research includes studies which are 'intimate, discreditable or incriminating'. Sensitive topics include personal experiences which may be related to deviance or social control and perspectives for dealing with 'difficult situations' (Williams & Ayres 2007: 656). The disclosure of their sensitive issues may put these individuals 'at risk for stigma or intolerance by others' and may also lead to 'feelings of isolation'. In this sense, research into topics like miscarriage, abortion, death, violence, sexual preferences and conduct, being gay or lesbian, children working as sex workers, the use and abuse of drugs, illegal activities, illness status, especially stigmatised ones such as HIV/AIDS and mental illnesses, to name a few, may be included within the definition of sensitive research (Liamputtong 2007; Williams & Ayres 2007; Dickson-Swift et al. 2008).

Vulnerable and marginalised people are closely related to sensitive issues. A vulnerable person is an individual who experiences 'diminished autonomy due to physiological/ psychological factors or status inequalities' (Silva 1995: 15). Based on this definition, vulnerable individuals are people who 'lack the ability to make personal life choices, to make personal decisions, to maintain independence, and to self-determine' (Moore & Miller 1999: 1034). Therefore, vulnerable individuals may 'experience real or potential harm and require special safeguards to ensure that their welfare and rights are protected' (Moore & Miller 1999: 1034). These vulnerable people then will include those who are 'impoverished, disenfranchised, and/or subject to discrimination, intolerance, subordination, and stigma' (Nyamathi 1998: 65). Based on these descriptions, we may include children, young people, older persons, ethnic minorities, immigrants, sex workers, the homeless, gay men and lesbians, and women. Historically, people suffering from chronic illness, the mentally ill and the caregivers of the chronically ill are also referred to as vulnerable populations (Nyamathi 1998: 65).

The term 'vulnerable' has also been referred to people with 'social vulnerability' (Quest & Marco 2003: 1297). Some population groups, including children, the unemployed, the homeless, drug addicts, sex workers, and ethnic and religious minority groups, face particular social vulnerability. Often, too, the term 'vulnerable' is used interchangeably with such words as 'sensitive', the 'hard-to-reach' and 'hidden populations' (Liamputtong 2007). Hence, we can include sex workers, bouncers and gang members. As Cecilia Benoit and others (2005: 264) suggest, sex workers are likely to be legally and socially labelled as '"outcast" – the whore stigma typically permeates all aspects of a sex worker's life'. Similar to other stigmatised people, women who sell sex services are discriminated and rejected by other societal members. Due to their social stigma, sex workers tend to be isolated from the community and society. This often weakens any support and social networks they have, and hence increases their vulnerability to stress, depression and other ill health (see Warr & Pyett 1999; Pyett 2001; Wojcicki & Malala 2001; Melrose 2002).

In this chapter, due to space limits, I will only refer to focus groups which are relevant to some sensitive topics, including sex and mental illness, and vulnerable groups, particularly children and adolescents, older people and people with disabilities. These groups of people are often perceived by researchers as 'invisible' populations in society (Stone 2003). Focus group research concerning ethnic minorities and in cross-cultural settings is dealt with in Chapter 8.

## THE USE OF FOCUS GROUP METHODOLOGY IN SENSITIVE TOPICS AND WITH VULNERABLE PEOPLE

Researchers have argued for the need to use focus group methodology when researching sensitive issues and working with vulnerable people (see Wilkinson 2004; Hyde et al. 2005; Warr 2005; Liamputtong 2007). These researchers suggest that focus group interviews allow group dynamic and shared lived experiences. Focus group researcher Jenny Kitzinger (1994a: 108, original emphasis) contends that 'group work ensures that priority is given to the respondents' hierarchy of importance, *their* language and concepts, *their* frameworks for understanding the world'. As such, focus groups access the element that other methods may not be able to reach. It permits researchers to disclose aspects of understanding that often remain hidden in the more conventional qualitative interviewing method. Feminist researchers Sharlene Hesse-Biber and Patricia Leavy (2010: 167) argue that group work is inviting to sensitive researchers 'working from "power-sensitive" theoretical perspectives' including feminism (see Chapter 2 in this volume). Group work may reduce the imbalance in power relationships between the researchers and participants that grants the researchers an 'authoritative voice'. This is an issue that most feminist researchers are concerned about. Focus groups, on the other hand, 'create data from multiple voices'.

Focus groups inexorably decrease the power and control of the researchers (Wilkinson 2004: 279; see also Chapters 1 and 2). Due to the number of participants instantaneously involved in the group interaction, the balance of power is transposed from the researchers. The authority of the researchers is 'diffused' in focus groups (Frey & Fontana 1993: 26). Because the goal of a focus group is to give opportunities for an interactive exchange of opinions, it is less influenced by the researchers. Focus group positions 'control over [the] interaction in the hands of the participants rather than the researcher' (Morgan 1988: 18).

The interaction between participants themselves substitutes their exchange with the researchers, and this leads to a greater focus on the points of view of the participants (Warr 2005; Hesse-Biber & Leavy 2010). Focus groups provide opportunities for researchers to listen to local voices (Murray et al. 1994). Jeanette Norris and others (1996: 129) too maintain that a focus group method is a research tool that gives 'a "voice" to the research participant by giving her an opportunity to define what is relevant and important to understand her experience'. The focus group methodology allows researchers to pay attention to the needs of 'those who have little or no societal voice' (Rubin & Rubin 1995: 36; see also Madriz 1998; 2000; 2003; Kossak 2005; Liamputtong 2007).

Focus groups allow 'peer group support and reassurance' (Lichtenstein & Nansel 2000: 120). As such, its structure empowers group members to share their views and experiences. This is especially crucial when the area of examination may be perceived as sensitive or uncomfortable for the respondents. Focus groups are seen as potentially effective tools for researching sensitive topics because the group process prompts participants to examine the issues in their own terms (Seymour et al. 2004). Focus groups help them to generate questions and priorities which are relevant to the areas under exploration and which could be further investigated during the research process. When carefully undertaken, focus groups allow crucial ways of gaining access in research to individuals who are relatively marginalised. Focus groups provide opportunities to 'open up' discussions on sensitive issues which are rarely referred to and not well understood (Seymour et al. 2004: 60).

Focus groups create layers of communications and, therefore, provide respondents with a safe environment where they can articulate their experiences, opinions and beliefs in the company of people who share similar experiences and hold similar beliefs. This results in a familiar atmosphere and it is helpful in encouraging people to discuss any difficult and unpleasant topics such as the stigma of living with mental illnesses and HIV/AIDS, or being street sex workers or having the experience of domestic violence (see Brownhill et al. 2005; Lichtenstein 2005; Davey et al. 2006; Pösö et al. 2008; Ahmad et al. 2009).

In sum, the focus group methodology has its suitability for examining 'sensitive' issues or its use in research involving vulnerable populations, because people may feel more relaxed about talking when they see that others have similar experiences or views (Frith 2000; Wellings et al. 2000; Liamputtong 2007).

## FOCUS GROUPS AND SENSITIVE TOPIC RESEARCH

The focus group methodology has been used in research concerning sensitive topics. In the following sections, I will provide in-depth discussions on the use of the methodology in two sensitive topics as a way of providing examples. These include sex-related research and mental health issues.

### Focus Groups and Sex-Related Research

Focus groups have been adopted in many sex-related research projects (see, for examples, Ngo et al. 2007; Sinha et al. 2007; Ha 2008; McClelland & Newell 2008; Merghati Khoei et al. 2008; Ragnarsson et al. 2008; Rodriguez G de Cortazar et al. 2009). As a researcher who has adopted focus groups in her own work, Hannah Frith

(2000) points to several major advantages of the methodology for researchers doing sex-related research. Because the focus group methodology provides environments which make individuals feel comfortable speaking about sexual experiences, this accommodates people to talk about sex. As a result, it allows the researchers to gain knowledge about the language used by participants in speaking about their sexual conduct.

Sex research has been predominantly conducted by large-scale surveys (see, for examples, Grunseit et al. 2005; Coleman & Testa 2006; Kirby et al. 2007). The use of highly structured research tools permits the researchers to generate data relating to the questions asked. The participants would respond only to those questions on the questionnaire and provide answers by selecting from a set of prepared answers. As such, to be able to construct a good set of questions, the researchers need to know what to ask and how to ask. Frith (2000: 277) argues that 'in order to formulate appropriate questions, a detailed knowledge of the area and a clear understanding of the information required is needed. When a topic is under-explored, detailed knowledge of this kind is not available. In such situations, focus groups can provide a useful alternative.' As I have also suggested in Chapters 1 and 6, the focus group method is a powerful approach for exploring topics about which little is known.

In their research examining women's perceptions of the threat of sexual aggression, Jeanette Norris and colleagues (1996: 129) suggest that focus groups offered a valuable means for understanding the experiences of the participants. This allowed them to develop hypotheses which could be tested in future research. Norris and associates argue that the focus group method is often employed in research such as their own project because it permits the researchers to generate diverse views, attitudes and experiences at the same time. Due to the relatively unstructured format of the method, it provides an opportunity for the revelation of unexpected matters. Although the researchers may have carefully prepared a question guide for their focus groups (see Chapter 5 in this volume), the lively discussions might lead to enigmatic areas of interest and this could markedly change the direction of the research.

In their focus groups on sexual risk taking, Elizabeth Vera and colleagues (1996) expected that issues relevant to teenage pregnancy and HIV infection would be the main concern of their participants. However, it took them by surprise when their 8- to 12-year-old participants spoke about women using sex as a means for bartering for gang protection and drugs. This unanticipated data provided invaluable information for the researchers to develop a complete picture of factors impacting on sexual risk taking among their participants. Frith (2000) argues that participant 'diversions' tend to emerge in focus group research because of the limit of control of the researchers. Due to the greater number of participants, and through persuasion and argument, they are able to influence each other and the direction of the discussion (see Chapters 1 and 2 in this volume).

According to Frith (2000: 282), the discussion of sexual matters is enhanced by the focus group methodology in three ways. First, an awareness of shared experiences among the participants in a group may provide them with confidence to speak about sensitive and difficult subjects. Second, an agreement between the respondents can assist the researchers to form a fuller and more elaborate picture of their perspectives. Last, disagreement between members of the group may make the participants wish to safeguard their opinions by providing further explanations. In Frith's work, young women met in focus groups to share their experiences of refusing sex. Frith (2000: 282) tells us:

> From stories of date rape and scorn at the coercive 'lines' men use, to debates about the relative merits of 'I'm on my period' and 'I don't know you well enough' as excuses for sexual avoidance, the lively conversations are punctuated by offers of sympathy, contested claims and howls of laughter. Focus groups can provide an opportunity for participants to talk about their own experiences and to hear the experiences of others.

As I have suggested in Chapters 1 and 2, focus groups provide safe environments for the group members to feel more secure in the company of others who share similar experiences. If the participants learn that other group members have similar experiences, it will allow them to be able to speak more freely about sensitive sexual matters such as infidelities, sexual risk taking, unsafe sexual practices, homosexual experiences, or any other socially disapproved forms of sexual matters. Shared experiences permit the participants to have more courage to speak about their 'fears, ignorances and prejudices' which are not too strange when they know that other people have the same feelings and experiences (Cooper et al. 1993: 327). Hence, many focus group researchers have found that their participants are willing to talk about highly intimate sexual conduct. For example, Zairean women in Judith Brown et al.'s study (1993) spoke about vaginal secretions and the methods they used in order to 'dry out' the vagina to make it 'tight'. The women described the use of wiping and washing procedures and 30 different substances, mostly leaves and powders, to insert into the vagina to produce the desired outcomes. In their focus group research with Australian women, Celia Roberts and colleagues (1995) showed us that the women had no difficulty in a group discussing their experience of faking orgasms. Rona Rubin (2004) found that men were willing to talk about erectile dysfunction and their attitudes toward the use of Viagra in focus groups in the UK. And young men in New Zealand in Louisa Allen's focus group research (2005) spoke intimately about their sexual and masculine identities.

Hannah Frith (2000: 283) suggests that disclosure of intimate sexual experience from one participant may encourage other members in the group to follow suit. More confident members of the group would normally 'break the ice' for shyer and reluctant participants. In Celia Roberts and colleagues' work (1995: 529–530), they show us that the admission of Jane about faking orgasms prompted Alison to reveal similarly:

| | |
|---|---|
| Interviewer: | Do the guys you know sort of worry about giving a girl an orgasm, like they sort of (oh yeah), or do they just … |
| Jane: | Oh yeah, did you get off, did you get off, did you get off. |
| Megan: | Yeah. |
| Jane: | 'Cos otherwise it says something about them I think. |
| Liz: | Yeah it does. |
| Jane: | And if I say 'No,' then that means like he wasn't good or … |

| Megan: | Yeah, they feel inadequate. |
| Jane: | So in a sense they're more worried about themselves. And so you think they're worried about you enjoying it but, I mean, (they're not) it's sort of, they're more worried about if they were good or not. |
| Megan: | Yeah. |
| Alison: | That's why I think girls fake it, so that they can sort of get it over with. |
| Jane: | I fake it sometimes. Just … 'cos my boyfriend gets really worried … because … he wants to know that he's giving me pleasure too. And so sometimes I'll just fake it, if I'm not really in the mood … |
| Alison: | Yeah, I used to do that a lot. |

When Alison knew that she was not alone in faking orgasms because Jane suggested that she had done it and girls in general do this too, she felt less inhibited about her own behaviour and revealed it in the group.

In Hannah Frith's research, one woman, Linda, said that she had been date raped: 'I said no and I said no and I said no, but I was forced.' Kate, another group member, revealed that she 'went through the same thing' at university. She then spoke about her own experience of date rape. After that other participants, one by one, talked about 'terrible situations' that they had to deal with, such as being pressured for sex by a boyfriend, being harassed at work and being trapped in a locked bedroom with a drunken man. Each woman would speak about her experience by making reference to what the person before her had said: 'I went through the same thing', 'on one occasion I did [get into a terrible situation], and that was a slightly different situation', or 'The only time it's ever come close for me …' (Frith 2000: 284). Clearly, according to Frith, the shared experience of being in 'terrible situations' could have made it easier for the women to share their stories of sexual harassment and abuse. Frith (2000: 290) contends that 'the unique features of focus group research – in particular, the collective discussion of topics and interaction between participants – give specific advantages to sex researchers'.

## FOCUS GROUPS AND MENTAL HEALTH RESEARCH

The focus group method has been adopted in many researches in the mental health area (see Schulze & Angermeyer 2003; Schilder et al. 2004; Brownhill et al. 2005; Lester & Tritter 2005; Davey et al. 2006). In their study on subjective experiences of stigma among schizophrenia patients in Germany, Beate Schulze and Matthias Angermeyer (2003) contend that focus groups permit entrance to research participants who may find face-to-face interaction in individual interviews to be intimidating. This is particularly so for people with schizophrenia who may be reminded of their therapeutic experiences in interview situations. Similar to Hannah Frith's arguments (2000) about the benefit of focus groups in sex research that I presented earlier on, the method creates 'multiple lines of communication' between group members (Schulze & Angermeyer 2003: 301) and hence provides a safe environment for the participants to share experiences, beliefs and viewpoints with others who have something in common with them. This safe environment also facilitates the respondents to speak about uncomfortable and formidable topics like stigma. As focus groups allow interaction among group members, the dynamics within the group reduce the influence of the researcher over the discussion process. As such, it provides the participants with an opportunity to speak more freely about their own concerns. The data that is generated would better reflect the social realities of the participants (Krueger 1994). Hence, the focus group methodology is seen by qualitative researchers as a sensitive approach to use in researching mental health issues.

In their own study, Beate Schulze and Matthias Angermeyer (2003: 301) stated that the focus group methodology was selected because it would allow them to investigate concrete stigmatisation experiences so that they could 'incorporate the lived experiences of those experiencing the stigma into understanding the stigma process and its effects'. Their study explicitly examined the stigma associated with schizophrenia. They wished to identify the concrete circumstances in which people living with a stigmatising condition are 'disqualified from full social acceptance' (Goffman 1986: 1), and how their everyday lives are affected by the stigma. They also gained further information from those in close contact with the participants including their family members and mental health professionals.

A set of focus group questions was created for the moderator. The questions were focused on three areas including concrete stigmatisation experiences, ideas about the causes of stigmatisation and suggestions for anti-stigma interventions. People living with schizophrenia were also invited to speak about the changes that occurred in their lives after they first developed the condition. Their aims were to uncover 'subjective views of stigma' from the perspectives of those who have concrete experiences of living with schizophrenia and those who have witnessed the circumstances of schizophrenic individuals in their everyday life. The focus group method that they selected 'has the advantage of affording a view of stigma which is informed by actual incidences of stigmatisation described by the patients, relatives and mental health professionals'.

Schulze and Angermeyer (2003: 301) contended that if attempts to fight against stigma are to be effective, direct information from people living with schizophrenia and family members is crucial. This will 'make a difference for the lives of those facing obstacles to their social integration on the basis of negative attributes associated with their illness'. The participation of these individuals and their families in anti-stigma programmes may provide them with a sense of empowerment. This will lead to an improvement in their self-esteem and skills for dealing with stigma. People living with schizophrenia and their relatives should form an important partnership in both research on stigma and in programmes to mitigate stigma and discrimination. This is in line with the guideline of the Global Programme against Stigma and Discrimination of the World Psychiatric Association which is based on the premise that mental health professionals must join forces with those who have to deal with stigma in their daily lives; that is, people suffering from schizophrenia and their families (Sartorius & Schulze 2005).

Helen Lester and Jonathan Tritter (2005) explored the experiences of people with serious mental illness using the focus group method. They suggested that individuals living with this condition experience 'both impairment (as embodied irrationality) which can, in itself, be oppressive, and also have to manage their lives within a largely disabling society' (p. 649). In this study, they provided some strategies which were adopted by people with serious mental illness to manage their situations in order to ensure that they could access and receive health services. Lester and Tritter showed us how these were a result of the complex relationship between disability and impairment. They based their research on the social model of disability framework since it provided a valuable means for understanding and making sense of the experience of people living with serious mental illness.

Lester and Tritter conducted 18 focus groups in six Primary Care Trusts (PCTs) across the West Midlands in the UK. The participating PCTs included South Birmingham, Solihull, Cannock, Coventry, Worcester and West Bromwich. The most common diagnoses of the participants in this study were schizophrenia, bipolar disorder and recurrent depression with a mean duration of illness of 8.8 years (range 1–32 years). They had been seen by their general practitioners (GPs) within the past 12 months, and 38 out of 49 participants were in receipt of shared care at the time the focus groups were conducted. They were recruited from day hospitals, patient groups and voluntary sector organisations. All focus groups were held at day centres. Each focus group took between 60 and 90 minutes. This was followed by an additional 30 minutes for refreshments and informal discussion. In focus groups with individuals living with mental illness, additional questions were asked about their experiences. The researchers also conducted focus groups with 39 GPs and 8 practice nurses.

Additionally, focus groups which combined individuals with mental illness and health professionals were held one week after the focus groups of separate participants had been held. These groups comprised approximately half of the individuals with mental illness and health professionals who had attended the separate groups. The second focus group commenced with a presentation of the key issues which emerged in the separate focus groups, followed with discussions on confirmation and elaboration. The rest of the time in the combined group allowed the participants to discuss in great depth issues which individuals with mental illness felt to be of value and relevant to them as well as deliverable by health professionals. These combined groups also examined the roles and responsibilities of both the users and health care professionals and their views about how to improve health services.

The results revealed the importance of the impact of mental illness and the interactions between their impairment and sociocultural relations and processes. These individuals were 'treated as less than equal citizens' (p. 665). Compulsory detention and medical treatment given without consent within the community were constraints on the legal and civil rights of these people. Those who had been in psychiatric hospitals for long periods were denied the opportunity to vote. Also, the social exclusion which was experienced by many people with mental illness severely affected their social and economic rights.

Lester and Tritter suggested that viewing the experiences of people with serious mental illness using a disability discourse is helpful in developing a good understanding about serious mental illness. This may encourage discussion about the position of people with mental illness within society. Lester and Tritter concluded that the results of their research suggest that if the users of mental health services are empowered to be perceived and treated as citizens instead of patients, the social model of disability would offer a valuable foundation for understanding and making sense of their experiences. This framework would offer a means for understanding how larger society responds to people living with serious mental illness and provide a theoretical ground for guiding policy and practice.

## FOCUS GROUPS AND VULNERABLE PEOPLE

Focus groups have also been used in research with vulnerable people. In this section, I will discuss the use of focus groups with three vulnerable groups in order to provide more in-depth discussion and examples for readers. The groups include children and young adults, people with disabilities, and older persons. Ethnic minority or cultural groups will be discussed in Chapter 8.

### Focus Groups and Children and Young Adults

Focus groups have increasingly been seen as a useful method for researching children (see Hennessy & Heary 2005; Hyde et al. 2005; Gibson 2007; Long 2007; Bisol et al. 2008; Ezekiel et al. 2009; Rodriguez G de Cortazar et al. 2009). It is only in the last 10 years that we have started to witness its use in children and young people in the areas of health education and health psychology (Hennessy & Heary 2005; Gibson 2007).

The focus group methodology is especially useful when working with disempowered groups, such as children and young people who may be reluctant to express their concerns in a one-to-one environment (Peterson-Sweeney 2005). Focus groups allow the interaction and stimulation of thought to occur during group process and this can produce rich data which is difficult to generate in an individual interview. When interviewed individually, children and young adults may feel pressured to respond in a particular way as they think that is what the researchers want them to do. Youths may also be reluctant to speak about their true feelings with an adult researcher, or may be too timid and frightened to discuss these in an individual interview. In contrast, focus group discussions are more relaxed as they provide a more natural environment than that of an individual interview. The participants share common experiences relevant to the discussed issues and they are encouraged to share their perspectives in a group atmosphere.

Focus group researchers Jeffrey Borkan and others (2000: 209) also suggest that focus groups offer 'an enjoyable forum for interaction' among the participants and permit some control of the quality of data because 'extreme views are often muted or marginalized by the majority'. They also offer to respondents the possibility for connecting with others and the continuous establishment of opinions during the group sessions, something not permissible in an in-depth interview. In their research on sexuality among school children in Ireland, Abbey Hyde and colleagues (2005: 2593) used focus groups to elicit information from these young people. Hyde and colleagues

(2005: 2588) argue that interactions in focus groups allow the young people to challenge each other 'on how aspects of their sub-culture are represented within the focus group, in a way that is normally beyond reach within individual interviews'. Interactions can also reveal vulnerabilities of some participants, and when this happens the others will share their vulnerabilities. The following is an example from Hyde and colleagues' work (2005: 2593). When the young people in one focus group were asked 'What would be the biggest fears around having sex?', the group responded this way:

P:    That you have a small willie.
P:    Yeah like fellas think more about that than getting the girl pregnant … when you're actually doing it than getting a disease.
P6:   Yeah, you do think more of, 'Oh crap what if I have a small willie?'
P4:   But you can't help it can you, not saying I have or anything!

Hyde and colleagues (2005: 2593) argue that focus groups potentially permit participants to bring their fears, vulnerabilities and uncertainties to the surface. It is extremely unlikely that in everyday conversations among young men themselves, their fears and vulnerabilities about the size of their penises will be shared. They may also be unaware that performance anxiety is a typical source of anxiety among young boys of their age.

Samantha Punch (2002), in her research about young people's perceptions of problems, their coping strategies and their help-seeking behaviour in central Scotland, used both focus group and individual interviews with these young adults. They were asked to suggest which method they liked better and the reasons for their preferences. About three-quarters of the participants liked the focus group interviews more than an in-depth interview. Punch (2002: 46) tells us that the main reason that the young people gave for their preferences of the focus group interviews was because 'they were in the supportive company of peers'. For example, Robert suggested that 'I preferred the group discussion because it was easier to talk with friends there'. The group environment was seen by the young people as valuable for them to generate confidence with other group members and to explore the topics broadly. John said 'because you can think together', and Janet remarked that 'you could look at things from more points of views'. For Karen, the group was 'more fun' and 'more humorous'. It was useful for establishing rapport as the young people became familiar with other group members and the researcher. Lastly, the young adults suggested that 'they enjoyed hearing what others had to say about the questions asked'.

Many of the principles and practices of conducting focus groups that I have discussed in previous chapters are applicable to children and young people in focus groups. However, some issues need to be modified or more carefully considered when working with children and young adults. These include, for example, group size, locations of the focus group sessions, flexibility, incentives, and power relationships between the young people and adult moderators/researchers. Here, I would like to point to one of the important considerations in focus groups involving children and young people. It is recommended that some activities should be incorporated in focus groups with children and young people (see also Chapters 4 and 8 in this volume). For focus group research with children, creativity is crucial (Punch 2002: Hennessy & Heary 2005). Samantha Punch (2002) suggests that employing flexible techniques is an efficient means for managing children's different abilities and preferences. The inclusion of activities or exercises, according to Faith Gibson (2007: 480), is 'an excellent strategy to maintain children's concentration and interest as well as enabling participants to work together. They can also be helpful as a fun warm-up session when children first arrive at a group.' As children cannot maintain their concentration for too long, activities and exercises can prolong their concentration period. Also, these activities can offer the young people an alternative means for expressing their perspectives and for researchers to gain access to the meanings that children have, particularly in areas of sensitive issues.

Focus group researchers have used a number of exercises and activities to stimulate discussion among children and young adults. Some techniques which are applied often within participatory research methods, such as drawing, role-playing, puzzles, visual prompts and fantasy wishes, can be used (see Kennedy et al. 2001; Coad & Lewis 2004; Veale 2005). In their work, Malcolm Hill and colleagues (1996) employed various developmentally appropriate techniques, including role-playing, brainstorming, artwork and visual prompts to examine children's emotional experiences and well-being. Faith Gibson (2007) has used drawings from a young man with cancer which depicted his thoughts on fatigue to encourage young adults to articulate what fatigue might mean to them. Ellis Hennessy and Caroline Heary (2005) suggest that sentence completion techniques can also be an effective way of maintaining attention on the topic among young people. Each participant has to complete the task and later discuss their ideas with other group members. This exercise is useful for stimulating deeper discussion among the participants. It also functions as a way to get all participants involved in the focus group process.

Susan Bissell and colleagues (2000) carried out their research with working children in Bangladesh. At the beginning of the focus group session, they showed a documentary film, *Voices of Children*, which depicted working children in Bangladesh. This was a means to initiate and encourage the children to discuss the issue in the focus groups. The film *Voices of Children* portrays the story of six children. Three children worked in the garment industry but lost their jobs at the time of the threat of trade sanctions and were forced to seek other forms of employment. The three other children were self-employed. One was selling flowers, one singing on street corners with his brothers, and another one was in a family artisan business. After the film, the children and the researcher sat on the ground in a circle to discuss their opinions based on what they had seen in the film. Bissell and colleagues (2000: 177) tell us that 'being able to refer to the film clearly provided a common point of interest or "focus" in the group discussion'. They were able to talk with the children about specific children in the film. The children also felt confident to contribute to the group discussion.

In her research about young people's perceptions of problems, their coping strategies and their help-seeking behaviour in central Scotland, Samantha Punch (2002: 51) used a variety of stimulus materials including video clips, problem page letters and common phrases as a means to prompt further discussions about how they deal with their problems and their perceptions about the way adults react to their problems.

Three short clips from recent TV shows were edited and recorded onto a videotape. Each one lasted about two minutes and showed a problem with which young people were trying to cope. These included a student who was being picked on by a teacher in *Home and Away*, an argument between a mother and daughter about a boyfriend in *Neighbours*, and a teenage bullying incident from *The Bill*. The video clips were used as visual vignettes (see Finch 1987). Each clip was shown during the group session and the participants were asked to discuss the way the young people in the clips had dealt with the problems. Subsequently, they were asked about how they personally would have reacted to the problems, and whether they, or anyone they know, had experienced similar problems and how they had coped with them.

Samantha Punch also used problem page letters to stimulate discussion. Problem page letters can be a valuable means for encouraging more in-depth discussion with young persons (Hazel 1996). Punch searched through many recent copies of *Bliss*, *Just Seventeen* and *Mizz* and found three letters which she believed would be suitable for discussing sensitive problems, such as sexual activity, eating disorders and depression. Punch photocopied and enlarged each of the original letters and the editorial replies onto coloured cards. The young people were invited to read the teenager's letter first and later talked about what they thought the person concerned should do, and, if it were them, what they would do. The use of problem page letters was particularly suitable for the subject matter of her research project because it permitted an exploration of how young people solve their problems and how they differed from those of adults. Interestingly, the use of problem pages also generated a very useful discussion on why girls tend to write to problem pages, and how girls and boys differ in the ways in which they cope with problems.

## People with Disabilities

Over the past two decades, we have witnessed a shift in the role of people with disabilities within research (Gates & Waight 2007). Historically, people with disabilities 'have had research done to them – they have been subjects to the researcher; the studied, the analysed, but never the participant' (Gates & Waight 2007: 111). However, with the development of the concepts of participatory research leading to emancipatory research within the general disability field, the use of focus groups has been seen as an 'appropriate methodological approach' for researching people with disabilities (Gates & Waight 2007: 112; see also Chapters 2 and 6 in this volume). A number of researchers have adopted the focus group methodology in their research with people living with disabilities (see Cambridge & McCarthy 2001; Fraser & Fraser 2001; Seymour et al. 2002; Bollard 2003; Gates & Waight 2007; Bisol et al. 2008; Rhodes et al. 2008).

In the area of disability research, the focus group methodology has become popular because of its 'open format and flexibility of implementation' (Kroll et al. 2007: 690). Focus groups are especially valuable in research with individuals who, because of their disabling conditions, are often excluded in larger, quantitative research projects. Focus groups in disability research have the potential to generate the opinions, perceptions, experiences and preferences regarding a diverse range of topics in different locations. Often, large population surveys are not sufficiently tailored to allow full participation of people with disabilities (Kroll et al. 2007). Focus groups allow the researchers to obtain sufficient information to develop both content and feasible structures for their questionnaires. Focus groups also offer promise for use in mixed-method research with disabled people as the context of quantitative findings can be explored and clarified by the method (Kroll et al. 2005; see also Chapter 6 in this volume).

In engaging people with disabilities in research, the focus group methodology provides advantages over other methods. Many focus group respondents find their participation enjoyable, informative and, more importantly, empowering. From their research, qualitative researchers Thilo Kroll and colleagues (2007: 691) tell us that:

> Observations from our work suggest that many experience focus group sessions as an opportunity to learn from one another as well as to contribute to social and policy change. In addition, they provide a forum for the exchange of views and opinions in a collegial, supportive atmosphere, especially for people from otherwise socially marginalized groups.

In their research with deaf and hard of hearing people about their experiences in the courts in the United States, George Balch and Donna Mertens (1999: 267) point out that due to the nature of the focus group methodology, including 'group interaction, spontaneity and openness, peer support, descriptive depth, and opportunity for unanticipated issues to emerge', the approach is well suited to understanding unmet communication needs among individuals who are deaf and hard of hearing. In their research, the safe environment of focus group settings offered them a relatively fast means for learning about what their participants have experienced in the court system and ways of overcoming difficulties. This time-effectiveness would be sensitive to the needs of many people with disabilities.

Only in the last decade have people with learning disabilities begun to be seen as 'reliable informants, who have valid opinions with a right to express them' (Bollard 2003: 156). The focus group methodology is one potential approach which could be adopted to provide 'the opportunity for often "silent voices" to be heard' (Bollard 2003: 156). Focus groups provide people with learning difficulties with an individual and collective voice and hence can be a powerful tool for communicating experiences which are often invisible or hidden (Cambridge & McCarthy 2001). However, Bollard (2003) contends that the adoption of the focus group methodology with people with learning disabilities has been sparse.

Martin Bollard's own research (2000) involved the use of focus groups with people with Down's syndrome who had mild learning disabilities. Seven participants took part in the focus group, which explored their experiences of 'going to their doctors'. They were asked to think about their feelings 'before', 'during' and 'after' going to the last appointment with their doctors. The participants were able to interact with each other, listen and take turns. As the moderator, Bollard was cautious about not leading the discussion too much, but on occasions he had to make sure that all participants had an opportunity to participate. He says that 'this demanded careful prompting so as not to expose those who were not freely contributing, and at the same time not to alienate those readily willing to express their experiences' (Bollard 2003: 161).

The aim of Bollard's focus group was to invent 'a platform' for the participants to be able to speak about their feelings and experiences. Bollard (2003: 161) contends that mediating the participants in one location allowed them to '"collectivize" their personal experiences, while also being involved in the research process'. To Bollard, this is the possibility of utilising the focus group methodology with people with learning disabilities. The methodology is seen as a means to enhance substantially the collective and participatory constitution of the research. The participants in his research were well able to take part in a group session and take turns despite the fact that other researchers have suggested that the ability of people with learning disabilities to interact in a group could be limited.

Although the focus group methodology provides 'a powerful collective voice' (Goodman 1998; Cambridge & McCarthy 2001; Bollard 2003), there are also some limitations when applying the methodology with people with learning disabilities. The approach requires group members to be able to interact and there is an attempt to uncover the meaning underlining what others think. This needs a reasonable level of skills in interaction and expression by the participants. And these are areas which people with learning disabilities may find difficult (Booth & Booth 1996). Therefore, similar to researching children, it is suggested that some activities and exercises should be incorporated into focus groups with people with learning disabilities. In Goodman's research in the UK (1998), the focus group methodology was adopted to examine an understanding of the concept of complaining and the complaint procedure. Goodman suggests that focus groups could be adopted in research with people with limited communication skills. However, it is useful to include a range of techniques such as drawings, role-play, video and wall posters with these individuals. Martin and colleagues (1997) make similar suggestion. They point out that a number of communication methods are essential in focus groups to assist people with mild and moderate learning disabilities.

In their research with people with learning disabilities, Bob Gates and Mary Waight (2007) found that the use of pictures as a medium for assisting the participants to express their views was invaluable. They tell us:

> Asking people to identify emotions from pictures – what makes them happy, sad and/ or frightened, who would support them in such situations, and using this as a cue to name local resources (for example, hospitals) – were all central to enabling us to assist participants focus their discussion. (p. 119)

Additionally, they found that inviting the participants to create their own pictures, such as to draw the person to whom they would go for help, their ideal person for support, or their GP, was very fruitful. The participants were invited to take their own drawings home, and this was seen as an empowering process for the participants. One participant was very proud of being able to show her mother the drawing that she had done of herself.

George Balch and Donna Mertens (1999: 275) point out that conducting focus groups with people with disabilities, such as deaf or hard of hearing people, can be 'intellectually, logistically, physically, and emotionally' hard work. Certainly, in each session, it necessitates more planning and cooperation among different individuals, more time, more breaks, and patience. It also needs more feedback during and after each group discussion. But in their own research, they contend that the focus group method was very fruitful as it helped to identify crucial unmet communication needs among deaf and hard of hearing people in courts, which was particularly useful for the court system. This reconfirms David Morgan's (1996: 133) suggestion that focus groups can be used to 'give voice' to marginalised people. I have argued similarly in my own writings (see Liamputtong 2007; 2010a).

## Focus Groups and Older Persons

Increasingly, we have witnessed the adoption of the focus group method with older persons (see Barrett & Kirk 2000; Seymour et al. 2002; Vo-Thanh-Xuan & Liamputtong 2003; Liang et al. 2004; Ardalan et al. 2010; Cloos et al. 2010). Similar to researching with other vulnerable groups that I have suggested in previous sections, some modifications of traditional focus group methodology have to be devised to suit older participants. These include group size, space requirements, the length of a session and a highly flexible approach in running focus groups (Quine & Cameron 1995; Seymour et al. 2002). Jane Seymour and associates (2002; 2004) also recommend having two moderators working together in focus groups with older people (see Chapter 4). Despite some challenges, they also suggest that the focus group method can be an effective approach to explore any health and social issues with older participants. And Seymour and colleagues (2002: 519) contend, sensitively and carefully conducted focus groups with older persons 'provide an important means for accessing groups that are otherwise neglected by research'.

Some interesting focus group research which involved older persons is that of Jane Seymour and colleagues (2002; 2004) on end-of-life care in Sheffield, England. They conducted eight focus groups with 32 older persons recruited from six community associations in Sheffield. Instead of only asking the participants to discuss the questions posed, the researchers also used a computer-based (Microsoft PowerPoint) 'slide show' in their group discussions. Due to the interest in new health technology, Seymour and colleagues (2002: 522) realised that visual presentations are an effective and interesting means of exchange with their participants. They wished to make sure that their respondents had sufficient knowledge and information to talk about the issue. They also wanted to ensure that they had a way of 'bringing back' the discussion if it became out of their control. Hence, their PowerPoint 'slide show' offered 'a simple pictorial aide-memoire' that comprised the following themes (Seymour 2002: 522; 2004: 59):

- The best place to be cared for (for example, home, hospital, nursing home or hospice).
- The use of technology to extend life (for example, resuscitation and artificial feeding).
- The use of technology to provide comfort (for example, terminal sedation and morphine).
- Who makes decisions (for example, clinical staff, patient or relative, with material on communications and advanced care planning)?

One slide that Seymour and colleagues used to help the participants to talk about advanced care statements contained a photograph of a man with early Alzheimer's disease and a portrayal of his plan to end his life:

> I have decided that life will end for me when they try to use life support systems. You should think about this and act to define how things will work for you. Then you need to talk to others about your concerns while you are still able. Complete an advance directive and enduring power of attorney. (Leslie Dennis, a person with dementia) (Seymour et al. 2004: 59–60)

Although Seymour and colleagues acknowledged that their approach was rather structured and might not allow the participants to discuss other issues of concern, it was beneficial in many ways. For example, presenting potentially risky material using TV-like technology created a more comfortable situation and offered a 'frame' for subsequent discussions. They found that both the computer and projector equipment attracted curiosity and discussion and were valuable as icebreakers (2002). The material provided useful flexibility and the pace of the discussion could be varied. Particular images or words could be revisited or skipped over. If the discussion became too personal, it was sometimes necessary to be interrupted or stopped. The slides permitted this possibility. Seymour and others (2002: 522–523) remarked: 'By showing such material in this way, it may be de-personalised, and it clearly generates a lot of interest. They were most revealing, and gave us insight into the types of needs that people have for information about end of life care.'

At the conclusion of the session, the participants were debriefed over lunch. They were offered opportunities to follow up some discussions that had been raised by them shortly after the focus group discussion. They were also provided with the names and contacts of bereavement care organisations. Seymour and colleagues (2002: 524) concluded that most participants enjoyed the group sessions and found the discussions interesting and extremely informative. Hence, this allowed Seymour to collect valuable data for her project

Recently, Ali Ardalan and colleagues (2010) examined older people's needs following major disasters: a qualitative study of Iranian elders' experiences of the Bam earthquake. On 26 December 2003, an earthquake measuring 6.6 on the Richter scale struck the ancient city of Bam in southeast Iran and its surroundings. More than 26,000 of Bam's population were killed, 30,000 were injured and more than 45,000 were made homeless. The earthquake also destroyed the ancient city of Bam and Bam's citadel, the world's largest dried clay structure.

Being aware that older people are likely to be vulnerable to the consequences of disasters prompted Ali Ardalan and colleagues to conduct focus group research to allow older people to assess their own needs following the Bam earthquake. Ardalan and colleagues (2010: 12) wrote: 'We believed that a better understanding of elders' own expressions of their needs following a disaster would challenge taken-for-granted and stereotypical views of the relief they require, and that this would encourage and enable the provision of more suitable and effective services.' Potential participants who met the criteria of the project were invited to take part in a focus group discussion. Those who could not participate in a focus group were interviewed individually. In total, six focus groups of six to ten people and ten individual interviews were carried out. All the focus groups were conducted in the Bam District Health Centre and in the Persian language, the local language of all participants and the moderators.

The results revealed four main themes: feeling insecure, emotional distress, affronts to dignity, and inappropriate service delivery. Ardalan and colleagues contended that for a disaster-prone country like Iran, culturally sensitive plans must be appropriately prepared to meet the needs of those who suffer from their effects, and particularly the needs of older people. Their study showed that older people have unique needs which are not generally perceived as crucial or having a high priority in disaster relief. The needs of older people should not be disregarded during the immediate disaster response or in the recovery plan. Relief workers should also be aware that because of their conditions, which may limit their physical mobility and ability to respond, general relief is not suitable for older persons. The immediate needs of older people, such as appropriate food, clothes and medical care, and their long-term needs, including the rehabilitation of their affairs and coping with continuing emotional distress, must be addressed. Taking into account the needs of older persons would result in effective service delivery for this group of vulnerable people.

## CONCLUSION

This chapter has discussed the use of focus group methodology in sensitive topics and with vulnerable people. As we have witnessed, there are more vulnerable and marginalised people in every corner of the world. It is inevitable then that our research will involve this group of people. Focus group methodology allows the researchers to conduct their investigations in sensitive areas and with groups of people who, because of their conditions, may find other forms of research intimidating. Focus groups provide 'a forum for mutual support' (Kroll et al. 2007: 697). Hence, they are likely to offer safer environments for vulnerable people to be able to express their needs and concerns. As such, the methodology offers remarkable possibilities for diverse research applications with vulnerable people including children, people with disabilities and older people. However, they can also be challenging and sometimes fraught with difficulties.

## TUTORIAL ACTIVITIES

1 List at least five research areas which can be defined as sensitive topics and discuss how the focus group methodology can be used sensitively in these areas.

2  You are required to carry out a research project in a low-socioeconomic area which has a large number of unemployed and homeless people. You know that these people are not willing to take part in research as they tend to find it intimidating. You know that the focus group methodology will permit you to conduct your research, but you need to convince your manager about the appropriateness of this methodology. How will you design and run it? Discuss

## FURTHER READING

Allen, L. (2006). Trying not to think 'straight': Conducting focus groups with lesbian and gay youth. *International Journal of Qualitative Studies in Education* 19(2), 163–176.

Balch, G.I., & Mertens, D.M. (1999). Focus groups design and group dynamics: Lessons from deaf and hard of hearing participants. *American Journal of Evaluation* 20, 265–277.

Barrett, J., & Kirk, S. (2000). Running focus groups with elderly and disabled elderly participants. *Applied Ergonomics* 31, 621–629.

Bollard, M. (2003). Going to the doctor's: The findings from a focus group with people with learning disabilities. *Journal of Learning Disabilities* 7, 156–164.

Frith, H. (2000). Focusing on sex: Using focus groups in sex research. *Sexualities* 3(3), 275–297.

Gates, B., & Waight, M. (2007). Reflections on conducting focus groups with people with learning disabilities. *Journal of Research in Nursing* 12(2), 111–126.

Gibson, F. (2007). Conducting focus groups with children and young people: Strategies for success. *Journal of Research in Nursing* 12(5), 473–483.

Hyde, A., Howlett, E.H., Brady, D., & Drennan, J. (2005). The focus group method: Insights from focus group interviews on sexual health with adolescents. *Social Science and Medicine* 61(12), 2588–2599.

Kroll, T., Barbour, R., & Harris, J. (2007). Using focus groups in disability research. *Qualitative Health Research* 17(5), 690–698.

Morgan, M., Gibbs, S., Maxwell, K., & Britten, N. (2002). Hearing children's voices: Methodological issues in conducting focus groups with children aged 7–11 years. *Qualitative Research* 2(1), 5–20.

Pösö, T., Honkatukia, P., & Nyqvist, L. (2008). Focus groups and the study of violence. *Qualitative Research* 8(1), 73–89.

Punch, S. (2002). Interviewing strategies with young people: The secret box, a stimulus material and task-based activities. *Children & Society* 16(1), 45–56.

*(Continued)*

*(Continued)*

Rubin, R. (2004). Men talking about Viagra: An exploratory study with focus groups. *Men and Masculinities* 7(1), 22–30.

Schulze, B., & Angermeyer, M.C. (2003). Subjective experiences of stigma. A focus group study of schizophrenic patients, their relatives and mental health professionals. *Social Science and Medicine* 56, 299–312.

Seymour, J., Bellamy, G., Gott, M., Ahmedzai, S.H., & Clark, D. (2002). Using focus groups to explore older people's attitudes to end of life care. *Ageing & Society* 22, 517–526.

Sparks, R., Girling, E., & Smith, M.V. (2002). Lessons from history: Pasts, presents and futures of punishment in children's talk. *Children & Society* 16, 116–130.

# 8
# FOCUS GROUP METHODOLOGY IN CROSS-CULTURAL RESEARCH

## CHAPTER OBJECTIVES

In this chapter you will learn about:

- Focus groups as a culturally sensitive research method
- Cross-cultural focus groups and language issues
- Translation of focus group transcripts
- Cultural considerations
- Focus groups in cross-cultural settings: some practical considerations
- Focus groups and participatory activities in cross-cultural research
- Case examples of cross-cultural research using focus groups

Increasingly, the focus group methodology has been seen as a good approach for understanding cultural diversities and examining cultural differences. The focus group methodology is a culturally sensitive data collection method for research in cross-cultural settings and research with ethnic minorities since it permits the researcher to reach communications which people use in their everyday interactions, and reveals cultural norms and values.

Following on from the feminist and dialogical theories that I have presented in Chapter 1, it is argued that the focus group methodology permits possibilities of hearing the multiple and collective voices of the 'Others' (marginalised people in cross-cultural settings) 'as constructors and agents of knowledge' (Fine 1994: 75) and 'as agents of social change' (Madriz 2000: 840). At the data gathering stage, focus groups help the researchers to hear 'the *plural voices* of the participants' (Fine 1994: 75). In this chapter, I will discuss focus groups as a methodology which has been perceived as more culturally appropriate for collecting information in cross-cultural research. In particular, I will point to the need for collectively spoken methods of focus when working with different groups in diverse cultural contexts. It is argued that the collective nature of focus groups allows marginalised people to express their views and needs so that some culturally sensitive and appropriate interventions may follow. This chapter also includes a discussion regarding language, translation issues and cultural consideration. Practical issues in conducting focus groups in cross-cultural research are also covered. The chapter also provides some case examples from empirical studies relating to the focus group methodology in cross-cultural settings.

## FOCUS GROUPS AS COLLECTIVE TESTIMONY: A CULTURALLY SENSITIVE RESEARCH METHOD

An important facet of the focus group methodology which is situated within the feminist framework is its ability to generate and legitimise collective testimonies. Women have used these testimonies and narratives to unpack particular aspects of their 'daily existences, their feelings, attitudes, hopes, and dreams' which have received little attention in research (Madriz 2003: 365). Focus groups make up rooms for eliciting collective testimonies. These testimonies allow women, both as individuals and as a group, to search for and construct their own 'unique and powerful "voices"' (Kamberelis & Dimitriadis 2008: 384). Esther Madriz (2003: 369) points out that, 'through collective stories and resistance narratives' which are 'filled with cultural symbols, words, signs, and ideological representation that reflect different dimensions of power and domination that frame women's quotidian experiences', focus groups are especially appropriate for unveiling the everyday existence of women, particularly women of colour (see also Chapter 1 in this volume). As a Latina feminist, Esther Madriz (2003: 365) situates the focus group methodology within these 'collective testimonies and group resistance narratives'. As a form of collective testimony, a focus group can be 'an empowering experience' for women of colour (Madriz 2003: 375). The collective testimony offered by the focus group methodology can 'empower the participants and validate their views and experiences ... To be considered an "expert" can be empowering for many participants' (Ivanoff & Hultberg 2006: 127). Focus groups can be used by women 'to unveil specific and little-researched aspects of women's daily existences, their feelings, attitudes, hopes and dreams' (Madriz 2003: 365).

Because the voices of women of colour have been silenced in most research projects, the focus group methodology will permit women of colour to write their own culture together (Madriz 2003). Focus groups may help not only to expose the layers of oppression that have suppressed their expressions, but also to facilitate the forms of resistance that they use for dealing with such oppressions in their everyday life. Madriz (2003: 364) believes that the focus group methodology 'can be an important element in the advancement of an agenda of social justice for women, because they can serve to expose and validate women's everyday experiences of subjugation and their indi-vidual and collective survival and resistance strategies'. Through collective stories, focus group interviews are essentially appropriate for uncovering women's daily experiences. Madriz (2003: 376) writes: 'By speaking collectively, women of color not only reclaim their humanity but, at the same time, empower themselves by making sense of their experience of vulnerability and subjugation.' I contend that the term 'women of color' that Madriz uses can also be applicable to other groups of women such as women from ethnic minority groups, indigenous women and women from non-Western societies.

The focus group methodology is an enquiry approach which resembles 'the particularities and everyday experiences' of women from non-Western cultural groups (Madriz 2003: 370). Traditionally, women have employed conversations with other women as a means for them to resist oppression in their everyday life. Historically and collectively, women have formed groups to discuss issues important to them and to become involved in political activities. For instance, after slavery ended, churchwomen and teachers gathered to organise political work throughout the South in the United States (Gilkes 1994). In 1937, Chinese women who worked in San Francisco's Chinatown organised a group to strike against the garment factory owned by the National Dollar Store (Espiritu 1997). Similarly, Mexican women have been keeping their traditional practices by getting together to talk, to make food, to arrange birthdays, in order to keep their rich oral traditions alive (Behar 1993; Dill 1994). Even nowadays, sharing with other women has been an important way for African American, Latina and Asian American women to deal with their marginality. These examples clearly show that the gathering and sharing of women with other women can lead to 'actions and movements for social change' (Madriz 2003: 370).

The form of collective communication occurring in focus groups is very familiar to the way women connect with other. Women in many Latina families tend to gather in a kitchen to drink coffee, plan the meals and share their worries and stories. Sharing with other women has also been an important means in which African American women have had to deal with 'centuries of oppression and the legacy of slavery' (Madriz 2003: 375). Similarly, Asian American women 'kept many customs alive' by gathering together to cook traditional foods, exchange folk knowledge, organise cultural celebrations and practise traditional healing methods (Glenn 1986). This is still the case of many Hmong women in Australia and the United States (see Liamputtong Rice 2000). These activities are performed while participating in dialogue with other women.

For people who are part of 'communitarian cultures', such as ethnic minorities and indigenous people, 'individualistic research methods place them in artificial, unfamiliar, and even "unsafe" environments' (Madriz 2003: 383). According to feminist researcher Rina Benmayor (1991: 159), collective testimonies are capable of having a direct impact on 'individual and collective empowerment'. Focus groups have this potential for researching women's lives. Madriz (2003: 383) contends:

> the shared dialogue, stories, and knowledge generated by the group interview have the potential to help such women to develop a sense of identity, self-validation, bonding, and commonality of experiences. Focus groups tend to create environments in which participants feel open to telling their stories and to giving their testimonies in front of other women like themselves.

Therefore, the focus group methodology has great potential for discovering the complex layers which shape the individual and collective lived experiences of the research participants. The process of collective talk in focus groups renders it 'a culturally sensitive data gathering method', not only for women but also for other cultural groups such as ethnic minorities, indigenous people and other non–Western populations (Madriz 2003: 383).

Esther Madriz (2003), in her work with Latina and African American women of lower socioeconomic background, makes use of the focus group methodology in powerful ways. This is clearly seen in her book *Nothing bad happens to good girls* (1997). In this book, Madriz writes about how the fear of crime creates a latent form of social control on the lives of women. Fear of crime dictates certain rules about what women 'should' and 'should not' do in public so that they themselves can be protected. These ideas inevitably lead to debilitating perceptions about 'good girls' and 'bad girls'. Not only that, they severely constrain what will be available to lower socioeconomic Latina and African American women in their everyday practices.

Regarding the research methods, in this book, Madriz argues that most research relating to fear of crime among women has used a quantitative approach. The methods tended to be large survey studies and conducted with both men and women. This approach, Madriz argues, vigorously restricts the points of view and experiences that the participants are preparing to share. As such, research data only reveals partial and inaccurate accounts of the issue. She suggests that it is difficult to get women, particularly women of non–Western groups, to speak about sensitive issues like their fears of sexual assault or rape, in the context of oral or written questionnaires, when they had to do it either alone or with a single researcher.

Madriz argues that quantitative methods such as surveys tend to alienate the research participants. Individual interviews can also make the participants feel afraid, suspicious and intimidated. Hence, she employed the focus group methodology in her research as she attempted to obtain richer information with greater accuracy from the women. She also notes that focus groups offered a safe environment where the women could provide support to each other when speaking about their experiences of crime and their discomforts and fears about crime. One of Madriz's participants, Carmen, remarked that: 'When I am alone with an interviewer, I feel intimidated, scared. And if they call me over the telephone, I never answer their questions. How do I know what they really want or who they are?' (Madriz 1998: 6–7). The following excerpt is what Madriz (1998: 3) tells us about her choice of method in this research. Madriz (1998) believes that it was essential for her to 'listen to women's stories to understand the limitations that fear of crime imposes on their everyday lives'. She writes:

> Rather than addressing how many of these women are afraid because of crime or how much fear they feel, my particular study was aimed at exploring the images and representations that shape women's anxieties and fears at understanding the way in which their lives are limited by these fears. I simply asked them about their worries, anxieties, and concerns related to crime and about the strategies they use to feel safe.

## CROSS-CULTURAL FOCUS GROUPS AND LANGUAGE ISSUES

In qualitative research, including the focus group methodology, language is crucial not only to the research process, but also to the resulting data and its interpretation.

Language allows the research participants to identify meanings of the world. It permits the researchers and the participants to interact in order to produce an understanding of the social world of the participant and an interpretation of this context. Hence, language is a fundamental tool which allows researchers to understand human behaviour, sociocultural processes and cultural meanings (Watkins-Mathys 2006; Hennink 2007; 2008; Liamputtong 2010a).

In conducting cross-cultural focus group research, the role and influence of language in research is more complex. Many focus group research projects are undertaken by researchers who are not familiar with the language of the research participants. This can be seen in cross-national research where the language of the researchers is markedly different from that of the participants and they are seen as 'outsider' (Watkins-Mathys 2006; Thomas 2008). It can also be seen in national research where the researchers carry out research with minority groups such as immigrants who may prefer to speak in their own language (Culley et al. 2007; Liamputtong 2010a).

The most common difficulties encountered by 'outsider' cross-cultural researchers is an inability to speak the local or native language. It is advisable that cross-cultural focus groups should be conducted in the native language of the participants. Problems and difficulties can arise if the researchers and the participants do not share the same language. In such a case, a bilingual moderator is employed to lead the group discussion. If this moderator is not trained properly, does not have a full understanding of the particular research project, or has biased ideas, the quality of information obtained may be distorted. Jane Yelland and Sandy Gifford (1995) have documented this problem with their study on Sudden Infant Death Syndrome among some groups of Asian immigrants in Australia. However, intensive and proper training of the bicultural moderator can overcome this.

If the researcher needs to conduct focus groups in another language by him- or herself, a translator will be necessary. Although not all cross-cultural researchers would promote this strategy, I suggest that the researchers need seriously to consider their options. What is clear is that the natural flow of discussion will be affected as everyone must wait for the interpreter to interpret the conversation before proceeding further (Hennink 2007). Sometimes, a focus group discussion may turn into a group interview instead. When I first conducted focus groups on health issues in Beijing, I needed assistance from an interpreter. Each focus group took longer than anticipated, despite having allowed for extra time at the planning stage; the natural flow of the group discussion was continually interrupted. But later on when I trained a Chinese moderator to conduct focus groups, these problems were resolved.

Cross-cultural researchers have developed some ways where they can work with interpreters more appropriately. Francesca Giordano and colleagues (2009), in their research in Tegucigalpa, the capital city of Honduras, conducted two focus groups with 22 local women to discuss what sexual advice mothers would have for their daughters. They arranged to have two moderators working with each group and alternated asking questions. Both groups had one assigned interpreter. The translation was carried out simultaneously to facilitate communication between the moderators and the participants. Many of the participants were bilingual and they assisted the researchers with the translation as well. The interpreters were community leaders who formed part of the larger project in Honduras.

Nevertheless, what I believe would work better is that a bicultural (or bilingual) research assistant is employed to work on the research project to overcome linguistic barriers in cross-cultural focus group research. Bicultural researchers share not only the language with the participants but also many social and cultural aspects. They are people who are more likely to have the best of knowledge of the groups (Im et al. 2004; Davies et al. 2009). They are individuals who are able to 'convey the underlying cultural meanings of participants' words and expressions to the researchers' (Hennink 2008: 25). Bicultural researchers play a vital role 'in the creation of knowledge and its cultural interpretation', which are essential in qualitative research including focus groups (Hennink 2008: 25). In Lee and Ellenbecker's study with elderly Chinese (1998), they worked with a (bicultural) researcher who was able to speak both English and Chinese. Through the bicultural researcher, they were able to obtain more accurate information from the participants as they could tell their experiences in their own language. The bicultural researcher could also interpret meanings of some Chinese words which could not be translated exactly into English.

It has been suggested that researchers who undertake cross-cultural research should be an 'insider', meaning that only those who share the social, cultural and linguistic characteristics as the research participants would be suitable to do so (see Eckhardt 2004; Watkins-Mathys 2006; Culley et al. 2007; Liamputtong 2010a). This is what Hasmita Ramji (2008) refers to as 'cultural commonality'. Insider status will reduce cultural and linguistic barriers. Cultural insiders may be able to carry out research 'in a more sensitive and responsive manner' than researchers who are outsiders (Bishop 2008: 148). Conducting focus groups cross-culturally is no exception. Esther Madriz's writing (1998; 2003) provides a good example of this. She contends that sharing the same race and ethnicity as the participants assisted her in enhancing rapport and hence increasing the willingness of participants to respond to her research. According to Madriz (2003: 380), a moderator who has the same racial or ethnic background or shares common experiences as the participants will be able to contribute better to the feelings of the participants. She says that although this may apply to other qualitative methods, it is particularly crucial for the focus group methodology 'where establishing rapport with the participants is key to eliciting high-quality information'. See also Chapter 4 in this volume.

Regardless of whether an interpreter or a bicultural worker is employed, there is another salient issue that cross-cultural researchers need seriously to consider. According to focus group researchers Adriana Umaña-Taylor and Mayra Bámaca (2004), the type of language or expressions used by the moderators and the participants has a great impact on the discussion in the focus groups. In their own research with Latina families, they refer to the specific type of Spanish spoken. Despite the fact that Latinos share Spanish as a common language, the meanings of some expressions and words are unique to particular national origin groups. It is crucial that the moderators should be familiar with the regionalisms employed by participants so that they are able to follow the flow of the conversation. In one focus group, the note-taker was unable to follow a small part of the discussion because her nationality was different from that of the participants in the group. Umaña-Taylor and Bámaca

(2004: 265) recommend that 'being familiar with participants' Spanish is important to make them feel comfortable and to facilitate the flow of discussion. In an ideal situation, the facilitator and note taker would be familiar with the specific Latino group being examined (e.g., Mexican).'

Most importantly, the researchers must identify the language in which the participants would feel most comfortable to speak in the focus groups, and this can be the national language or a regional language of their country (Hennink 2007). Although in some countries there is only one common language spoken throughout the country, the linguistic traditions can vary between regions in others. For example, a study of contraceptive use in Zambia was carried out in two regions and two different languages were used by local people. In the copperbelt province, people speak the language of Bemba, but in the northwestern province, the languages of Luvale, Lunda and Kaonde are used (Benaya 2004). Similarly, in Thailand, although central Thai is used by most Thais, people in each region prefer to speak in their own local dialect. In the northeastern part (Isan), people converse in the Lao language, and in the north, *kam muang* (northern dialect) is spoken. Many words and expressions are different from the central Thai language and this can be problematic in focus group research if the moderators and the participants do not share similar regional languages. Hence, it is crucial to identify the language(s) spoken in the study areas when planning for focus group research and to recruit moderators who are able to converse in the local language or dialect.

## TRANSLATION OF FOCUS GROUP TRANSCRIPTS

Typically, the focus group discussions are transcribed for in-depth data analysis. Salient issues relevant to the transcription of focus group research in general will be discussed in greater detail in Chapter 10. However, I wish to raise the issue of translation of focus group transcripts in this section as it is relevant to cross-cultural focus group research.

Some focus group researchers may instruct their bicultural researchers first to transcribe the focus group discussions in the language of the discussion and then translate them into the language of the researchers, which, often, is English. Two versions of the transcripts are produced and hence the accuracy of the translation can be done easily. However, this may not be feasible for some focus group research as there are costs, time and resources involved in this process. Others may prefer their bicultural researchers to transcribe the interview data directly into the English language, instead of transcribing it into the local language and then translating (Hennink 2007). Doing it this way, there is the possibility that interpreter bias may be produced (Lopez et al. 2008). For example, Emma Pitchforth and Edwin van Teijlingen (2005) carried out qualitative research with Bangladeshi women with limited formal education who had recently used emergency obstetric care. The researchers worked with a lay interpreter who carried out the interviews. The interpreter was not professionally trained, but she had research interviewing experience, a health-related postgraduate qualification and been trained and worked full time with the research team for six months. The interviews were translated directly into English by the interpreter. For quality assurance purposes, Pitchforth and van Teijlingen arranged an independent bilingual interpreter to transcribe four interviews into English. The review of two transcripts revealed that the study interpreter did not translate the women's responses. Rather, she 'interpreted' the data. The level of detail which was provided by the study interpreter was also markedly different to that of the independent bilingual interpreter. She left out many details which led to a loss of some insight into the experiences of these women. Although Pitchforth and van Teijlingen contended that this did not significantly impact on the research in general, it could have caused some 'significant problems' with their research if they wished to analyse the issues which were not translated for them. Similar problems may occur in cross-cultural focus group research.

There are also important issues about the translation of focus group data. It is evidenced that concepts cannot always be translated across languages and cultures. As Lorraine Watkins-Mathys (2006: 224) contends, 'language is context and time bound, and creating shared meaning thus poses certain challenges because of its dependency on the way in which language is used within its context at a certain time'. Because of subtle differences in meaning, translating from one language to another can be very complex and problematic (Twinn 1998; Kapborg & Bertero 2002; Bujra 2006). Due to cultural differences or non-equivalent expressions, some words cannot be translated into English properly. Some of the common Western conceptual meanings can be difficult to understand in other cultures. This is also applicable in translating cultural meanings into English. Western researchers may not be able to appreciate the complexity of concepts which are common in other cultures.

Indeed, as Lorraine Watkins-Mathys (2006: 214) points out, individuals who speak different languages see the world from different perspectives because people 'construct it in different ways using different "word pictures" and "metaphors"'. It is problematic to obtain comparability, through word-for-word translation, or to strive for 'objective equivalence' since individuals and the language they use interact with their environment differently and meanings are produced from their own subjective perspective. And this interaction means 'localized understanding' occurs (Welch & Piekkari 2006: 431). Hence, cross-language research is no longer solely about the translation issue, but it is about the way that the researchers and the participants interact with the environment. This includes listening, asking for clarification about contents and stories, observation and the manner in which people are reacting to queries and interacting with others.

It is therefore important that researchers seriously consider translation issues in cross-cultural focus group research. Misinterpretation of meaning can be particularly problematic and at worse dangerous, and of course this has a great impact on the quality of data (Twinn 1998; Esposito 2001). Translation needs to transfer the meanings correctly from one culture to another. Therefore, meaning-based, instead of word-for-word, translation is crucial (Twinn 1998; Temple & Edwards 2002; Culley et al. 2007; Hennink 2007; Shklarov 2007; Irvine et al. 2008).

A literal translation of the words makes little sense. The translation should focus on transmitting the meaning of the discussed issues, concepts, ideas and expressions, and this may necessitate using entirely different words (Hennink 2007). For example, in the Chichewa language of Malawi, the word pregnant is referred to by many terms which may have different meanings, such as '*Wa Mimba* (someone with a tummy), *Wodwala* (sick woman), *Wa Pakati* (an in-between state, between life and death)'. To translate all of these terms as 'pregnant' may result in the loss of the subtle differences in vocabulary which is used to describe pregnancy and what these may imply (Hennink 2007: 216). Hennink (2007: 217) suggests that 'remaining sensitive to these issues will ensure that the transcript retains the richness and detail of the qualitative data'.

An important aspect of cross-cultural focus group research which I believe deserves greater attention is that of transcribing data in its original language. Often, interviews are not transcribed in the original language. As a result, 'possible differences in the meanings of words, or concepts across languages vanish into the space between spoken otherness and written sameness' (Temple 2002: 844). In order to reduce difficulties associated with the translation and interpretation of the verbatim data, focus group data should be transcribed in its original language (Twinn 1998). Many subtle issues have been lost in the process of translation by others than the researchers themselves.

Hence, if the researchers are also bilingual and carry out their focus groups themselves, the interview data may be transcribed in its original language in order to preserve the subtlety of the accounts generated in the focus groups. The researchers would only translate the participants' narratives into English if they use these in their subsequent writing (Liamputtong 2010a). In other cases, if the researchers are outsiders and do not speak the same language as the participants, and the focus groups are carried out by bicultural researchers, these bicultural researchers would transcribe and translate the interview data at the same time. In this case, they should be instructed to translate as closely as possible what the participants say. If there are some words or concepts which are difficult to translate into English, the original words should be retained and some brief or detailed explanation of such words or concepts should be provided. This way, the researchers will be able to interpret the participants' narratives and meanings in greater depth and more accurately.

Cross-cultural researchers have come up with strategies that they can use to ensure that the translation of their data will be carried out more accurately. In Azita Emami and Carol Tishelman's study on cancer with Iranian women in Sweden (2004), focus group interviews were conducted in the Farsi language. Emami, who is a native Iranian woman, transcribed and analysed the data in Farsi. Four transcripts were then translated into Swedish so that other members of the research team could access some of the data. The analysis done by Emami was then reviewed and discussed to verify the interpretation. Noreen Esposito (2001) suggests several strategies that could be followed. These include:

- having two translators to translate the material;
- adopting a back translation approach to convert one set of data into another language;
- using multiple focus groups for those involved to discuss the translation and process;
- making use of triangulation of participants, methods and researchers in the translation process;
- working with outside bilingual reviewers.

## CULTURAL CONSIDERATIONS

Cultural sensitivity is an important issue in conducting focus group research with people from different cultures. It is not feasible to list all cultural considerations in this text, and I do not intend to stereotype cultural norms as there are diversities in each cultural group. In what follows, I will point to some cultural considerations that previous focus group researchers have dealt with in their projects so that better considerations can be made by other researchers in the planning of their focus groups in cross-cultural settings.

According to cross-cultural researcher Giana Eckhardt (2004: 406), due to the strong influence of Confucian, Taoist and Buddhist philosophy within Chinese culture which influences the behaviour of individuals, the focus group method is an appropriate research tool in China. This influence is manifested in the respectful attitudes towards collective norms of the individuals. However, Chinese culture also values the importance of hierarchy and this is a crucial factor that the researchers need to take into account when making plans about group composition (see also Chapter 3 in this volume). A group should be composed of an 'appropriate peer group' (Watkins-Mathys 2006: 211). For instance, younger participants should not be in the same group as older respondents as they may feel the 'social pressure to agree with older respondents as a sign of respect' (Eckhardt 2004: 407). In addition, because of the strong commitment of individuals to the collective norms within Chinese society, this tends to discourage individuals from speaking about their true inner feelings and thoughts. As such, Eckhardt (2004) recommends that focus group researchers in China need to incorporate other qualitative methods such as in-depth interviews and participant observations during the research fieldwork. This will allow the researchers to triangulate their data and provide opportunities for generating wider perspectives from the participants.

Another important issue is that in some groups, due to their cultural norms, the participants may not say anything until it is their turn to speak. In Pacific Northwest Indian communities, as June Strickland (1999: 192) points out, tribal elders, particularly men, will not speak until others have spoken. Hence, it is essential to 'allow time at the end of a discussion and silence for the elders to speak'. Additionally, in the first group meeting, traditional people and elders in these communities will not speak until the end of a meeting. This means that the researchers need to invite them more than once to make sure that they can contribute.

In many cultures, the social positions of people are based on a hierarchy which will determine who can speak first and/or last. From their experience of conducting focus group research regarding infant care practices with Maori, Tongan, Samoan and Cook Islands caregivers in Auckland, New Zealand, Sally Abel and colleagues (2001: 1142) point out that a cultural expectation regarding traditional speaking customs in the Pacific groups could result in situations which may have implications for the selection of participants from these communities and for the interpretation of the findings. Often, the participants kept their views until those who were older or of higher status had spoken. This suggests that, to encourage free discussion in focus groups, participants who are of equivalent age and social status should be preferred. But in the focus groups in the rural Junagadh district of Gujarat, India, the elders or the participant who has the most legitimate authority would speak last (Vissandjée et al. 2002). In addition, Bilkis Vissandjée and colleagues (2002) contend that lower caste women would not speak in front of women who are from a higher caste or have higher education. However, the exclusion of this group of women would have impacted on the participation of many others and would have jeopardised the quality and reputation of their research. They therefore conducted individual interviews with these women in order to compensate for their silence during the focus groups. Also, the status of women within the family can be another important factor impacting on the silence of women in the focus groups. Vissandjée and colleagues (2002: 833) write:

> Freedom of expression among rural Gujarati women is based on familial position. Daughters-in-law hold the lowest level of autonomy and freedom of expression, followed by daughters and mothers-in-law, respectively. The sociofamilial status of the mother-in-law decrees that her word is usually final, and those who have not yet attained this role seem to have less legitimate authority when speaking.

In Tonga, men are culturally required to adhere to *fevaitapui*, which is a custom that men are prohibited from talking about their wife's personal life with her brothers or male cousins. Where men's relationships with other male participants are uncertain, this can restrict the discussion in focus groups (Abel et al. 2001). In Samoan culture, there is a similar practice among Samoan men. Interestingly, however, in Abel and colleagues' own research, there was no evidence that this had any impact on the discussion in the focus group with Samoan men. This cultural practice does not reduce the benefit of focus groups in these communities, but rather they are factors to consider when selecting potential participants (Abel et al. 2001).

Cultural norms also dictate the place of individuals in a group setting. For example, in a group discussion in Fiji, research participants may be seated according to their status. This means that those with a higher status will be seated in the front and those with less status will be placed in the back. This may create some problems with interaction in the group. Hence, the moderators may need to use their special skills to ensure full participation from all members of the group regardless of where they are seated. In running focus groups in cross-cultural settings, Glenn Laverack and Kevin Brown (2003: 341) suggest that Western researchers need to have a good 'understanding of the fluid social dynamics and complex balance of relationships that occur between research participants'. Some local practices may be seen as non-significant by researchers, but they can have a great impact on the participants. In Laverack and Brown's research, a practice of the seating arrangement for different groups of people was important for the Fijians, and they had to observe this rule when carrying out their research.

In cross-cultural research, the concept of cultural insider and outsider has a great impact on the research process. In China, Lorraine Watkins-Mathys (2006: 212) suggests, the insider and outsider status is conceptualised within the *guanxi* concept. Guanxi plays a crucial role in all facets of Chinese life. An accepted hierarchy and process within *guanxi* networks requires an insider to introduce outsiders into a particular *guanxi* network. Familial ties are the bases of these networks. Without an introduction from a trusted insider to a network, the outsider will not be admitted into the world of those who see themselves as belonging to that network. In Confucianism as operated in Chinese culture, the individuals as well as their positions within the society are determined by their relationships to others. Although Western researchers are perceived as having a relatively high status, they are seen as outsiders. They need to establish relevant networks in order to create what Ann Ryen (2002) calls 'an environment of trust' through the introduction of insiders. This can be done by working with local research partners who are fluent in both English and the local language and have a good understanding of the focus group method (Eckhardt 2004). According to Giana Eckhardt (2004: 413), 'using a cultural insider to assist with the interpretation of the data will lead to the most meaningful understanding of the data … [and] … implies a high level of trust in terms of verifying the interpretations'.

In different cultures, the concept of time can have different meanings (Laverack & Brown 2003). This factor can have an influence on the interpretation of the participants about the time that the focus group commences. The moderator and observer must be flexible and patient in this regard. Although those who turn up late may have some difficulty in participating in the group discussion, to exclude them can jeopardise the trust of the participants towards the research team (Ekblad & Bäärnhielm 2002)

The participants may be late in turning up at the interview sites and the procedure may go slowly. This may be due to a perception of time in a cultural setting. In their research in Fiji, Glenn Laverack and Kevin Brown refer to this as 'Fiji time'. Accordingly, Fiji time signifies that:

> priorities are different in different cultural contexts. The social ceremonies and customs of Fiji are of great importance and can take precedence over 'just getting things done'. A casual pace is taken as a normal part of rural Fijian life, and plans can be changed at short notice. (Laverack & Brown 2003: 340)

Laverack and Brown suggest that researchers working in a cross-cultural context must be flexible in order to accommodate an uncertain and different timeframe of the local cultural group.

Esther Madriz (1998: 5) too suggests that Latinas hold a different perception of time and punctuality than white people do, and therefore may turn up late for their sessions. In her research, it is usual for Latina women to commence 30 minutes late or even later. Madriz suggests that one solution is to invite the women half an hour before the group is scheduled to start so that the delays can be minimised. Similarly, June Strickland (1999: 193) points out that in the Pacific Northwest Indian communities people are rarely at the designated place on time; they tend to arrive for meetings over a period of 15 to 30 minutes. Some participants might arrive an hour after the event has commenced. Additionally, in these communities, storytelling is the format that people use for communicating with others, and this may take a lot of time. However, the stories they tell are related to the topic of investigation and often provide concrete examples. Also, the communities practise some rituals such as prayer songs and 'give away' ceremonies and it takes time to go through these. It is essential that the researchers should not rush through the focus group sessions. The people themselves expect to stay 3–4 hours for a session. Hence, the time allocated to conduct focus groups in these communities should be set around four hours.

The provision of food, and perhaps traditional food, is also an essential part of conducting focus groups in cross-cultural settings. Since food is a focal point for sharing experiences for many Latina women, in her research on fear of crime, Esther Madriz (1998: 6) provided snacks and coffee for the adult women and pizza and soft drinks for the teenagers. Many participants continued to share their experiences with crime and fear of crime after the group discussion had finished, while having coffee and eating. Similarly, Adriana Umaña-Taylor and Mayra Bámaca (2004) recommend the provision of food for Latino focus group participants because hospitality is very important to these people. The researchers contend that this helps the participants to feel welcome and comfortable. They also highly recommend the provision of traditional foods for the Latino population. In their study with Emirati women, Wendy Winslow and colleagues (2002) provided snacks to their participants as in the tradition of Arab hospitality. Luciana Ruppenthal and colleagues (2005: 743), in their research concerning reproductive health needs of immigrant women in Canada, selected hot, sit-down meals instead of cold finger foods as this promotes 'a culturally warm environment for participants to become acquainted'. Gerald Berthelette and colleagues (2001: 17) employed focus groups in their research to evaluate the effectiveness of their diabetes education programme with Aboriginal families living with type 2 diabetes. The importance of food in Aboriginal communities was discussed and they ended up providing a menu which met Aboriginal tastes and included wild rice soup and bannock. In their research with Mexican migrant farmworkers in Oregon, Marie Napolitano and colleagues (2002: 179) took into account the social value of providing food for their participants. Mexican food or pizza (for convenience) was served either before or after the focus group. However, Mexican food was the preferred choice among the participants. The researchers eventually ordered Mexican food from a restaurant which turned out to be not too expensive and the pickup time could be managed to coincide with the schedule of the group sessions. The times that the researchers and the participants spent together during the consumption of food resulted in discussions about the participants' personal experiences with work and pesticides. The researchers contend that eating together provided them with additional insights and 'the time was socially rewarding'.

In Pacific Northwest Indian communities, traditional foods including salmon and fry bread should be served. It is also expected among the participants that extra food is provided for them to take home after the session. In these communities, generosity is an essential value. This requires that extra food preparation should be done. According to June Strickland (1999: 194), it is also crucial to provide gifts as a 'give away' ritual. Culturally, this ritual requires that gifts are distributed by hand after the meal. It is also important that all participants must receive several gifts and these gifts must be handmade by community members. The gifts which are well received in these communities include beadwork, baskets, pottery and buckskin medicine bags.

Selecting an appropriate time for the group discussion is essential in some cultural groups. In Wendy Winslow and colleagues' study (2002) in the United Arab Emirates, they used a focus group method to elicit information from the women. As many

Emiratis rest during the intense heat of the afternoon, focus groups should be conducted during the morning or evening. Additionally, women pray five times each day and hence the time chosen for research should not interfere with these daily prayers. However, Winslow and others also contend that prayer time can be seen as a natural break during a group discussion as the women in their study were able to resume the group discussion easily since they perceived prayers as part of the natural rhythm of their day.

Monique Hennink (2007: 70–71) cautions us about using culturally appropriate questioning strategies in cross-cultural focus groups. In certain groups or settings, some questioning approaches could be inappropriate or cause offence to the participants. This is particularly so in focus groups that examine sensitive issues in settings where certain topics are not openly discussed or are illegal, for instance abortion, sexuality, sexual behaviour or domestic violence. If the research project involves discussion about sexual matters, the researchers need to be cautious about asking questions in the group. In most Asian cultures, sex is regarded as taboo, a formidable matter, not something that should be talked about with other people (Liamputtong 2010a). The question guide (see Chapter 5 in this volume) should be carefully constructed and reviewed so that any inappropriate questions can be modified. In their research with migrant farmworkers in Oregon, Marie Napolitano and colleagues (2002: 181) contend that the questions should not be constructed using the word 'you', for instance 'tell me what you do to protect yourself from pesticides'. The participants seemed to take these personally and would not answer what was obvious. More useful information was generated when the question was changed directly to 'a person' or to 'one', such as 'what can a person do to protect him- or herself from pesticides?'

I argue that sensitivity to the culture is good, but this is still not good enough. Knowledge of the culture is essential so that the researchers can work more effectively with members of the community. A good example is from research regarding maternal health practices in India which examined women's health concerns during pregnancy (Kauser 2001). The pregnant women participants did not wish to discuss problems which might occur during pregnancy because they believed that talking about these problems might put their pregnancy at risk. This cultural belief is a well-known taboo among the local people, but it was unknown to Kauser and the research team. Hence, it was not possible to ask the women to discuss their concern about the potential problems related to pregnancy. The researchers had to develop a different strategy to obtain the information from other sources (Kauser 2001).

Failure to recognise and include many of the cultural considerations that I have provided in this section in the conduct of the focus group sessions is likely to 'result in the loss of valuable information and potential conflict with participants' (Halcomb et al. 2007: 1006). I would like to point to the work of Bilkis Vissandjée and colleagues (2002: 841) who provide some basic steps for culturally competent focus groups which readers may wish to adopt in their research:

- Researchers must be flexible and expect the unexpected in terms of time and cultural difference.
- Researchers must take the time to understand local customs and respect them during data collection. Do not disregard local customs as this could lead to the

alienation of yourself and your research from the people from whom you intend to learn.

- It is wise to consult other researchers in the area who have carried out similar research. Their successes and failures will help you to develop your approach appropriately and highlight areas of caution that you may avoid.
- Local community members should be engaged in the research design, choice of methodology, planning, and implementation of your focus groups.
- Researchers must be prepared to adapt literature or previous experience with focus groups in cross-cultural settings and look for new techniques which are more culturally appropriate in your research.
- It is wise to share information about yourself with the participants. This helps to increase their trust and rapport and is a good strategy for inviting people to share their experiences with you.

## FOCUS GROUPS IN CROSS-CULTURAL SETTINGS: SOME PRACTICAL CONSIDERATIONS

Many of the issues that I have discussed in Chapters 3 and 4 are applicable to focus groups in cross-cultural research. However, I would like to point to other salient areas which need to be taken into account if the researchers wish to see their focus groups proceed smoothly when working cross-culturally.

### Venue of Focus Groups and Outdoor Locations

In traditional focus group research, it is suggested that the venue must be at a neutral place (see Chapter 4 in this volume). However, very often in other cultural settings, particularly in small villages or communities, the researchers may be invited to conduct their focus groups at the home of a community leader (Hennink 2007). The appropriateness of using this venue and the effect that it may have on participants' contributions to the group discussion have been debated among focus group researchers. Some suggest that it is important to accept the offer of the community leader as this is a way to show respect for his or her hospitality. It may also be the most practical place for the focus group because the participants would feel more comfortable in this venue since it is the usual place for having community meetings. However, others argue that the venue may produce 'a power dynamic, whereby participants feel obliged to respect the views of the community leader on the topic of discussion rather than voice their own opinion' (Hennink 2007: 161). Additionally, the community leader may join in the group discussion at any time and this could have an effect on the hierarchy within the group discussion and the quality of the data. It is crucial that the researchers must be aware of the possible influence of certain types of venues for their focus groups.

Most focus groups are held indoors as it should be quiet enough for the participants to concentrate on the discussion. The need for confidentiality also dictates indoor locations. But in some contexts, and particularly when carrying out focus groups in developing countries, it is appropriate to hold focus groups in outdoor settings (Vissangdée et al. 2002; Hennink 2007). Generally, a focus group is conducted outdoors when it needs to be organised close to where the participants live or work, such as fields in agricultural areas, or when there is no suitable indoor venue available for use (Hennink 2007).

Conducting focus groups outdoors requires some modifications and compromises as it may have an impact on the quality of the data generated in the group. Excessive noise, interruptions, distractions, lack of privacy and the risk of onlookers are typical problems associated with outdoor focus groups and these can affect the group dynamics (Hennink 2007). Also, the tape-recording of outdoor discussion groups would pick up the sounds of others in the surroundings, such as children crying and playing, street vendors selling food, people carrying out their everyday chores and vehicles passing by. It could be problematic for transcribers to differentiate the voices of the focus group participants from those of others in the background. Therefore, it is crucial that the researchers should find a relatively quiet location and ensure that a note-taker is present to record the discussion. However, as I have said in Chapter 5, nowadays there are digital tape-recorders that researchers can use. The digital tapes can screen out background noises so that the discussion is still audible even if the focus groups are held where there is a noisy background.

Outdoor focus groups also attract the attention of onlookers or passers-by. This can impact on the concentration of the participants and may distract them from the topic under discussion (Hennink 2007). It is important to try to run the focus groups away from any central community areas. For example, focus groups can be held behind a wall or hedge or in a courtyard and under a distant tree. All these will provide a shield from interruptions by onlookers or passers-by (Vissandjée et al. 2002; Hennink 2007).

## Seating

When holding focus groups in outdoor settings, it is crucial to arrange seating in such a way that the participants can effectively interact with each other. Chairs may need to be carried to the outdoor location but these can be replaced easily with ground sheets or straw mats (Hennink 2007). It is essential to observe cultural norms regarding seating of the local people. For instance, if it is culturally required that older individuals are to be seated on chairs and younger persons to sit on mats, the researchers should arrange seating accordingly so that the participants feel comfortable and relaxed in the group discussion (Hennink 2007). According to June Strickland (1999), in Pacific Northwest Indian communities, the circle symbolises unity. Circles are used in ceremonies, room arrangements and community activities. It is, therefore, important that the researchers organise a circular seating arrangement in their focus groups with these communities.

Often, in cross-cultural focus group research, the participants sit on the floor (see Bissell et al. 2000; Vissandjée et al. 2002; Winslow et al. 2002; Borghi et al. 2007; Hennink 2007). In their research regarding the influence of rural women's social, economic and political autonomy on their health status and household welfare in rural Gujarat, Bilkis Vissandjée and colleagues (2002: 831) suggest that it is crucial for them to consider how their participants would sit. The custom in rural India is 'to sit on the ground, shoes off and legs crossed'. Hence, they adopted the same custom during their focus groups in order to allow the participants to focus on the discussion rather than thinking about how they were sitting. Similarly, women in the Arab world are accustomed to sitting cross-legged in a circle on a rug with shoes off. In Wendy Winslow and others' study with Emirati women (2002), they point out that this allowed the women to have a natural involvement and interaction which might not have occurred if the women were sitting at tables and on chairs.

## FOCUS GROUPS AND PARTICIPATORY ACTIVITIES IN CROSS-CULTURAL RESEARCH

Commonly, in carrying out focus groups with poor and marginalised people in resource-poor countries, other participatory activities are built into the group discussions. Focus groups offer an excellent context for more innovative participatory techniques during the group session (Lloyd-Evans 2006). Some stimulus materials such as image display boards and music have been used to encourage discussions among the group participants. As Sally Lloyd-Evans (2006: 159) suggests, 'visual exercises provide a focus for talking about issues and they also play a useful role in encouraging quieter members of the group to take part in the research'. Often, it is a good strategy to encourage the participants to 'put their ideas on paper, draw images or maps, devise flow charts, respond to images, take their own photographs with disposable cameras, or use ranking exercises'.

The free-listing method, where participants are invited to list all elements of the topic under discussion, is often used in cross-cultural focus groups (Colucci 2007, 2008). Other participatory activities such as pile and picture sorting can also be used in cross-cultural focus groups. In a study in India (Kauser 2001), the researcher utilised a pile-sorting activity. The participants were provided with a pile of cards with an illness written on them and asked to put them in different piles according to their understanding of the severity of the illness.

Participants may also be invited to create a story around the issue under study. This strategy is particularly appropriate when the researchers aim to gain a 'real-life situation' from the participants. Storytelling in focus groups can provide particularly interesting information (see Strickland 1999). The inclusion of some participatory activities in focus groups is extremely useful for reducing language barriers that some participants may encounter. This is because the participants do not have to rely on oral language to express their ideas. The participatory activities also make the experience of taking part in focus groups more enjoyable and less threatening (Colucci 2007, 2008).

In their research regarding feeding of young children in school shelters among indigenous mothers in Mexico, Bernardo Turnbull and colleagues (2006: 507) carried out a series of workshops with the mothers. These workshops functioned very similarly to focus groups. In the workshop, the mothers were asked to discuss the nutrition of their children both at home and at the shelter. Turnbull and colleagues also used 'mapping to locate food sources within their communities'. They asked the mothers to bring food from their homes and to display possible combinations on the table. The mothers were also asked to score a food matrix for nutritional value, its price and acceptability.

## CASE EXAMPLES OF CROSS-CULTURAL RESEARCH USING FOCUS GROUPS

Focus group interviews have been increasingly adopted in cross-cultural research. Gisele Maynard-Tucker (2000) conducted focus groups regarding knowledge of AIDS among high-risk groups, sex workers and STD patients in Antananarivo, Madagascar, for the World Bank/Futures Group International in 1996. Focus group discussions with sex workers and their clients were planned to be carried out in a private room in a restaurant in the red-light district. For six days, focus groups were organised from noon to 2 pm. Sex workers were informed about the research in the streets and bars the night before by a health promoter who was known to the women. Many promised to attend, but few actually turned up. Later, it became clear that these women spent all night working and they would sleep in the morning. In the end, women were recruited from the streets and bars closer to the research venue. The choice of restaurant where focus groups were held with the women assisted recruitment as it was convenient for them to attend. Lunch was served after the session and it was during this lunch time that the women talked freely about their lives, expectations, difficulties and sexual behaviour. The women felt more at ease during a social gathering than in a formal focus group discussion.

As part of the project called 'Reducing Pesticide Exposure in Minority Families', Marie Napolitano and colleagues (2002) carried out focus groups with Mexican migrant and seasonal farmworkers (MSFW) in Oregon. The main objective of their research was to develop an effective and culturally appropriate pesticide exposure educational intervention for migrant farmworker families. The focus group methodology was employed to obtain the community's viewpoints on pesticide exposure, the effectiveness of educational messages, and preferences regarding types of interventions. The researchers used the results of the focus groups to develop a culturally appropriate pesticide exposure video which addressed the major ways that the children of farmworkers are exposed to pesticides and the preventative methods which can reduce these exposures.

In planning their research with migrant farmworkers, the focus group methodology was seen as the most feasible and productive way to generate information from the parents about pesticide beliefs and practices and pesticide education. Napolitano and colleagues (2002: 178) suggested:

> These migrant farmworker parents would only be available for short periods of time during the crop season. Their workdays are long and usually six days per week. Therefore, focus groups that could gather sufficient numbers of parents together for as short a period of time as possible were deemed our best choice.

The focus groups were carried out during the 1997 and 1998 harvesting seasons in five communities in the state of Oregon. Fifty-nine parents aged 21–30 years took part in the focus groups. All were Mexican born and about half had five years or less of education. The participants comprised 25 females and 34 males. Each focus group took about 70 minutes.

Apart from being able to use focus groups to obtain information about pesticides so that it could be used for the development of an educational tool, the focus groups offered several secondary outcomes. The participants perceived the focus groups as 'beneficial educational time' (p. 182). Additionally, they appreciated being asked to take part in the research. One participant remarked that 'our answers are not so good because no one had asked our opinions before' (p. 182). Lastly, the focus group methodology was an effective means for the development of educational tools which would be culturally appropriate and meet particular needs in the target group.

In research with Aboriginal mothers who experienced fetal alcohol syndrome/ fetal alcohol effects (FAS/FAE) in Candana (2007), Amy Salmon invited the women to take part in her research and asked them to choose if they wished to be interviewed individually or in a group. All of the women selected a group interview because they felt that it would provide them with 'support, encouragement, and an increased sense of safety and trust' in a situation where the researcher was not previously known to them (Salmon 2007: 985). Salmon, therefore, undertook two group interviews with each of the women. The grouping of these women remained the same for both interviews. Although Salmon did not use the term 'focus groups' as such, it falls within the collective testimony of focus group methodology that I am discussing in this chapter.

By participating in the focus group interviews, the women were able to share their individual experiences with others. Through the group discussion, the women were also able to see that their experiences were similar to, different from, or related to the experiences of others in the group. As such, the focus group interviews 'provided a venue through which participants could give voice to collective experiences that are often privatized in health policy texts as the failings or shortcomings of individual mothers acting alone' (Salmon 2007: 988).

The focus group interviews permitted the women to build on and articulate their collective experiences as mothers. This method allowed the women to talk about their lack of knowledge (such as the intake of caffeine and aspartame), which was crucial for their ability to make informed decisions about not only their own health, but also the health of their children. The focus group interviews also showed that the women were 'standing alongside one another as mothers, actively seeking out information to protect and promote their children's health to incorporate consciously into their mothering practice' (p. 990).

Francesca Giordano and colleagues (2009) examined the hopes and dreams of Honduran mothers about the sexuality of their daughters in Tegucigalpa, the capital city of Honduras. The study aimed to explore beliefs and attitudes regarding sexuality that Honduran women wished to transfer from generation to generation. Two focus groups were conducted with 22 local women. They were asked about advice regarding sexual beliefs and behaviour which mothers would have for their daughters. In conducting research on sexuality issues with Honduran women, Giordano and colleagues realised that it could be difficult for the women to speak about them openly. This led them to make a decision on several important points which would allow them to generate the data they needed.

Prior to the conduct of focus groups, the moderators and translators were trained in the basics of carrying out focus groups and met as a group to review the interview protocol. The emphases of the training were placed on the creation of a safe and comfortable environment for discussion, the use of open-ended questioning techniques to allow free-flowing discussion, and the provision of accurate, immediate and colloquial translation. In the focus groups, the translation was conducted simultaneously in order to facilitate communication between the moderators and the participants. One of the researchers, who is a native Honduran Spanish speaker, prepared both the Spanish transcripts and English translations.

All participants were asked to sign a consent form which was in Spanish. At the commencement of each focus group, the women were invited to introduce themselves informally, for example they talked about their marital status, their children and how long they had lived in Honduras. There was no formal demographic data collected at the beginning. The focus group interview protocol was composed of open-ended questions including comfort with their bodies, identification as girls, choosing a husband, sex and sexual pleasure, sexual violence and reproductive health. The emphasis in the discussion was on their experiences in providing advice to their daughters and other young Honduran women. Giordano and colleagues also used several follow-up questions to elicit the women's views and these included how sexual and gender-identification information was first learned, how advice was communicated, difficulties and supports, and their experiences of joys, regrets and taboos.

In each focus group, two moderators worked together and asked questions alternately. Both groups had one designated interpreter who was a community leader and worked as part of the larger Honduran research project. Food was provided to both groups and small surprise gifts were also given at the conclusion of each session as a way of thanking the participants for their time.

Francesca Giordano and colleagues (2009) contended that the value of a focus group as a data collection method is the use of group processes and interpersonal interactions as a means for eliciting detailed worldview perspectives from the participants. With the use of focus groups in their research, it was revealed that 'hope lies within the power of the relationship that mothers forge with daughters'. They concluded:

> From a feminist and social constructionist perspective, mothers provide a central role model, facilitate the creation of cultural knowledge and, therefore, can be the source of cultural change. The voices of these Honduran women suggest the strength and richness of the relationship Latina mothers, whether native or immigrant, have with their daughters. (p. 1007)

## CONCLUSION

Because the focus group methodology was developed particularly for use with Anglo-Celtic populations, some researchers have raised questions about the appropriateness of the methodology in cross-cultural research (Yelland & Gifford 1995). Others, however, have demonstrated that the methodology is a culturally sensitive research approach (Madriz 1998; 2003; Napolitano et al. 2002; Culley et al 2007; Halcomb 2007; Thomas 2008; Davidson et al. 2010). As Lorraine Culley and colleagues (2007: 103) suggest, focus groups 'do not discriminate against people who cannot read or write and who are, therefore, often excluded from more formal channels of communication'. These issues are often relevant to poor people in resource-poor settings. Hence, the method is appropriate for carrying out research in many cross-cultural settings. Additionally, as Andrew Thomas (2008: 87) contends, focus groups permit cultural values and norms of the participants to have 'breathing space'. The methodology provides an opportunity for 'empathic collection of deep data from the local context' because it underscores participation, supportive environments, interaction between group members and interaction between the researchers and group members in a relatively naturalistic setting. These characteristics are normalised aspects of many cultural groups. As such, focus groups are seen as a culturally sensitive data collection method in many cultures that value collective traits.

Similar to conducting any qualitative research cross-culturally, the use of focus groups in cross-cultural settings can also be challenging. Lorraine Watkins-Mathys (2006: 223) contends that engaging in the focus group methodology using different languages and in different cultural contexts 'makes understanding much more difficult and complex and depends on cultural insiders and dialectic processes which are time consuming and open to misunderstandings or gaps'. However, conducting focus groups cross-culturally provides 'enriching experiences' for the researchers, who would be able to obtain different insights into the topic under investigation. It also helps the researchers to acquire a 'new level of understanding' (Watkins-Mathys 2006: 223) as they attempt to 'make sense of the unfamiliar' (Welch & Piekkari 2006: 434).

## TUTORIAL ACTIVITIES

You are a research student who needs to produce a thesis as part of your degree. You wish to conduct your research on the experience of living with disability in a resource-poor country in Asia or Africa. You feel that the focus group methodology would be an ideal method to use in your research, but you need to convince your supervisor about the methodology and whether its use is viable.

1  How would you explain the value of the focus group methodology in cross-cultural research?
2  What salient issues do you need to plan in carrying out this piece of research?
3  What are the likely difficulties that you can anticipate and how would you go about overcoming these difficulties?

## FURTHER READING

Culley, L., Hudson, N., & Rapport, F. (2007). Using focus groups with minority ethnic communities: Researching infertility in British South Asian communities. *Qualitative Health Research* 171, 102–112.

Hennink, M.M. (2007). *International focus group research: A handbook for the health and social sciences.* Cambridge: Cambridge University Press.

Liamputtong, P. (2007). *Researching the vulnerable: A guide to sensitive research methods.* London: Sage.

Liamputtong, P. (2010a). *Performing qualitative cross-cultural research.* Cambridge: Cambridge University Press.

Madriz, E. (2000). Focus groups in feminist research. In N.K. Denzin & Y.S. Lincoln (eds.), *Handbook of qualitative research*, 2nd edition (pp. 835–850). Thousand Oaks, CA: Sage.

Thomas, A. (2008). Focus groups in qualitative research: Culturally sensitive methodology for the Arabian Gulf? *International Journal of Research & Method in Education* 31(1), 77–88.

Vissandjée, B., Abdool, S.N., & Dupéré, S. (2002). Focus groups in rural Gujarat, India: A modified approach. *Qualitative Health Research* 12(6), 826–843.

Watkins-Mathys, L. (2006). Focus group interviewing in China: Language, culture, and sensemaking. *Journal of International Entrepreneurship* 4, 209–226.

Willis, E., Pearce, M., & Jenkin, T. (2005). Adapting focus group methods to fit Aboriginal community-based research. *Qualitative Research Journal* 5(2), 112–123.

# 9
# VIRTUAL FOCUS GROUPS

## CHAPTER OBJECTIVES

In this chapter you will learn about:

- Introduction to virtual focus groups
- Types of virtual focus groups
- Group dynamics, interaction and expression in virtual focus groups
- Moderating virtual focus groups
- Case example of virtual focus group research

In recent years, virtual or online focus groups have become increasingly visible in health and social science research. Conducting focus group research online 'represents attempts within the research community to adapt conventional methodological approaches to keep pace with advances in communication technology' (Fox et al. 2007: 539). Additionally, it provides another means for carrying out research with people who are unable or unwilling to participate in orthodox focus groups or may just prefer to participate online.

In this chapter, I will detail the principles and practices of conducting virtual focus groups including an introduction to virtual focus groups and types of virtual focus group research. I will outline some discussions on dynamics, interactions and expression in online focus groups along with details on moderating online focus groups. The chapter also includes some examples drawn from empirical research in the areas of health and social sciences. It must be noted here that, due to space limitations, I am unable to include many aspects of conducting focus groups online, for example how to recruit potential participants online, ethical considerations, deception in virtual research and general benefits and challenges of online research. These aspects have been documented in many other publications (see Mann & Stewart 2000; Bloor et al. 2001; Franklin & Lowry 2001; Johns et al. 2004; Liamputtong 2006; Whitehead 2007; Fielding et al. 2008; O'Connor et al. 2008).

## VIRTUAL FOCUS GROUP METHOD

Despite resistance from some focus group researchers (Greenbaum 2001), virtual focus group interviews have been used and become more popular in the health and social sciences. The virtual environment offers a new possibility for researchers to carry out their focus group research (Gaiser 2008). Undertaking focus group in a virtual setting provides many benefits. It provides an opportunity to carry out focus group research which is relatively inexpensive. Often, a wider range of potential participants can be accessed by the technique and diverse information can be generated in a shorter period of time. The technique offers 'more specific framing' of research topics and concerns by the participants, hence reducing the bias of researchers (Gaiser 2008). Data collection can be done among small groups of participants from different distant locations simultaneously (Gaiser 2008). Virtual focus groups can generate individual perspectives and group similarities (Murray 1997). It is more likely that participants' inhibitions are reduced and anonymity is enhanced. Hence, not only ideas and solutions but also critical comments from the participants can be captured. Due to the anonymity of virtual focus groups, they can increase personal disclosure and this can lead to an increase in the interaction among the participants. Practically, virtual focus groups can help to overcome some difficulties such as arranging face-to-face groups, bringing together divergent groups, and the costs of transportation, rental of facilities and transcription that occur in traditional focus groups (Mann & Stewart 2000; Valaitis & Sword 2005; Liamputtong 2006; Gaiser 2008). In traditional focus groups, interaction between the participants is essential (Morgan 1997; see also Chapter 3). However, by facing other participants, individuals may be pressured to conform, and this can restrict overall interaction and the quality of the collected data. In virtual focus groups, it is likely that the pressure to conform may be markedly reduced. Hence, this offers a possibility for generating data which can be more difficult to obtain in face-to-face focus group interactions (Gaiser 2008).

But are they focus groups? Virtual focus group researchers Kate Robson and Matthew Williams (2005: 396) ask 'to what extent online focus groups can truly be considered to belong to the focus group method'. In orthodox focus groups, a group discussion is organised around a particular topic and is facilitated by a researcher. The explicit use of group interaction to produce data is the distinguishing feature of a focus group. To facilitate more open discussion, a setting which is familiar, comfortable and unthreatening for the participants is essential. Will these essential features be catered for by the virtual focus group? Some of these questions have been discussed in the literature concerning the use of virtual focus groups. Most published research projects in the health and social sciences have employed asynchronous, or non-real-time, groups which include discussion groups and bulletin boards, where messages which are posted in a folder are examined and responded to by other participants (see a later section). Offering an asynchronous mode can be advantageous for people who cannot type fast, it can overcome time zone differences, and it can generate detailed and reflective responses (Fox et al. 2007). However, there has been some debate about whether this modality is actually a real form of a focus group method (Bloor et al. 2001). But Kate Robson and Matthew Williams (2005: 397) argue that 'the acceptance of computer mediated variations on a whole range of research methods, including focus groups, is appropriate to contemporary technological developments'.

## VIRTUAL FOCUS GROUPS: TYPES

Generally, there are two different types of virtual focus groups which have been used by social science researchers: synchronous (real-time) and asynchronous (non-real-time) focus groups. However, recently another type has arisen: virtual focus groups making use of 3D graphical environments (see Williams 2003; Williams & Robson 2004; Robson & Williams 2005). I will outline them below.

Each type of virtual focus group technique has its own prominent characteristics. Hence, depending on a given research project, each method can be more or less appropriate (Robson & Williams 2005; Gaiser 2008). Researchers need to ask whether or not their research should be done in synchronous or asynchronous modality (Gaiser 2008). Each form has strengths and challenges. Depending on whether group members are temporally co-present or not, discussions may differ considerably. Synchronous or real-time focus group discussions are fast moving and chaotic, but are also more similar to face-to-face discussions in traditional focus groups (Robson & Williams 2005). But organising these can be a challenge. Asynchronous focus groups provide the participants with time to consider their responses, and are usually lengthier than those in synchronous focus groups. They are also easier to arrange.

### Synchronous Focus Groups

Synchronous focus groups resemble conventional face-to-face focus groups since they allow real-time interaction between the moderator and participants, but rather than real venues, chatrooms or focus group conference software are used (Oringderff 2004; Gaiser 2008; O'Connor et al. 2008). In synchronous focus groups, all the participants are online at the same time and the transmission of texts between them is instantaneous. What one participant composes at his or her keyboard is immediately sent to the group as a whole. Other participants can read the text as it is typed or as soon as the 'send' or 'return' button is hit. The participants can 'reply' immediately to any message once it arrives at their computer (Mann & Stewart 2000: 101). Synchronous focus groups 'can be fast, furious and highly interactive'. As the participants do not need to wait for others to 'respond before sending further messages, those who are most proficient at typing have the "power" to "say" the most' (Mann & Stewart 2000: 102).

As such, focus group researchers who have employed the synchronous form commonly agree that group interactions are characterised by 'dynamism and immediacy' (Fox et al. 2007: 539). The transient co-presence allows online interactions to be intensified, and hence creates an environment where discussions can thrive (Robson & Williams 2005). This immediacy of synchronous communication resembles that of conventional discussions in focus groups.

There are various synchronous modes of communication and they are progressing very quickly. The more popular forms are Internet Relay Chat (IRC), AOL's chatrooms, and instant messaging programs such as MSN Messenger and Yahoo Instant Messenger or Skype chat (Robson & Williams 2005; O'Connor et al. 2008). However, a commonly used approach is to facilitate synchronous focus groups via conferencing software. For example, in their virtual focus group research concerning young people and health risks, Fiona Stewart and colleagues (1998) made use of conferencing software packages, for example 'Firstclass Conferencing', which was available for online and distance teaching purposes at Deakin University in Australia.

However, nowadays there are less familiar forms of online communication. These are synchronous modes of communication which permit both text-based and graphical interaction. They have appeared because of higher bandwidths and faster processor speeds. They emanated from the MUDs (Multi-User Dungeons or Domains) and MOOs (object-oriented MUDs) which continue to be very popular modes of text-based real-time communication (see also a later section) (Robson & Williams 2005: 404).

There are other popular shareware and freeware options including mIRC and XChat. Typically, they are free for a trial period. The users are then expected to register and pay a small fee. GChat and DigiChat are also available for use. They permit storage and download of the discussion text. Listings of freeware and shareware applications are easily accessible online (Gaiser 2008: 301).

## Asynchronous Focus Groups

The most widely adopted modes of virtual group interaction are asynchronous, text-based message board or email facilities. Asynchronous discussions can be email based, or Web based. Asynchronous discussions do not require the participants to be online at the same time to communicate (Valaitis & Sword 2005). The participants can log in and respond to discussion topics in their own time. Asynchronous focus groups offer the ability to deal with global time differences, provide time for participants with limited typing skills, and let participants have more time to focus and reflect on their responses (Oringderff 2004). In a virtual focus group which is carried out asynchronously, there is a significant amount of control that the participants have on how, when and what they articulate (Gaiser 2008). Hence, asynchronous focus groups offer useful forms of communication aiming at increasing participation and reflective responses (Oringderff 2004).

Asynchronous focus groups can be carried out using emails and email group lists. Distribution lists are 'email-based discussion groups, with a central email address to which all contributions are sent before being automatically forwarded to those subscribed' (Robson & Williams 2005: 404). Early virtual focus group researchers made use of these distribution lists as a means to access potential participants and conduct their research. Participants experience these types of asynchronous focus groups similar to how they use their emails (Gaiser 2008). Distribution lists have several administration options which make them especially valuable for research purposes (Robson & Williams 2005). The list subscriptions can be stopped. This permits the list owner to select the subscribers who can participate in the discussion, and who can have access to information generated from the discussion. The researchers can also moderate the lists. Hence, the researchers can remove any identifying information, arrange the order of messages into different threads, and pose their questions and prompts similar to what a 'real-life' focus group moderator would do (Robson & Williams 2005). Distribution lists are easy and straightforward to set up and run. They do not require any specialist software or expertise. They also make it easy for research participants to take part.

Web-based asynchronous focus groups are usually undertaken through web-boards. Web-boards are located on websites and the contributors are required to use browser software to visit the sites. The users write messages on online forms and submit them through the browser. For some web-boards, the users must register prior to reading or contributing to discussions. Others permit anyone to read or contribute freely, but most require some kinds of registration to contribute or 'post'. For virtual focus group researchers, web-boards which necessitate registration have many benefits, especially in relation to issues of identification (see Prandy et al. 2001). Through the registration process, the researchers are able to obtain relevant background information on the participants and, more importantly, maintain control of the composition of the groups. Because the participants have registered to the web-board, they only need to identify themselves on the board by a user name. This means that their real names, emails or IP addresses cannot be identified by others apart from the researchers. Hence, the researchers have greater control in protecting the identities of the participants. However, it can be confusing to use web-boards, whereas email-based modes of group communication are still a familiar medium for most people (Robson & Williams 2005). Because contributions are done online, there may be a time pressure for those who use a dial-up Internet connection since they have to pay for it (although this is increasingly less of an issue for many with expanding rates of broadband uptake). This is not an issue when writing emails offline. And compared with other email-based modes of discussion, a higher degree of technical competence is required in setting up and running the boards (Robson & Williams 2005).

## Online Focus Groups in Virtual Graphical Environments

A recent development in online technology has begun to lead to a new means for social interaction. This is referred to as networked virtual reality (VR), but is more commonly known as graphical MUDs (Robson & Williams 2005; Fox et al. 2007). Until recently, these visual graphical environments were only an 'imagined' world within textual MUDs. They are 'platforms where multiple users are not only able to communicate via text in a synchronous fashion, but are also presented with a graphical representation of the world within which they are communicating' (Robson & Williams 2005: 406). Currently, there exist several platforms online which are different in their visual representation.

In Mathew Williams' graphical online focus group (2003), the virtual reality platform was three dimensional. Similar to an offline environment, it permitted the participants to move around in a space. Kate Robson and Matthew Williams (2005: 406–407) provide a detailed description of this virtual focus group in the following excerpt:

The participants were represented by avatars, a graphical version of the person behind the home computer. If preferred, each participant could alter the appearance of their avatar by choosing from a list containing a myriad of alternative forms. These forms ranged from male to female avatars of differencing dress and demeanour to inanimate and fantasy characters more analogous to the gaming genre that inspired the creation of many of these worlds. Once a suitable visual representation had been chosen, communication occurred via text which was displayed in a window beneath the graphical interface. This combination of graphics and text in a communications medium led to an entirely different experience of conducting an online focus group.

Robson and Williams (2005: 406) suggest that a networked VR provides the participants with the feeling of 'being somewhere'. Since a networked VR exists in both physical (graphical/visual) and textual (in some cases also verbal/audible) locales, it permits more engaging discussions among the participants: 'Not only are discussions heightened in the textual sense, but also forms of visual communication allow for a richer form of social interaction.' These new 'physical' online environments have provided answers to some of the pitfalls of Internet research, particularly the lack of use of space and body movement characters which usually assist in the analysis and interpretation of data in the offline environment. In this system, each avatar is credited with a set of animated emotions. If a person in the group disagrees with what is said, he or she can shake his or her head. And if the person is in agreement with the statement of another avatar, he or she can jump for joy. According to Robson and Williams (2005: 406), 'such forms of communication through gesture and body language adequately mirror their offline equivalents allowing for a more thorough interpretation of emotion and opinion within the online group'.

As I have discussed in Chapter 4, the venue where a focus group is conducted has an impact on the interaction in the group. In a virtual setting, Robson and Williams (2005) contend, there is no difference. Any selected graphical environment can have different meanings which could impact on the way the participants interact with each other. In Williams' research (2003), due to the 'flexible' character of networked VR platforms, he managed to select a multitude of possible environments. These ranged from 'the conventional four-walled virtual seminar room (with virtual tea and biscuits for that added comfort) to a quiet open field on a bright sunny day, or to the extreme of an underwater fantasy world' (Robson & Williams 2005: 407).

Additionally, many networked VR platforms allow the members to build their own properties within existing worlds. And to some extent, the platforms advocate the building of totally new worlds to suit the purposes of their members. This offers the researchers a distinctive possibility to build settings which would reflect both their and the participants' needs and circumstances. Ideally, this would reduce the influence of the venue on the collected data (Robson & Williams 2005). However, there can be some difficulties associated with the use of VR in comparison with the more familiar options of email or web-boards, if the participants are not familiar with it.

Whatever types of virtual focus groups and software that the researchers may wish to adopt, it is essential to have support services. Many institutions have excellent websites and support services that researchers may be able to tap into when using this type of focus group research. For example, Amanda Kenny (2005) used WebCT or LMS at La Trobe University in Australia to carry out her research. Lyn Turney and Catherine Pocknee (2005) also conducted their virtual focus group via Blackboard at Swinburne Institute of Technology in Australia. And a virtual focus group that Fiona Fox and colleagues (2007) undertook was done with the help of an IT technician from her faculty and hosted by the university.

## GROUP DYNAMICS, INTERACTION AND EXPRESSION

It has been suggested that group dynamics are a problematic factor for virtual focus groups. Group interactions do happen online, although interactions among the participants in a text-based focus group may not resemble those of face-to-face groups (Hughes & Lang 2004). However, one well-known dynamic, the domination of the discussion by one or several participants (see Chapter 5 in this volume), is unlikely to occur online. In virtual focus groups, the voice of each participant will be heard because they do not need to wait for their turn; they can jump in any time. Having said that, however, there are different kinds of virtual focus group participants who interact in different ways. From the nature of the chat interface in their study, Jerald Hughes and Karl Lang (2004: 99) compile a list of participant behaviours:

- Monologuing – participants who type a series of posts on a solitary thread, without responding to others, and the others do not respond to them.
- Dittoing – participants who contribute by mostly agreeing with others' views.
- One-Liners – participants who provide statements with relatively brief content. The nature of the interface in Blackboard and in many other chat systems encourages this type of participation because the input section shows only one line of text several dozen characters long.
- Essays – participants who compose comments as complete paragraphs which usually consist of multiple, orderly and grammatical complete sentences. The Essayist tends to contribute fewer posts because of the time it takes to conceptualise and type in these paragraphs. But it also means that the Essayist provides deeper contents than the One-Liner.
- Challenging – participants who tend to closely monitor the contributions of others, and challenge disagreement in the groups.

Researchers will have to decide how to deal with each type of participant (see Chapter 5).

Most studies have generally found that virtual focus group participants feel freer to detect other people's faults (Reid & Reid 2005). This leads to more disagreements and criticism than in face-to-face focus groups. This is in fact not a bad thing in focus groups as disagreement and conflict to a certain degree can enhance the generation of better ideas.

The lack of verbal and visual interaction in virtual research has been seen as another salient limitation of the use of virtual focus group as a research tool. This lack of verbal communication can be problematic for both researchers and participants. Much tacit information that could be observed in face-to-face research is lost in virtual research (Selwyn & Robson 1998). Similarly, in virtual focus groups, as Ted Gaiser (2008: 299) points out, 'the nuances of subtle visual interactive cues are lost'. Jerald Hughes and Karl Lang (2004: 99) contend that virtual focus groups which are carried out in text-based form only do not offer 'the media richness and social presence of face-to-face focus group sessions'.

However, virtual researchers can use non-verbal expressions and emotional icons, commonly known as emoticons, which people can use to express their emotion and emphases as a means to compensate for the visual loss in virtual research (Murphy & Collins 1997; Mann & Stewart 2000; Gaiser 2008). According to Ted Gaiser (2008: 299), these non-verbal expressions offer 'a communicative replacement for lost emotional context in social interactions'. These substitute expressions have already become standardised and familiar to virtual users (Hughes & Lang 2004). Such emoticons are presented in the following box.

---

**BOX 9.1   EMOTICONS USED IN ONLINE SETTINGS AND RESEARCH**

:-) (happy)

;-) (wink)

:-( (feeling sad)

:((( (feeling very sad)

:-# (my lips are sealed)

:-o (surprised)

:-] (sarcasm)

@:-) (wearing a turban) (you need to tilt your head towards your left shoulder to see this properly)

*Source*: Walston and Lissitz (2000: 462–463)

---

Often, according to Jill Walston and Robert Lissitz (2000: 462–463), virtual group members employ 'notations or intentional misspelling' to convey messages which normally would be expressed with tone of voice or facial expressions in a face-to-face interaction. Some of the strategies which are utilised to show emphases include repeating vowels ('Noooo way'), repeating punctuation (!!!!! or ?????) and all capital letters (That was GREAT!). However, it must be noted too that all capital letters signify shouting when online and hence this can be considered rude if overused. A pause in the discussion is represented by extra spaces or repeating periods (full stops) between words. Text expressions such as 'hmmmm', 'yuk-yuk', or 'whoa', which would have been expressed with sounds in face-to-face interactions, and some abbreviations such as 'lol' (laughing out loud), 'AFAIK' (As Far As I Know), 'BTW'

(By The Way), 'TIA' (Thanks In Advance), 'HTH' ([I] Hope This Helps) and 'IMO' (In My Opinion), are also used in a virtual environment (Mann & Stewart 2000; Hughes & Lang 2004; Fox et al. 2007).

## MODERATING VIRTUAL FOCUS GROUPS

Moderating virtual focus groups can be more challenging than the face-to-face ones. It necessitates 'finesse and skill' (Gaiser 2008: 299). The nature of the virtual environment can make it difficult, and sometimes impossible, for the moderator and the participants always to be present. Hence, Ted Gaiser (2008: 299) asks: 'Is it always necessary for a moderator to facilitate a group for it to function well as a group?' Reducing the moderator's involvement during the life of the research can be problematic, as this could be perceived by the participants as lacking facilitation and guidance (Gaiser 2008). Additionally, due to the lack of visual and verbal cues, this may make the participants confused about what they are meant to do. And this could derail discussion and restrict the overall success of the focus group. However, group independence can also offer a fertile environment for virtual focus groups. It can generate productive data for virtual researchers, or allow the discussion to commence and continue easily (Gaiser 2008).

Similar to traditional face-to-face focus groups, virtual group moderating is also essential, and in order to sustain the work of the groups, the moderators should provide some leadership to the group. They should be attentive and keep the group focused. They should also gently remind the participants that the core aim of the group is to interact with others (Gaiser 2008). In virtual focus groups, the moderators simply need a different set of skills, based on the possibilities of online communications, including non-standard uses of text such as emoticons, in order to bring the group activity to the desired level.

A valuable way for the commencement of a virtual focus group is via an introduction exercise (Gaiser 2008). It is a useful means for assisting the participants to begin to connect with each other (Gaiser 2008). In traditional focus groups, individuals can start the connection by physical appearance and a greeting process such as having a cup of coffee or tea together before the group commences. The participants can see each other and have a chat about each other's participation. But in virtual focus groups, this opportunity is not available. Hence, it requires other ways for people to connect.

In moderating virtual focus groups, researchers can employ many of the emoticons to express feelings and concerns (see earlier section on emoticons). But lack of visual cues could generate some interesting data that might not have emerged if the participants could see, through body languages, that the researchers are not interested in what they say (Gaiser 2008). The non-visual interaction might make the participants continue to delve deeper into a topic or expand into other interesting areas.

In synchronous focus groups, fast typing skills and some experiences with the style of real-time discussion are necessary. The dynamics of synchronous modes can be 'fast, furious, and chaotic' (Fox et al. 2007: 542–543). The differentiation between sending and replying is blurred since the participants do not have to wait for their turn to respond (Mann & Stewart 2000). Interactions between the participants can be complex and result in a chaotic transcript which can be difficult to make sense of. However, this fast pace can also result in a 'surprisingly enjoyable process'.

There are also occasions when silences occur in virtual focus groups. This may be because the participants are thinking, typing or refusing to respond (O'Connor & Madge 2003). It can be a challenge for the moderators to decide if they should move forward by prompting or asking more questions, or to wait because the participants might be busy typing a long response (Fox et al. 2007).

Additionally, the number of participants in a group is important for the moderators' sense of control. In her work, Fiona Fox (in Fox et al. 2007) recruited at least six participants for each discussion, but ended up with only three. However, synchronous online discussion with three participants was manageable for her to moderate and provided sufficient input for lively discussions. Due to the high speed of dialogue in synchronous focus groups, important issues can be rushed through if there are too many participants. Fiona Fox and colleagues (2007) suggest that virtual focus groups that comprise more than five participants may require a second moderator. This person can type while the other focuses on the content and flow of the discussion.

## CASE EXAMPLE OF VIRTUAL FOCUS GROUPS

Recently, there have been several studies utilising virtual focus groups. In this section, I will focus on some examples as a means to illustrate the many salient points that I have covered in this chapter. I will focus only on examples from synchronous and asynchronous focus groups. To my knowledge, there is only one study that employed networked virtual reality focus groups (see Williams 2003) and I have included several aspects of this study in the earlier sections.

Wendy Seymour (2001), using asynchronous focus groups, examined issues relating to technology, disability and risk among people with disabilities in Adelaide, Australia. Seymour (2001: 151–152) explored several options in order to select a suitable Internet interview capacity for her research. These included ICQ ('I Seek You', a chat program from Mirabills for Windows 95), AOL (America Online), Common Ground Bulletin Board which was commenced in 1991 by the Disability Information and Resource Centre, Adelaide, South Australia, and the threaded discussion online site provided by the Flexible Learning Centre at the University of South Australia. She selected the last option because it appeared to be most sensitive to the needs of her project. Despite being unable to undertake real-time interviews, the site offered many advantages. The participants could get in and out as frequently as they wanted. Over time, it allowed them to expand on a specific issue, to provide clarity of their responses, or to delete certain issues that they did wish to be used in the research. They could also trace the history of interactions through reading each message in a threaded discussion. This facility provided the participants with a generous opportunity to articulate their perspectives, which could impact on the research outcomes.

Seymour selected the threaded interview site over other Internet resources because of the assurance of ready support from an in-house provider. Being able to log into the discussions gave her the chance to shape the course of the interview. Practically, the major advantage was the cost of carrying out the project. Since the interviews could be directly transferred into Word documents for the analysis of data, it reduced the time-consuming process and expensive cost of data transcription.

The participants were recruited electronically through an available disability listserver which had a wide circulation among its members. Ethically, an in-house provider prevented many of the ethical issues which could be problematic by working through an external Internet site or server. This was because confidentiality of the participants could be better ensured. A consent form which outlined the content and nature of the interview was sent via email to the invited participants. The form included their names and the date of the request. The participants were requested to type 'yes' or 'no' in the designated area on the form as an indication of their understanding of the nature of their participation. Then it was printed, signed by Seymour and securely kept with other research materials.

Since the participants were invited to respond when it suited them, Seymour had to accommodate this freedom into the planning of her research. The data collection period was quite long. The shortest interview was carried out over 22 days, and the longest spanned 75 days. The average time of the interviews in her study was 42.6 hours.

Among the 20 participants, 7 participated exclusively through the threaded discussion site, but 5 participants changed to using email during the research process; 6 participants opted for email from the start. Due to difficulties in accessing the web page, 1 participant decided to use email and the other chose a face-to-face interview instead.

Although the participants had basic knowledge and skills regarding use of a computer and the Internet, they were not equally competent. In response to 'quietness' in the web page and due to its immediate qualities, sometimes Seymour decided to make contact with the participants via email. This, however, made the participants think that it was an incentive for them to continue the interview by email. Once they chose to move from the threaded discussion site to email, all subsequent discussion happened in this form.

The most common reason given for moving from the primary site to an email interview was familiarity with the email technique. However, the design of the web page was problematic for some participants – it was too distracting. The technique distracted them from the research questions. Some found cutting and pasting the questions and answers into a single response space difficult. The size of the response box and the small text font decreased their concentration and influenced their responses. Although some participants used their own strategies to overcome difficulties using the threaded discussion site, the task was time consuming. Even those who completed their interview through the site said that they preferred email because it was simpler to use and they were familiar with it.

Despite some technical difficulties in carrying out this research, Seymour (2001: 162) contended that:

> investigating disability and technology demanded a methodology to fit the topic. Disability is a time-consuming lifestyle and conducting the research online removed the need for the participants to leave their home environment. Addressing the physical impediments associated with space and time were significant advantages in this study.

Lyn Turney and Catherine Pocknee (2005: 2–3) conducted three virtual focus groups as part of their twelve focus groups which were undertaken following two large random surveys of public attitudes towards a range of new technologies. The virtual focus groups consisted of males and females who had a personal interest in DNA paternity testing and a patient special interest group from a stem cell study.

The virtual focus group method was adopted in these three groups because the participants were people who were difficult to access. This was mainly due to their geographical separation. Several recruitment strategies, including email, telephone and the snowball method, were employed in order to access them from around Australia. Recruitment of men for the paternity testing stakeholder focus groups was especially challenging. Turney and Pocknee were informed that generally men who were involved in fathers' rights groups were unwilling to talk with outsiders. But eventually, they were able to gain access to these men from across Australia through the assistance of the leader of a fathers' rights group, snowballing from the original contact, and posting notices on related online sites and in chat groups.

The female participants were recruited through a flier which was posted by the Council for Single Mothers and Their Children, notices in related online chat groups and publicity related to the survey. These mothers and their children had been ordered to have a test in order to have the father's name on the child's birth certificate and/or to meet the conditions for making a claim for child support payments. Because they were single mothers with young babies, it was difficult for them to participate in a face-to-face focus group. Virtual focus groups were an appropriate means that enabled them to participate in this project.

Similarly, the participants in the stem cell study patient group were also recruited through email and the posting of notices on related online sites and chat groups. They all were living with a medical condition (Parkinson's disease or a spinal injury) which had the potential to be alleviated or cured by the outcomes of stem cell research. They too had difficulties participating in a face-to-face focus group because of their restricted mobility, medication and need for care.

When setting up the group, Turney and Pocknee made several direct contacts via telephone and/or email with each participant (using their real identity) to discuss possible time and availability, and to select a pseudonym password for their virtual identity. Hence, although they were anonymous to others in the group, they all knew that the space between their online and offline identities was mediated by the researchers and this would protect them from identity deception.

The three virtual focus groups were carried out through an Internet discussion board on Blackboard which involved an asynchronous form of communication for one week. In all three groups, the virtual setting allowed the participants in each group to talk openly and anonymously about a personally and politically sensitive issue, which would have been more difficult to do in conventional focus groups. This Blackboard was run by the university's IT department and was programmed to permit access only to university-approved personnel. It provided staff and students with an environment which contains extensive communication facilities, Internet access, security features, password protection and automated data collection. It was hosted on internal university servers in order to ensure security. All research conducted through this system was required to meet the university's quality, security and privacy procedures.

The participants were given a guarantee that their personal information and perspectives would be secure and would not be accessible by unauthorised personnel. Therefore, two password-protected websites, one for male and one for female participants, were developed in 2003. A third site for the stem cell research group was set up in early 2004. Each website had a discussion forum, an online chatroom and email and announcement facilities.

Turney and Pocknee selected the discussion forum as their virtual focus groups. The moderator posted a series of text-based questions and probes, and the participants had the opportunity to respond in text format. Their responses were later downloaded for data analysis. They could fully access the site for a one-week period in order to respond to the questions, read the probes of the moderator and other participants, and post their comments.

Technologically, Turney and Pocknee (2005: 8) highly recommended the use of university learning management systems such as Blackboard and WebCT for undertaking virtual focus group research. Turney and Pocknee also suggested that this method should be considered for use when researching hard-to-reach individuals, particularly when it involved individuals or groups who, for whatever reason, are reluctant or unable to take part in face-to-face focus groups. For many hard-to-reach groups, the opportunity to participate in research from the comfort and privacy of their own homes is an attractive option. Their comfort is also enhanced by the secure, safe and anonymous environment offered by the online technology. This certainly would enhance higher participation among these groups of people.

Fiona Fox (in Fox et al. 2007: 540) undertook virtual focus group research in order to investigate appearance-related concerns among young people who have chronic skin conditions. Virtual focus groups were selected for this study in order to generate group discussions among young people. Seven synchronous focus groups were conducted with young people aged between 11 and 18 years. Traditional face-to-face focus groups could present some challenges for these young people, including personal arrangement, access to transport and their confidence in meeting strangers in an unfamiliar space. It has been suggested that having to meet strangers in a strange place could prevent individuals with a visible difference from participating in research.

Through her work with young people and the use of the Internet, Fox realised that synchronous communication through tools such as instant messaging and chatrooms is a prolific means for communication online in her research). She believed that synchronous chat might be attractive to her participants and allow discussions which could be similar to face-to-face dynamics. She also believed that by meeting her participants in an environment which was familiar and interesting to them, she would be able to gain access to better understanding about issues which had previously been a hidden aspect of their life.

Fox recruited her participants through health websites. Since most young people use the Internet as a source of health-related information and are familiar with synchronous online chat, she was confident that this would increase the chance for recruiting the participants online. Her research website was also linked to the advertising pages designed for young people posted by skin care charities and support organisations.

In conducting a synchronous focus group, a virtual venue such as a chatroom is essential. Fox found that the virtual spaces offered by external providers were inflexible and too expensive. She also believed that networked virtual reality or graphical MUDs, which allow both synchronous text communication and a graphical environment (Stewart & Williams 2005; see earlier section), would be too distracting for the aims of her study. In the end, she decided that an IT technician from her faculty would set up an online forum hosted by the university. This was to provide a reassurance to the young people and their parents that the research was carried out by a member of a reputable institution instead of an unknown identity. For security purposes, the installation of password-protected access for both moderator and participants was organised.

Arranging a suitable date and time for a group of young people was particularly challenging. In synchronous communication, having participants from diverse locations and across nations, time zone differences created some difficulties. In her research, suitable times for running the groups were restricted by the participants' school or college commitments. Fox decided to separate UK and international groups because of problems in trying to arrange a mutually convenient time to host a mixed group. She eventually conducted four virtual focus groups with British participants and three with participants from outside the UK.

For Fox, the use of synchronous online communication offered insight into a social space which is familiar to many young people. She felt that synchronous communication 'fostered a sense of ease and enjoyment, which, in turn, facilitated candid and insightful dialogue' (p. 544). The method would also be useful for research involving people who have other appearance-related issues, people with restricted mobility, or people who do not have the confidence to take part in face-to-face focus groups. Fox contended that virtual focus groups are 'an important development in the focus group tradition'. And in her own study, synchronous communication proved to be 'successful in fostering insightful and engaging exchanges' among the participants and the researcher.

## CONCLUSION

The advance of the Internet and networked communications has provided focus group researchers with a new opportunity to conduct their research in 'new social spaces, devoid of physicality' (Robson & Williams 2005: 413). As readers have seen in this chapter, virtual focus groups offer many benefits which allow the researchers to conduct research with diverse populations, across nations and from different time zones. Yet, as in any research method and technique, virtual focus groups also present some difficulties.

Ted Gaiser (2008: 304) reminds us that the change of technologies is rapid. Even now, we have witnessed an opportunity for conducting focus groups in a virtual reality environment. Some video conferencing applications such as Skype and iSight are becoming more widely available. It will not be too long before focus groups are undertaken in a video conference environment. However, the experiences of running these kinds of focus groups are still different from traditional face-to-face interviews. As they become more widely adopted for carrying out focus groups in the future, it is crucial that the researchers consider the implications of new technologies and how they can influence the research experience of both participants and researchers.

## TUTORIAL ACTIVITIES

1  Virtual focus groups have been adopted in the health and social sciences and many researchers have suggested that they are useful in many aspects, but they also have their own pitfalls. Discuss some of the benefits and limitations from your own point of view.
2  You have been asked to conduct a research project on the perceptions of euthanasia and its legal implications among young people in different nations.

   - What would be the best way to carry out this research?
   - How would you go about doing it?
   - What resources would you need?
   - What difficulties may occur in carrying out this research method?

## FURTHER READING

Fox, F.E., Morris, M., & Rumsey, N. (2007). Doing synchronous online focus groups with young people: Methodological reflections. *Qualitative Health Research* 17(4), 539–547.

Gaiser, T.J. (2008). Online focus groups. In N. Fielding, R.M. Lee, & G. Blank (eds.), *The Sage handbook of online research methods* (pp. 290–307). London: Sage.

Hughes, J., & Lang, K.R. (2004). Issues in online focus groups: Lessons learned from an empirical study of peer-to-peer filesharing system users. *Electronic Journal of Business Research Methods* 2(2), 95–110.

*(Continued)*

*(Continued)*

Kenny, A.J. (2005). Interaction in cyberspace: An online focus group. *Journal of Advanced Nursing* 49(4), 414–422.

Mann, C., & Stewart, F. (2000). *Internet communication and qualitative research: A handbook for researching online*. London: Sage.

O'Connor, H., & Madge, C. (2001). Cyber-mothers: Online synchronous interviewing using conferencing software. *Sociological Research Online* 5(4). Retrieved on 14 April 2009, from www.socresonline.org.uk/5/4/o'connor.html

Robson, K., & Williams, M. (2005). Researching online populations: The use of online focus groups for social research. *Qualitative Research* 5(4), 395–416.

Seymour, W. (2001). In the flesh or online? Exploring qualitative research methodologies. *Qualitative Research* 1(2), 147–168.

Turney, L., & Pocknee, C. (2005). Virtual focus groups: New frontiers in research. *International Journal of Qualitative Methods*, 4(2), Article 3. Retrieved on 12 April 2009, from www.ualberta.ca/~iiqm/backissues/4_2/pdf/turney.pdf

Underhill, C., & Olmstead, M. G. (2003). An experimental comparison of computer mediated and face-to-face focus groups. *Social Science Computer Review* 21(4), 506–512.

Williams, M. (2003). *Virtually criminal: Deviance and harm within online environments*. Doctoral dissertation, University of Wales, Cardiff.

# 10
# MANAGING AND MAKING SENSE OF FOCUS GROUP DATA

## CHAPTER OBJECTIVES

In this chapter you will learn about:

- Transcribing data derived from traditional focus groups
- Data analysis methods
- Analysis of virtual focus group data

In any piece of research, there will be a time when the researchers have to manage the data they have collected and begin making sense of it. Focus group research is no exception. In this chapter, I will discuss how researchers can manage their focus group data, in particular how to transcribe the data from traditional focus groups including the Jeffersonian transcribing conventions. I will also present analytic approaches including thematic analysis and analysis of group interaction. A brief discussion regarding the management and analysis of virtual focus groups is also included.

## TRANSCRIBING TRADITIONAL FOCUS GROUP DATA

Group discussions which have been audiotape-recorded (see Chapter 5) need to be transcribed to enable data analysis. In traditional face-to-face focus groups, transcription transforms an oral text to a written one. Transcription permits further analysis and provides 'a permanent written record of the interviews' which the researchers can share with others who are interested in the research (Stewart et al. 2009: 602). Transcribing the interviews is in fact an initial data analysis. However, transcribing large amounts of material is a time-consuming process and often can be tiring and even stressful. For an hour-long focus group interview, it may take an experienced transcriber 4–8 hours to transcribe (Bloor et al. 2001).

Similar to other qualitative methods, there are several salient issues to consider when transcribing focus group interviews. First, who should perform the transcription of the focus group interviews? I suggest that the researchers or the moderators should transcribe their own group discussions. Not only will they learn about their moderating style, but also 'to some extent they will have the social and emotional aspects of the interview situation present or reawakened during transcription, and will already have started the analysis of the meaning of what was said' (Kvale 2007: 95). The researchers will also become familiar again with the data that they have heard. This will certainly help with the further analysis of the data.

Some researchers may prefer to have a research assistant or pay someone else to transcribe the focus group interview. To me, this is not a preferred option as it can also be challenging to both the transcriber and the researcher (see Tilley 2003), but it can be done occasionally. The researchers must ensure that the transcriber transcribes verbatim, and pauses, laughs or crying must be indicated on the transcripts (Poland 2002; Rapley 2007). This will assist the researchers to make better sense of the interview and hence help with the analysis. Kerry Daly (2007: 217) suggests that if the transcription is carried out by a transcriber or research assistant, the researchers should:

- discuss with the transcriber the transcription techniques used and this may include the techniques they use to record pauses, expressions and grammatical conventions; and
- as soon as one transcription is done, the researchers should listen to the tape and review the transcript. This will allow the researchers to suggest a modification in style or technique to the transcriber.

Lynne MacLean and colleagues (2004) provide several suggestions for ensuring that the focus group interview transcripts are transcribed more accurately. Due to the many problems that the researchers may come across in transcription, they also recommend working with transcribers as part of the research team.

Second, how should the focus group interviews be transcribed? Since there are multiple players in a focus group, it is much more complicated to transcribe focus group discussions and hence more time consuming than transcribing other qualitative interviews. This is due to the fact that researchers must take into account not only what is said, but *who* is saying it in the session. This can be problematic because it is not easy to distinguish individuals' voices (Bryman 2008: 476). Additionally, people often talk over each other, and this can make it more difficult to transcribe. Deborah Warr (2001: 126) too contends that it can be difficult to 'portray turn-taking and interruptions in the exchanges and to note the pauses and moments of laughter, especially if the discussion becomes rowdy'.

Nevertheless, there are ways that researchers can manage their focus group interview data. Blake Poland (2002: 641) recommends that interview transcripts should be transcribed verbatim. The transcript should represent the accounts of what actually happened in the interview. It should not be edited or 'tidied up' to make it 'sound better'. I too suggest that each focus group interview be transcribed word by word and that the transcript includes all the informal conversation style and emotional expressions, including pauses, emphases, laughter, sighing and sounds like 'hm', 'oh', 'ah'. Both the questions and answers should be transcribed. What questions, how the researchers ask the questions and answers from the participants are all important in the focus group interview (Liamputtong 2009). This may sound tedious, but it will assist the researchers when trying to make sense of the data. Some emotional expressions like laughter and crying may indicate how the participant feels when referring to the issue that prompts him or her to laugh or cry.

How much the researchers edit the transcripts is a matter of preference (Stewart et al. 2009). Because not all transcripts will be complete, the researchers may attempt to fill in missing words and gaps, or to correct the spelling of typographical errors. David Stewart and associates (2009: 602) contend:

> Although editing may increase readability, it is important that the character of the respondents' comments be maintained, even if at times they use poor grammar or appear to be confused. Because one use of focus group interviewing is to learn how respondents think and talk about a particular issue, too much editing and cleaning of the transcript is undesirable. Too much editing and cleaning tends to censor ideas and information, often based on the [researchers'] preconceived ideas.

In Table 10.1, I present some instructions that Blake Poland (2002: 641) has developed for transcribing the interview data, which I believe are also applicable to data obtained by the focus group method.

TABLE 10.1    TIPS FOR TRANSCRIBING FOCUS GROUP INTERVIEW DATA

| | |
|---|---|
| **Pauses** | Specify short pauses during talking by a series of dots (…), the length of which depends on the amount of time elapsed. For example, two dots for less than half a second, three dots for one second, four dots for one and a half seconds. Indicate longer pauses with the word pause in parentheses. Use '(pause)' for two- to three-second breaks and '(long pause)' to indicate a pause of four seconds or more. |
| **Laughing, coughing, and so on** | Signify in parentheses; for example, '(coughs)', '(sign)', '(sneeze)'. Use '(laughing)' to indicate one person, '(laughter)' to mean several laughing. |
| **Interruptions** | Denote when someone's talk is broken off midsentence by including a hyphen (-) at the point where the interruption takes place, for example 'How did you-'). |
| **Overlapping speech** | Employ a hyphen to signify when one speaker intersperses into the conversation of another, include the speech of the other with '(overlapping)'. Then return to where the original speaker was interrupted (if he or she continues). For instance: <br><br> R:   She said that was impos- <br> I:    (overlapping) Who, Mary? <br> R:   No, Sonja. |

*(Continued)*

TABLE 10.1 (CONTINUED)

| Garbled speech | If guessing what was said, signal words that are not clear with square brackets and question mark, for example 'At that, Emma just [doubled? Glossed?] over'). |
| --- | --- |
| | Use x's to indicate passage which cannot be elucidated at all. Number of x's should symbolise approximate number of words which cannot be clarified. For example, 'Zoe went xxxxx xxxxx, and then [came? Went?] home.' |
| **Emphasis** | Strong emphasis can be represented with capital letters, for instance 'You did WHAT?' |
| **Held sounds** | Repeat the sounds which are held, separated by hyphens. If they are emphasised, capitalise them too. For example, 'No-o-o-o, not really' or 'I was VER-r-r-y-y-y excited.' |
| **Paraphrasing others** | When a participant employs a voice which indicates that he or she is imitating someone else's speech or is expressing his or inner voice, use quotation marks and/or indicate with '(mimicking voice)'. For example: |
| | R: Then you know what he came out with? He said (mimicking voice) 'I'll be damned if I'm going to let YOU push ME around.' And I thought to myself: 'I'll show you!' But then a little voice inside said 'Better watch out for Susan.' Sure enough, in she came with that 'I'm in control now' air of hers. |

As an example, I present the example that Tim Rapley (2007: 53–54) developed from his interactions with his friends when they were cooking in a large kitchen and found that the cucumber was frozen. He terms this short transcription as 'the politics of cucumber':

| Tim: | Is it all frozen? |
| --- | --- |
| Mary: | No, this part of it's fine. Okay, when you peel it |
| Ben: | Uh huh |
| Mary: | slice it in four lengthways |
| Ben: | Oh and then just ((overlap)) |
| Mary: | a n d t h e n just take the seeds out |
| Tim: | Or alternatively slice it in half and use a teaspoon and run it along |
| Mary: | You can choose whichever method you prefer |
| Tim: | And obviously there is going to be politics ((Mary laughs)) depending on which method you choose |
| Mary: | Absolutely. No there won't |
| Ben: | Secretly there will be though |
| Mary: | Heh? |
| Ben: | Secretly there will be ((Mary laughs)) |

In the following section, I will introduce the Jeffersonian transcript system which has been widely adopted in conversation analysis, and which some researchers have also used in managing and analysing their focus group data. In the 1960s, Gale Jefferson developed a particular style of transcription notation which was designed to use symbols on a typewriter in order to represent certain aspects of speech which are used in everyday interactions (Rapley 2007: 59). The main features which researchers conducting conversation analysis have employed are adopted from Jefferson (2004) and summarised by Tim Rapley in Box 10.1 (Rapley 2007: 59–60).

### BOX 10.1    SIMPLIFIED JEFFERSONIAN TRANSCRIBING CONVENTIONS

| Symbol | Example | Explanation |
|---|---|---|
| (0.5) | That (0.5) is odd? | **Length of silence** measured in tenths of a second. |
| (.) | Right (.) okay | Micro-pause, less than two-tenths of a second. |
| ::: | I:::: I don't know | Colons indicate **sound-stretching** of the immediately prior sound. The number of rows indicates the length of prolonged sound. |
| _____ | I know that | Underlining indicates speaker's **emphasis or stress**. |
| ( | T: (Well at's<br>R: (I mean really | Left parenthesis indicates the point at which one speaker overlaps another's talk. |
| = | You know=I fine | Equals sign indicates that there is **no hearable gap** between the words. |
| WORD | About a MILLION | Capitals, except at beginnings, indicate a marked **rise in volume** compared with the surrounding talk. |
| ° | °Uh huh° | Words in degree signs indicate **quieter** than the surrounding talk. |
| > < | >I don't think< | Words in 'greater than' then 'less than' signs are delivered at a **faster pace** than the surrounding talk. |

*(Continued)*

(Continued)

| Symbol | Example | Explanation |
|---|---|---|
| < > | <I don't think> | Words in 'less than' then 'greater than' signs are delivered at a **slower pace** than the surrounding talk. |
| ? | Oh really? | Question mark indicates **rising** intonation. |
| . | Yeah. | Full stop (period) indicates **falling** intonation. |
| hhh | I know how.hhh you | A row of h's prefixed by a dot indicates an **inbreath**, without dot an **outbreath**. The number of h's indicates the length of the in- or outbreath. |
| ( ) | What a ( ) thing | Empty parentheses indicate **inability to hear** what was said. |
| (word) | What are you (doing) | Word in parentheses indicates the **best possible hearing**. |
| (( )) | I don't know ((coughs)) | Words in double parentheses contain **author's descriptions**. |

According to Tim Rapley (2007: 61), it is often difficult to make sense of the text and see what the speech sounds like when researchers first experience transcripts written in this system. Rapley himself would say the lines out loud and attempt to understand how the symbols represent the sound and pace of words. It requires some practice. However, after a short period of time, the texts will become more and more readable and intelligible. Additionally, it makes more sense when the researchers can listen to a recording of the interview in parallel to reading a transcript. Using the excerpt 'the politics of cucumber' that I presented above, Rapley provides an example of this type of transcription that he deliberately developed for his writing as follows:

Tim:    Is it all frozen?
Mary:   No. this part of it's fine. Okay, when you peel it,
Ben:    Uh huh
Mary:   Slice it in four lengthways (a n d t h e n)
Ben:    (Oh and then just)
Mary:   Just take the seeds out

| | |
|---|---|
| Tim: | Or alternatively slice it in ha::lf, and use a teaspoon, ((banging sound)) and run it along. (0.3) |
| Mary: | You can <u>ch</u>oose whichever method you, pre:<u>fer</u>.= |
| Tim: | =(And) obviously there is gonna be politics. (.) (depending on which method you choose)= |
| Mary: | (.h u h< h e h h e h h e:h ) =<u>Absolutely.</u> ((rustling sound)) (0.4) |
| Mary: | No there won't.= =((banging sound)) (0.8) ((rustling sound))= |
| Ben: | =Secretly there will be though (0.4) |
| Mary: | Heh? |
| Ben: | SECRETLY THERE WILL BE= =ehh °heh heh heh° |

Compared with the previous transcription, Rapley (2007: 62) contends that this type of transcription provides 'a more textured re-description of the scene' of interactions in the kitchen where Tim, Mary and Ben are cooking. It certainly provides readers with 'a sense of the quite artful and beautiful ways that we all routinely interact'.

Lastly, the tone of voice also has significant meanings. According to Richard Krueger (1998: 33), the words 'This was good', for example, can have different meanings depending on tone. Considering the following:

| Comment | Translation |
|---|---|
| This was GOOD! | (It was good) |
| This was GOOD? | (It was supposed to be good but wasn't) |
| THIS was good! | (This one was good, but others were not) |
| This WAS good. | (It used to be good, but not any more) |

Nevertheless, researchers can have their own reasons for the way they manage the text and may decide on a different approach. In their focus group research *Animals Future* in the UK, Phil Macnaghten and Greg Myers (2004: 73) tell us that the interviews were transcribed by Kate Lamb, who has become highly skilled at 'puzzling out overlapping talk and attributing turns to speakers'. Kate was asked to follow some simple instructions:

- All words are transcribed, using conventional spelling (not using the spelling to indicate the pronunciation in any way).
- Repeated words, broken-off words and back-channel utterances (uh-huh, mm) are ignored.
- Uncertain or inaudible passages are indicated.
- There are no indications of pauses, overlap, stresses, volume, pace or intonation, except in conventional punctuation.

Macnaghten and Myers (2004: 73) point out that their practices not only save transcription time, but also make the transcripts readable. Some extra features which are used in some other transcription conventions can make the text unreadable (see above). However, they also point out that this practice of transcription was influenced by the way that Phil Macnaghten wanted to analyse the data. Macnaghten wished to look for themes. He needed to know what the participants said in order to find key issues. The polished transcription allowed him to undertake thematic analysis. However, Greg Myers wanted to carry out a discourse analysis on the interview transcripts. Because that necessitates the details which indicate interaction, for example pauses, overlaps and emphasises, Myers revisited the audiotape and added them in. See the previous examples of this type of transcription.

## ANALYSING FOCUS GROUPS RESULTS

There has been some debate regarding an appropriate way to analyse focus group data. Some suggest that data generated from the focus group method can be analysed similarly to other qualitative methods, particularly thematic analysis (Conradson 2005; Kitzinger 2005; Davidson et al. 2010). Others argue otherwise (see Wilkinson 2004; Morgan 2010). For example, Andrew Parker and Jonathan Tritter (2006: 34) contend that it is inadequate to analyse focus group data as in other conventional qualitative research. They advocate that 'attention must be paid to the dynamic aspects of interaction within the group, for it is this dynamic nature which is at the heart of focus groups and which endows them with the power to generate insight often negated by other methods'.

Additionally, researchers have discussed whether the analysis of focus group data should only be conducted at the level of the group and how much attention should be paid to the comments expressed by individuals within groups (Barbour 2007). For Rosaline Barbour, there is no straightforward answer. Often, researchers will simultaneously carry out several different analyses. Barbour suggests that it is useful to analyse data at the individual level because this can assist researchers in further exploring differences within the group. Barbour (2007: 131) contends: 'Focusing on individual voices, however, is particularly helpful in determining the extent to which a perspective is a collective one'.

According to feminist focus group researcher Sue Wilkinson (2004: 287), focus group data can be situated within 'either essentialist or social constructionist interpretations'. Within the essentialist interpretation, the researchers are more interested in hearing the voices of individual participants (who may speak with, or in contrast to, other participants). For researchers working within this framework, focus groups offer a valuable means to understand 'the individual in social context' (Rubin & Rubin 1995: 95). Hence, focus group data represents more 'authentic' or 'closer to the essential meanings of participants' lives' than data generated by other research methods. Within the social constructionist framework, focus group data is constructed (Crossley 2002). Within this framework, the focus group methodology allows access to 'the patterns of talk and interaction through which the members of any group constitute a shared reality' (DeVault 1990: 97). The focus of this analytical approach is on 'the construction and negotiation of persons and events, the functions served by different discourse'.

Following Wilkinson's paradigm I will introduce two different types of data analysis in focus group research: thematic analysis and the analysis of interaction within groups.

## Thematic Analysis

There are significant similarities between the analysis of focus group and other qualitative data. Commonly, the researchers are interested in the themes which emerge from the data. Thematic analysis is referred to as 'a method for identifying, analysing and reporting patterns (themes) within the data' (Braun & Clarke 2006: 79). It is perceived 'as a foundational method for qualitative analysis' (Braun & Clarke 2006: 78; Liamputtong 2009).

The techniques used for analysing data in thematic analysis and grounded theory are broadly similar. The main difference between grounded theory and thematic analysis is that grounded theory includes theoretical sampling (see Chapter 4), whereas thematic analysis does not. For thematic analysis, the researchers do not need to 'subscribe to the implicit theoretical commitments of grounded theory if they do not wish to produce a fully worked-up grounded theory analysis' (Braun & Clarke 2006: 81).

There are two main steps in doing thematic analysis. First, the researchers need to read through each transcript and try to make sense of the interview data. Then, as part of a collective set, the researchers need to examine the transcript and make sense of what is being said by the participants as a group (Minichiello et al. 2008). Thematic analysis 'involves searching across a data set – be that a number of interviews or focus groups, or a range of texts – to find repeated patterns of meaning' (Braun & Clarke 2006: 86). Coding plays a major part in thematic analysis and, as in grounded theory, the researchers need to perform initial and axial coding in order to deconstruct data, code it up and find links between the data. Axial coding is the step that will allow the researchers to connect different codes that they have identified in the initial coding. Axial coding is 'a way of organising the data together by making connections between a major category and its sub-category' (Minichiello et al. 2008: 280). This allows the researchers to find themes in the data.

Some qualitative researchers have provided useful strategies or steps for coding that we can follow. Victor Minichiello and colleagues (2008: 268), for example, suggest that when experienced researchers develop codes, one strategy they tend to use is to ask the question 'What is this thing (or things) I have before me?' A good example is the work of Erving Goffman (1961) who was interested in the study of mental institutions. He used this question to document particular characteristics of mental hospitals. By further asking 'What are the general features of mental hospitals?', Goffman produced 'total institutions' theory that many qualitative researchers continue to apply in their work today.

Uwe Flick (2006: 300) suggests the following list of basic questions that qualitative researchers, including focus group researchers, can use as their coding strategies. He also suggests that the researchers should examine the text regularly and repeatedly with these questions. Using these questions, Flick contends, the researchers will be able to identify the themes.

---

**BOX 10.2   BASIC QUESTIONS USED FOR CODING STRATEGIES**

| | |
|---|---|
| What? | What is the concern here? Which course of event is mentioned? |
| Who? | Who are the persons involved? What roles do they have? How do they interact? |
| How? | Which aspects of the event are mentioned (or omitted)? |
| When? How long? Where? | Referring to time, course and location: When does it happen? How long does it take? Where did the incident occur? |
| How much? How strong? | Referring to intensity: How often is the issue emphasised? |
| Why? | Which reasons are provided or can be constructed? |
| What for? | What is the intention here? What is the purpose? |
| By which? | Referring to means, tactics and strategies for achieving the aim: What is the main tactic here? How are things accomplished? |

---

Within thematic analysis, it is essential that the researchers attempt to differentiate between the views of individuals and the actual group collective perspectives. Hence, deviant case analysis is important; that is, 'attention must be given to minority opinions and examples which do not fit with the researcher's overall theory and attention given to silenced voices' (Kitzinger 2005: 66).

## Analysing Focus Groups and Interaction

Several researchers have suggested that focus group researchers tend to neglect analytical consideration of social interaction within groups (see Wilkinson 1998; 1999; 2004; Hydén & Bülow 2003; Warr 2005; Lehoux et al. 2006; Halkier 2010). Many focus group researchers manage focus group data similarly to what they do with data from individual interviews; that is, representing single voices rather than positioning comments within the group discussion (Crossley 2002; Robinson 2009; Willis et al. 2009). Interactions among the participants in the group, Sue Wilkinson (2004: 286) contends, are 'rarely reported, let along analyzed'. And more commonly too, the analysis focuses on the content generating from the group instead of the process of interaction. As I have suggested earlier, the social constructionist framework emphasises the co-construction of realities between people and the dynamic negotiation of meaning in context. Situated within this framework, it is essential that focus group researchers examine the interaction between participants in the data analysis.

According to focus group researcher Janet Smithson (2008: 365), the main issue of analysis in focus groups should not be on what each participant says in a group context, but more on the discourses or themes that are produced within the group context. As such, interactive effects and group dynamics should be a focus of the analytical approaches that the researchers select to analyse their data. Sue Wilkinson (1998: 197) argues that there is a considerable potential for developing new, and better, approaches for analysing focus group data than examining emerging themes. These analytical approaches will allow the researchers to see how themes or discourses are jointly formed by the participants in the group. Similarly, Karen Willis and associates (2009: 133) argue that focus group data has three layers: 'the individual, the group, and the group interaction'. In order to analyse these three slices properly, it is necessary to pay attention to the forms and scopes of expressions (both verbal and non-verbal), the interactive nature of the discussion, the context in which interaction occurs, and the contents which are produced by the group. This way reveals not only the dynamics of the discussion which can inform the strength of perspectives held by the participants and the level of agreement or disagreement in the groups, but also how the agreement or disagreement is derived.

As I have discussed in Chapter 4, the participants in focus groups may employ humour in expressing their points and concerns rather than speaking about them directly. Jenny Kitzinger and Clare Farquhar (1999) suggest that these 'sensitive moments' may deepen understanding of issues which are seen as 'private, sensitive and controversial'. If researchers do not pay close attention to dynamics in the groups, perspectives which deviate from the group norm or those which are not expressed explicitly may be silenced (Kitzinger 1994b; Wellings et al. 2000). Hence, considerable attention is necessary so that the researchers can learn about the strategies that participants adopt to deal with perspectives which are difficult to express. Kaye Wellings and associates (2000: 264) argue that rather than seeing the dynamics of the group as problematic, they should be treated as data. If the researchers aim to represent accurately the perspectives of the participants, it is necessary to consider the interpretation of both direct and indirect data, particularly around sensitive issues. Hence, both verbal and non-verbal expressions, the tactical use of humour, interruptions in interaction, and disagreement between participants, must be included in the analysis of focus group data (Willis et al. 2009: 260). An illustration in the research on sexual behaviour conducted by Kaye Wellings and colleagues (2000: 261) is used here to show the analysis of how humour is used by the participants to separate themselves from what they perceived as 'behaviours or identities'. In one of the focus groups, often male participants referred to themselves as heterosexual and assumed that the other males in the group would also be heterosexual. But this assumption was jokingly challenged by one male participant whose remark led to uproar in the group:

> M:    How do you know I'm not gay, I might come out of the closet in a minute …
> 'Ooh hello ducky' (group uproar).

By analysing and interpreting both sets of data (content and interaction), the researchers do not need to be too overtly concerned whether the data obtained from the participants is 'objectively true' (Willis et al. 2009). They can be more concerned about the way that such data is exchanged within the group and how group dynamics may confirm or challenge individuals' claimed perspectives (Warr 2005). For example, rather than trying to prove if people have misperceptions about the use of medicinal drugs, paying attention to both the content and the interaction in the group may allow us to understand more about what influences people to use medicinal drugs and how decision-making is made, which can be valuable for the promotion of safe use of drugs in communities.

If researchers want to claim that the focus group method is an appropriate approach for researching collective identity, they must capitalise on the opportunity offered by the method to analyse process as well as content (Munday 2006). This means paying attention not only to the interactions which occur among the participants, but also to that which takes place between the participants and the moderator. The presence and behaviour of the moderator play a crucial role in forming the context in which discussion is constructed and cannot be written out of the analysis (Myers & Macnaghten 1999; Warr 2005).

Karen Willis and colleagues (2009: 133) use the list of analytic questions that Patricia Stevens (1996: 172) has developed for the analysis of the interactions and examination of meaning at the group level to characterise some important elements of analysis, as given in Table 10.2.

TABLE 10.2   ANALYSING GROUP INTERACTION

| Group component | Aspect of interaction for analysis |
| --- | --- |
| What? | What topics/opinions produced agreement? |
| | What statements seemed to evoke conflict? |
| | What were the contradictions in the discussion? |
| | What common experiences were expressed? |
| | Did the collective interaction generate new insights or precipitate an exchange of information among participants? |
| Who? | Whose interests were being represented in the group? |
| | Were alliances formed among group members? |
| | Was a particular member or viewpoint silenced? |
| How? | How closely did the group adhere to the issues presented for discussion? |
| | How did group members respond to the ideas of others? |
| | How did the group resolve disagreements? |
| | How were emotions handled? |
| | How were non-verbal signs and behaviours used to contribute to the discussion? |

I recommend that readers may wish to consult the analytical template that Pascale Lehoux and colleagues (2006: 2101) have developed in their research regarding the patients' view. The template allows researchers to understand group interactions in focus groups not only amongst the participants themselves but also between the participants and the moderator. Janne Moen and colleagues (2010) have adopted this template in their recent publication.

At this point, I will provide some examples which illustrate many points that I have discussed above. The following example, taken from Janine Munday's work (2006: 100), demonstrates how paying attention to the process of interaction can provide understanding into how collective identity is formed. It demonstrates that this formation would not have been revealed if content alone had been considered. The example is about a discussion of the nude charity calendar that was produced by the members of Rylstone Women's Institute (WI) and was about the episode of making the calendar which was portrayed in the film *Calendar Girls*. Munday included the question: 'Thinking about the nude charity calendar that was produced a few years ago by a WI group, what do you think this says about the WI and its members?' She assumed that this question would allow the women to speak about the negative image about the WI among people outside the organisation. Munday also expected that the women would feel defensive or worried as membership of the WI was important to these women and played a crucial role in constructing their collective identity. However, she found that although the women acknowledged the negative image of the WI, it did not particularly upset them. As shown in the following excerpt, the women themselves believed that such an image was false. They had no real aspiration to challenge it because it was seen as something that was too difficult to succeed (p. 100).

| Moderator: | Do you think it sort of … maybe dispelled a certain image that people have … of WI members … I mean dare I say Jam and Jerusalem? |
| Mary: | Mmm yeah could be. |
| June: | think it might be a bit difficult to dispel don't you? |
| Mary: | Well |
| June: | it's quite entrenched isn't it? |

Rather, the women spoke about the calendar in relation to the group who produced it, and about their identities as women. The women who produced the calendar were criticised for turning a fun and good idea into a serious matter by permitting their story to be made into a film and by involving the media. They believed that the episode had a damaging effect on the women who were involved and Rylstone WI. They also criticised these women for attracting attention from the media. This was seen as improper behaviour for all women and to WI members. As a consequence of their involvement, some of the women had marriage breakdowns. This was greeted by dismay and disapproval by the participants. One participant, Jane, did not know about the problems that followed production of the calendar. But by the end of the group discussion, Jane was also criticising the women who produced the calendar. This was mainly because the group drew on pre-existing beliefs about marriage and how women should behave, and this persuaded Jane willingly to express her agreement with the views of the others. Through analysing both content and process, Munday (2006: 101) contends, it becomes clear that 'gender identity, more than WI membership, plays the crucial role in informing the collective identity of this group of women'. This example illustrates the importance of taking interaction into account in the analysis of focus groups because it helps to 'reveal an already existing consensus about gender identity that is shared by the group' (p. 101).

The following example underlines the importance of analysing process and content and the way that the expression is constructed and influenced by the context in which the interactive processes are situated. Munday (2006: 102) suggests that content of the discussion cannot be well analysed without making reference to its context. This example is taken from an interaction which occurred towards the end of the session, when the participants openly expressed their disagreement. Up to this point, the women had been expressing their strong sense of cohesion and unity. However, in response to a question about what the women found to be the most important part of WI membership, one participant, June, immediately said it was 'friendship'. Three other women automatically agreed with June's response, but then June challenged this notion. June contended that the WI provided more opportunities to women than just friendship, for example the possibility of studying at Denman, the WI college which offers many courses and arranges some outings for members. However, she eventually agreed with the majority view that it was friendship which really counted:

> June: There's an awful lot you can do.
> Jane: You wouldn't join the WI just to go to er Denman to learn something.
> June: No but you might join the WI if it were a big one so that you could ... do some of the things small ones cannot afford.
> Jane: Yes.
> June: Um you know I should think ( ) they can go on outings.
> Mary: That's right.
> June: Theatre visits.
> Mary: Yes because they've got the numbers to do it.
> June: So it does open up a lot of avenues but you wouldn't go if you didn't want to be friends with other women.

The excerpt shows that June attempted to defend her view, trying to justify it to the other participants who appeared to agree with her view. Although June eventually expressed her view which conceded the majority consensus, it does not necessarily mean that she changed her opinions. Rather, she was prepared to 'express conformity with the group'. Munday contends that 'through careful consideration of both the content of the talk, and the interactive processes through which it was produced, it is possible to analyse how these women work together to construct their own sense of collective identity'.

## VIRTUAL FOCUS GROUPS AND DATA ANALYSIS PROCESS

I have suggested in Chapter 9 that data generated from virtual groups does not need to be transcribed as in traditional focus groups. The production of a text file is instantaneous in virtual research (Strickland et al. 2003; Liamputtong 2006). There is no need to set aside a budget for transcribing machines or transcription costs. The immediate production of a text file also eliminates delays caused by transcription. Neil Selwyn and Kate Robson (1998: 4) say that not only does it save the researchers time and money, but it also 'eliminates any errors introduced through incorrect transcription'. In focus groups using email, for example, the data which is eventually analysed is precisely what the participants have written. From a researcher's perspective, this is a major advantage of virtual focus group (Kenny 2005). In her research, Amanda Kenny (2005: 419) did not need to transcribe any data since it was automatically stored in WebCT.

As I have suggested in Chapter 9, virtual focus groups are often criticised for their lack of non-verbal data such as expression, movement and environment. According to Kate Robson and Matthew Williams (2005: 409–410), text-only virtual data is 'all-inclusive text'. This makes it difficult to identify different elements of non-verbal data. In traditional face-to-face focus group interactions, these elements can be easily observed and are useful for making sense of the data (see previous section). However, Robson and Williams (2005: 409–410) suggest three characters of virtual focus group data which are comparable with those in conventional focus groups: content, form and style. Content refers to the words that the participants use to express themselves. It is similar to the verbal expressions of traditional data. Form resembles 'context' in conventional focus group research. Style is comparable with non-verbal cues in orthodox focus group research. Meanings are conveyed through idiomatic forms of expression such as emoticons, line width, use of capitals, colour and font that I have presented in Chapter 9. Hence, the analytic approaches that I have discussed earlier in this chapter are applicable to the analysis of virtual focus groups. Both the content and interaction through non-verbal expressions such as emoticons can be analysed using thematic and/or interactive data analysis methods. Similar to the analysis of traditional face-to-face focus groups, researchers need carefully to consider what type of data analytic approach is better suited to the aim and nature of their research.

## CONCLUSION

Robert Bogdan and Sari Biklen (2007: 172–173) write that: 'You have just finished typing the fieldnotes from your final observation of the study and you proceed to file them. There, facing you, is all the material you have diligently collected. An empty feeling comes over you as you ask, "Now what do I do?"' This is very true for most qualitative researchers and I would say that focus group researchers do not escape this type of 'empty feeling' either. There is a time when we must begin thinking about managing our focus group data that we have 'diligently collected' and how to make sense of it. In this chapter, I have discussed how researchers can manage their focus group data, particularly how to transcribe the data from traditional focus groups, and I have introduced the Jeffersonian transcribing conventions. I have also presented two major analytic approaches, including thematic analysis and analysis of group interaction, and provided some examples to illustrate the many points introduced. I have also included a brief discussion regarding the management and analysis of virtual focus groups in this chapter. We must remember that the management and analysis of our data will lead to how we interpret and present our results. This interpretation and presentation are the means by which we represent the voices of our research participants. Hence, they are also an important aspect of our focus group research that we must seriously consider in our research endeavours.

## TUTORIAL ACTIVITIES

Read through this short focus group transcript:

Manee:      People in community tend to see this disease as promiscuous disease. As women, we can have only one partner or one husband. But, for those who have HIV/ AIDS, people tend to see them as having too many partners and this is not good. They are seen as bad women. And they will be discriminated against more than men who have HIV/AIDS.

Sinjai:      I also know that men who live with this disease are not seen as bad as the women are. If you are women and have HIV/AIDS, it is worse for you.

Natharee:   This is what has happened to me. People in my community knew that I have got AIDS, and they have been treating me like I am a bad woman. They did not even ask me where I got AIDS from and they assumed I got it from being a bad woman.

- What sense can you make of this data?

Form a group of three with your colleagues and do the following tasks:

1  Perform coding on this transcript.
2  Using thematic analysis, what is the main theme of this short transcript?
3  Compare your coding and theme with your colleagues and discuss similarities and differences of your analysis.

---

### FURTHER READING

Braun, V., & Clarke, V. (2006). Using thematic analysis in psychology. *Qualitative Research in Psychology* 3, 77–101.
Gibbs, G.R. (2007). *Analyzing qualitative data*. London: Sage.
Grbich, C. (2007). *Qualitative data analysis: An introduction*. London: Sage.
Hydén, L.-C., & Bülow, P.H. (2003). Who's talking? Drawing conclusions from focus groups – some methodological considerations. *International Journal of Social Research Methodology* 6(4), 305–321.

Kitzinger, J., & Farquhar, C. (1999). The analytic potential of 'sensitive moments' in focus group discussions. In R.S. Barbour & J. Kitzinger (eds.), *Developing focus group research: Politics, theory and practice* (pp. 156–173). London: Sage.

Lehoux, P., Poland, B., & Daudelin, G. (2006). Focus group research and 'the patient's view'. *Social Science and Medicine* 63, 2091–2104.

Morgan, D.L. (2010). Reconsidering the role of interaction in analyzing and reporting focus groups. *Qualitative Health Research* 20(5), 718–722.

Munday, J. (2006). Identity in focus: The use of focus groups to study the construction of collective identity. *Sociology* 40(1), 89–105.

Rapley, T. (2007). *Doing conversation, discourse and document analysis.* London: Sage.

Smithson, J. (2000). Using and analysing focus groups: Limitations and possibilities. *International Journal of Social Research Methodology* 3(2), 103–119.

Sparks, R., Girling, E., & Smith, M.V. (2002). Lessons from history: Pasts, presents and futures of punishment in children's talk. *Children & Society* 16, 116–130.

Tilley, S.A. (2003). 'Challenging' research practices: Turning a critical lens on the work of transcription. *Qualitative Inquiry* 9(5), 750–773.

Warr, D.J. (2005). 'It was fun…but we don't usually talk about these things': Analyzing sociable interaction in focus groups. *Qualitative Inquiry* 11(2), 200–225.

Willis, K., Green, J., Daly, J., Williamson, L., & Bandyopadhyay, M. (2009). Perils and possibilities: Achieving best evidence from focus groups in public health research. *Australian and New Zealand Journal of Public Health* 33(2), 131–136.

# IN CONCLUSION

In the past decade, focus group methodology has become popular and evidence points to its valuable approach for qualitative data collection. Despite this, the methodology is still under scrutiny as a 'soft' option by researchers outside qualitative disciplines. It is true that although focus groups have invaluable benefits and may offer many useful insights, they of course have some pitfalls, as do other research methods.

I have demonstrated in previous chapters that focus group methodology is invaluable in generating in-depth information for researchers in the health and social sciences. Researchers may argue that focus groups are efficient since they generate large amounts of data from multiple individuals within a relatively short timeframe. But they are not an easy option. Some focus groups can be complex and the data generated can be bulky. As Karen Willis and associates (2009: 136) sum up: 'Far from being a quick and easy way of obtaining qualitative evidence, focus groups are demanding of time and resources'. But for Jenny Kitzinger (2005: 68), although the data that focus groups generate can be overburdened, they are also 'rich and complex'. The methodology is not intimidating for either the participants or the researchers.

In this volume, I have introduced focus group methodology and its history. I have covered several theoretical frameworks within which the focus group method is situated. Ethical considerations in conducting focus group research are also discussed. The principles and practicalities of undertaking focus group research have been included in great depth. I have shown the use of focus group methodology in differently ways, for example as a self-contained method, in mixed-method research, in multi-method studies, in needs assessment and as part of community-based participatory action research. I have also pointed to the use of the methodology with different groups of people, including vulnerable people and in cross-cultural settings. The application of the methodology in online research has also been discussed in the book. Lastly, I have discussed ways that focus group researchers can manage and make sense of their data. I believe this volume is comprehensive and will provide great insights for students and researchers who wish to embark on focus group research.

I also believe that focus group methodology can provide a window into the complexity and richness of social life and health behaviours of individuals and groups from whom we wish to learn and understand. There are many benefits that our research participants can gain from taking part in focus group research. There are also diverse ways in which we can adopt the methodology. But one that I believe has, and will continue to, become magnified in the health and social sciences is to use the methodology more radically. Focus group methodology, Lori Peek and Alice Fothergill (2009: 55) contend, benefits research participants not only socially, but also has 'a socio-political nature'. Advocating for a more radical use of focus groups based on the dialogic focus group theories of Paulo Freire (1970/1993) (see Chapter 2), Alan Johnson (1996: 525) contends that focus group methodology can even 'rupture … underlying social relationships of exploitation and oppression'. This is because it can cultivate the 'sociological imagination' among research participants by assisting them to link their personal troubles to wider social structures. Indeed, Johnson argues, focus groups are capable of producing a 'collective will for change' where the group members move from individual troubles to 'socialized solutions' (p. 532). As Johnson (1996: 535, original emphasis) writes:

> What the radical focus group can offer is precisely the opportunity to explore the collective character of that experience and foster a *collective* will for social change. Certainly the reported experiences of focus group practitioners suggest that *people are quite capable of viewing their own experience in a wider optic than that of the individualizing ideologies of the day.*

These benefits, empowerment, social support, development of the sociological imagination, and envisioning social change (Peek & Fothergill 2009), would become even more momentous when working with vulnerable groups and marginalised people.

In sum, focus group methodology has 'enormous power and potential' (Peek & Fothergill 2009: 56). It offers many advantages for social scientists to adopt this qualitative methodology in their research settings. I agree with Madeleine Jowett and Gill O'Toole (2006) and Lori Peek and Alice Fothergill (2009), who suggest that focus groups may not be an appropriate method for every research project. Therefore, researchers who wish to consider using this methodology must carefully identify the research topic of interest and, once decided, be sensitive to the many issues that I have included in this volume.

# REFERENCES

Abel, S., Park, J., Tipene-Leach, D., Finau, S., & Lennan, M. (2001). Infant care practices in New Zealand: A cross-cultural qualitative study. *Social Science and Medicine* 53(9), 1135–1148.

Ahmad, F., Driver, N., McNally, M.J., & Stewart, D.E. (2009). 'Why doesn't she seek help for partner abuse?': An exploratory study with South Asian immigrant women. *Social Science and Medicine* 69(4), 613–622.

Alexander, C.S., & Becker, H.J. (1978). The use of vignettes in survey research. *Public Opinion Quarterly* 42, 93–104.

Allen, K.R., & Walker, A.J. (1992). A feminist analysis of interviews with elderly mothers and their daughters. In J.F. Gilgun, K. Daly, & G. Handel (eds.), *Qualitative methods in family research* (pp. 198–214). Newbury Park, CA: Sage.

Allen, L. (2005). Managing masculinity: Young men's identity work in focus groups. *Qualitative Research* 5(1), 35–57.

Angrosino, M. (2007). *Doing ethnographic and observation research*. London: Sage Publications.

Ardalan, A., Mazaheri, M., Naieni, K.H., Rezaie, M., Teimoori, F., & Pourmalek, F. (2010). Examining older people's needs following major disasters: A qualitative study of Iranian elders' experiences of the Bam earthquake. *Ageing & Society* 30(1), 11–23.

Avis, M. (2003). Do we need methodological theory to do qualitative research? *Qualitative Health Research* 13(7), 995–1004.

Bailey, A. (2008). Let's tell you a story: Use of vignettes in focus group discussions on HIV/AIDS among migrants. In P. Liamputtong (ed.), *Doing cross-cultural research: Ethical and methodological perspectives* (pp. 253–264). Dordrecht: Springer.

Balch, G.I., & Mertens, D.M. (1999). Focus groups design and group dynamics: Lessons from deaf and hard of hearing participants. *American Journal of Evaluation* 20, 265–277.

Barbour, R. (2007). *Doing focus groups*. London: Sage.

Barbour, R., & Kitzinger, J. (eds.) (1999). *Developing focus group research: Politics, theory and practice*. London: Sage.

Barrett, J., & Kirk, S. (2000). Running focus groups with elderly and disabled elderly participants. *Applied Ergonomics* 31(6), 621–629.

Basch, C.E. (1987). Focus group interviews: An underutilised research technique for theory and practice in health education. *Health Education Quarterly* 14(4), 411–448.

Beauchamp, T.L., & Childress, J.F. (2001). *Principles of biomedical ethics*, 5th edition. New York: Oxford University Press.

Behar, R. (1993). *Translating woman: Crossing the border with Esperanza's story*. Boston, MA: Beacon Press.

Benaya, K. (2004). *Factors influencing contraceptive use and method choice among women among men in Zambia*. PhD thesis, University of Southampton.

Bender, D.E., Harbour, C., Thorp, J., & Morris, P. (2001). Tell me what you mean by 'si': Perceptions of quality of prenatal care among immigrant Latina women. *Qualitative Health Research* 11(6), 780–794.

Benmayor, R. (1991). Testimony, action research, and empowerment: Puerto Rican women and popular education. In S.B. Gluck & D. Patai (eds.), *Women's words: The feminist practice of oral history* (pp. 159–174). New York: Routledge.

Benoit, C., Jansson, M., Millar, A., & Phillips, R. (2005). Community-academic research on hard-to-reach populations: Benefits and challenges. *Qualitative Health Research* 15(2), 263–282.

Berglund, C. (2007). *Ethics for health care*, 3rd edition. Melbourne: Oxford University Press.

Bernard, H.R. (2006). *Research methods in anthropology: Qualitative and quantitative approaches*, 4th edition. Lanham, MD: Rowman & Littlefield Publishers, Inc.

Berthelette, G., Raftis, Y., & Henderson, G. (2001). A culturally appropriate format for a focus group? *The Aboriginal Nurse* 16(2), 17–18.

Bhana, D. (2009). 'AIDS is rape!' Gender and sexuality in children's responses to HIV and AIDS. *Social Science and Medicine* 69(4), 596–603.

Billig, M. (2005). *Laughter and ridicule: Towards a social critique of humour*. London: Sage.

Bishop, R. (2008). Freeing ourselves from neocolonial domination in research: A Kaupapa Māori approach to creating knowledge. In N.K. Denzin & Y.S. Lincoln (eds.), *The landscape of qualitative research*, 3rd edition (pp. 145–183). Thousand Oaks, CA: Sage.

Bisol, C.A., Sperb, T.M., & Moreno-Black, G. (2008). Focus groups with deaf and hearing youths in Brazil: Improving a questionnaire on sexual behaviour and HIV/AIDS. *Qualitative Health Research* 18(4), 565–578.

Bissell, S., Manderson, L., & Allotey, P. (2000). In focus: Film, focus groups and working children in Bangladesh. *Visual Anthropology* 13(2), 169–184.

Black, E., & Smith, P. (1999). Princess Diana's meanings for women: Results of a focus group study. *Journal of Sociology* 35(3), 263–278.

Bloor, M., Frankland, J., Thomas, M., & Robson, K. (2001). *Focus groups in social research*. Thousand Oaks, CA: Sage.

Blumer, H. (1938). Social psychology. In E. Schmidt (ed.), *Man and society* (pp. 144–198). New York: Prentice Hall.

Blumer, H. (1969). *Symbolic interactionism: Perspective and method*. Berkeley: University of California Press.

Bogdan, R.C., & Biklen, S.K. (2007). *Qualitative research for education: An introduction to theories and methods*, 5th edition. Boston, MA: Pearson Education.

Bollard, M. (2000). *Going to the doctor's: The expectations of people with Down's syndrome, their carers and general practitioners*. MA dissertation, University of Warwick.

Bollard, M. (2003). Going to the doctor's: The findings from a focus group with people with learning disabilities. *Journal of Learning Disabilities*, 7, 156–164.

Booth, T., & Booth, W. (1996). The use of depth interviewing with vulnerable subjects: Lessons from a research study of parents with learning difficulties. *Social Science and Medicine* 39(3), 415–425.

Borghi, J., Shrestha, D.L., Shrestha, D., & Jan, S. (2007). Using focus groups to develop contingent valuation scenarios – A case study of women's group in rural Nepal. *Social Science and Medicine* 64(3), 531–542.

Borkan, J., Reis, S., Hermoni, D., & Biderman, A. (1995). Talking about the pain: A patient-centered study of low back pain in primary care. *Social Science and Medicine* 40(7), 977–988.

Borkan, J.M., Morad, M., & Shvarts, S. (2000). Universal health care? The views of Negev Bedouin Arabs on health services. *Health Policy and Planning* 15(2), 207–216.

Bourdieu, P. (1977). *Outline of a theory of practice*. Cambridge: Cambridge University Press.

Bradby, H., Varyani, M., Oglethorpe, R., Raine, W., White, I., & Helen, M. (2007). British Asian families and the use of child and adolescent mental health services: A qualitative study of a hard to reach group. *Social Science and Medicine* 65(12), 2413–2424.

Brannen, J., & Pattman, R. (2005). Work-family matters in the workplace: The use of focus groups in a study of UK social services department. *Qualitative Research* 5(4), 523–542.

Braun, V., & Clarke, V. (2006). Using thematic analysis in psychology. *Qualitative Research in Psychology* 3, 77–101.

Brondani, M.A., MacEntee, M.I., Ross Bryant, S., & O'Neill, B. (2008). Using written vignettes in focus groups among older adults to discuss oral health as a sensitive topic. *Qualitative Health Research* 18(8), 1145–1153.

Brown, J.E., Ayowa, O.B., & Brown, R.C. (1993). Dry and tight: Sexual practices and potential AIDS risk in Zaire. *Social Science and Medicine* 37(8), 989–994.

Brownhill, S., Wilhelm, K., Barclay, L., & Schmied, V. (2005). 'Big build': Hidden depression in men. *Australian and New Zealand Journal of Psychiatry* 39, 921–931.

Bryman, A. (2008). *Social research methods*, 3rd edition. New York: Oxford University Press.

Bujra, J. (2006). Lost in translation? The use of interpreters in fieldwork. In V. Desai & R.B. Potter (eds.), *Doing development research*. London: Sage.

Burman, M.J., Batchelor, S., & Brown, J.A. (2001). Researching girls and violence. *British Journal of Criminology* 41, 443–459.

Callaghan, G. (2005). Accessing habitus: Relating structure and agency through focus group research. *Sociological Research Online* 10(3). Retrieved on 16 January 2010, from www.socresonline.org.uk/10/3/callaghan.html

Cambridge, P., & McCarthy, M. (2001). User focus groups and best value in services for people with learning disabilities. *Health and Social Care in the Community* 9(6), 476–489.

Campbell, R., & Wasco, S.M. (2000). Feminist approaches to social sciences: Epistemological and methodological tenets. *American Journal of Community Psychology* 28(6), 773–791.

Carey, M.A., & Smith, M. (1994). Capturing the group effect in focus groups: A special concern in analysis. *Qualitative Health Research* 4(1), 123–127.

Carlson, E.D., Engegretson, J., & Chamberlain, R.M. (2006). Photovoice as a social process of critical consciousness. *Qualitative Health Research* 16(6), 836–852.

Carpenter, C., & Suto, M. (2008). *Qualitative research for occupational and physical therapists: A practical guide*. Oxford: Blackwell.

Charmaz, K. (2006). *Constructing grounded theory: A practical guide through qualitative analysis*. London: Sage Publications.

Cho, J., & Trant, A. (2006). Validity in qualitative research revisited. *Qualitative Research* 6(3), 319–340.

Christians, C.G. (2008). Ethics and politics in qualitative research. In N.K. Denzin & Y.S. Lincoln (eds), *The landscape of qualitative research*, 3rd edition (pp. 185–220). Thousand Oaks, CA: Sage.

Cleland, J., & Moffat, M. (2001). Focus groups may not accurately reflect current attitudes. (Letter) *British Medical Journal* 322(7294), 1121.

Cloos, P., Allen, C.F., Alvarado, B.E., Zunzunegui, M.V., Simeon, D.T., & Eldemire-Shearer, D. (2010). Active ageing: A qualitative study in six Caribbean countries. *Ageing & Society* 30, 79–101.

Coad, J., & Lewis, A. (2004). Engaging children and young people in research: A systematic literature review for The National Evaluation of The Children's Fund. Retrieved on 27 March 2010, from www.ne-cf.org.

Coleman, L., & Testa, A. (2006). Experience of sexual intercourse and reported risk behaviour among an ethnically diverse sample of young people. *Sexual Health* 3, 166–177.

Collins, P.H. (1986). Learning from the outsider within: The sociological significance of black feminist thought. *Social Problems* 33(6), S14–S32.

Colucci, E. (2007). 'Focus groups can be fun': The use of activity-oriented questions in focus group discussions. *Qualitative Health Journal* 17(10), 1422–1433.

Colucci, E. (2008). On the use of focus groups in cross-cultural research. In P. Liamputtong (ed.), *Doing cross-cultural research: Ethical and methodological perspectives* (pp. 233–252). Dordrecht: Springer.

Conradson, D. (2005). Focus groups. In R. Flowerdew & D. Martin (eds.), *Methods in human geography: A guide for students doing a research project* (pp. 128–143). Harlow: Pearson Prentice Hall.

Cook, I., & Crang, M. (1995). *Doing ethnographies.* London: Institute of British Geographers.

Coomber, R. (1997). Using the Internet for survey research. *Sociological Research Online* 2(2). Retrieved on 12 March 2010, from www.socresonline.org.uk/socreson line/2/2/2.html

Cooper, P., Diamond, I., & High, S. (1993). Choosing and using contraceptives: Integrating qualitative and quantitative methods in family planning. *Journal of the Market Research Society* 35(4), 325–339.

Couch, D., & Liamputtong, P. (2007). Online dating and mating: Perceptions of risk and health among online users. *Health, Risk & Society* 9(3), 275–294.

Couch, D., & Liamputtong, P. (2008). Online dating and mating: The use of the Internet to meet sexual partners. *Qualitative Health Research* 18(2), 268–279.

Crigger, N.J., Holcomb, L., & Weiss, J. (2001). Fundamentalism, multiculturalism, and problems conducting research with populations in developing nations. *Nursing Ethics* 8(5), 459–469.

Crossley, M.L. (2002). 'Could you please pass one of those health leaflets along?': Exploring health, morality and resistance through focus groups. *Social Science and Medicine* 55(8), 1471–1483.

Crowe, T.V. (2003). Using focus groups to create culturally appropriate HIV prevention material for the deaf community. *Qualitative Social Work* 2, 289–308.

Culley, L., Hudson, N., & Rapport, F. (2007). Using focus groups with minority ethnic communities: Researching infertility in British South Asian communities. *Qualitative Health Research* 171, 102–112.

Daly, K.J. (2007). *Qualitative methods for family studies & human development.* Thousand Oaks, CA: Sage.

Davey, S.J., Dziurawiec, S., & O'Brien-Malone, A. (2006). Men's voices: Postnatal depression from the perspective of male partners. *Qualitative Health Research* 16(2), 206–220.

Davidson, P., Halcomb, E., & Gholizadeh, L. (2010). Focus group in health research. In P. Liamputtong (ed.), *Research methods in health: Foundations for evidence-based practice* (pp. 61–76). Melbourne: Oxford University Press.

Davies, B., Larson, J., Contro, N., Reyes-Hailey, C., Ablin, A.R., Chesla, C.A., Sourkes, B., & Cohen, H. (2009). Conducting a qualitative culture study of pediatric palliative care. *Qualitative Health Research* 19(1), 5–16.

Dawson, S., Manderson, L., & Tallo, V.L. (1993). *A manual for the use of focus groups.* Boston, MA: International Nutrition Foundation for Developing Countries (INFDC).

Dean, R., & Gregory, D. (2005). More than trivial: Strategies for using humour in palliative care. *Cancer Nursing* 28(4), 292–300.

Denzin, N.K. (1989). *Interpretive interactionalism.* Newbury Park, CA: Sage.

Denzin, N.K. (1995). Studies in symbolic interaction, vol. 16. New York: Jai Press.

DeVault, M.L. (1990). Talking and listening from women's standpoint: Feminist strategies for interviewing and analysis. *Social Problems* 37, 96–116.

Dew, K. (2007). A health researcher's guide to qualitative methodologies. *Australian and New Zealand Journal of Public Health* 31(5), 433–437.

Dickson-Swift, V., James, E., & Liamputtong, P. (2008). *Undertaking sensitive research in the health and social sciences: Managing boundaries, emotions and risks*. Cambridge: Cambridge University Press.

Dill, B.T. (1994). Fictive kin, paper sons, and compadrazgo: Women of color and the struggle for family survival. In M.B. Zinn & B.T. Dill (eds.), *Women of color in US society* (pp. 149–169). Philadelphia, PA: Temple University Press.

Duggleby, W. (2005). What about focus group interaction data? *Qualitative Health Research* 15(6), 832–840.

Dunbar, C., Rodriguez, D., & Parker, L. (2002). Race, subjectivity, and the interview process. In J.F. Gubrium & J.A. Holstein (eds.), *Handbook of interview research: Context & method* (pp. 279–298). Thousand Oaks, CA: Sage.

Easter, M.M., Linnan, L.A., Bentley, M.E., DeVellis, B.M., Meier, A., Frasier, P.Y., Kelsey, K.S., & Campbell, M.K. (2007). 'Una mujer trabaja doble aquí': Vignette-based focus groups on stress and work for Latina blue-collar women in eastern North Carolina. *Health Promotion Practice* 8(1), 41–49.

Eckhardt, G. (2004). The role of culture in conducting trustworthy and credible qualitative business research in China. In R. Marschan-Piekkari & C. Welch (eds.), *Handbook of qualitative methods for international business research* (pp. 402–420). Cheltenham: Edward Elgar.

Edwards, R. (1990). Connecting method and epistemology: A white woman interviewing black women. *Women's Studies International Forum* 13(5), 477–490.

Ekblad, S., & Bäärnhielm, S. (2002). Focus group interview research in transcultural psychiatry: Reflections on research experiences. *Transcultural Psychiatry* 39(4), 484–500.

Emami, A., & Tishelman, C. (2004). Reflections on cancer in the context of women's health: Focus group discussions with Iranian immigrant women in Sweden. *Women & Health* 39(4), 75–95.

Espiritu, Y.L. (1997). *Asian American women and men: Labor, laws, and love*. Thousand Oaks, CA: Sage.

Esposito, N. (2001). From meaning to meaning: The influence of translation techniques on non-English focus group research. *Qualitative Health Research* 11(4), 568–579.

Esterberg, K.G. (2002). *Qualitative methods in social research*. Boston, MA: McGraw-Hill.

Eysenbach, G., & Till, J.E. (2001). Ethical issues in qualitative research on Internet communities. *British Medical Journal* 323(7321), 1103–1105.

Ezekiel, M.J., Talle, A., Juma, J.M., & Klepp, K.-I. (2009). 'When in the body, it makes you look fat and HIV negative': The constitution of antiretroviral therapy in local discourse among youth in Kahe, Tanzania. *Social Science and Medicine* 68(6), 957–964.

Fern, E. (2001). *Advanced focus group research*. Thousand Oaks, CA: Sage.

Fielding, N., Lee, R.M., & Blank, G. (2008). *The Sage handbook of online research methods*. London: Sage.

Finch, J. (1987). The vignette technique in survey research. *Sociology* 21(1), 25–34.

Fine, M. (1994). Working the hyphens: Reinventing self and other in qualitative research. In N.K. Denzin & Y.S. Loncoln (eds.), *Handbook of qualitative research* (pp. 70–82). Thousand Oaks, CA: Sage.

Fine, M., & Gordon, M. (1989). Feminist transformation of/despite psychology. In M Crawford & M. Gentry (eds.), *Gender and thought: Psychological perspectives* (pp. 146–174). New York: Springer.

Flick, U. (2006). *An introduction to qualitative research*, 3rd edition. London: Sage.

Flicker, S., Haans, D., & Skinner, H. (2004). Ethical dilemmas in research on Internet communities. *Qualitative Health Research* 14(1), 124–134.

Folch-Lyon, E., & Trost, J.F. (1981). Conducting focus group sessions. *Studies in Family Planning* 12(2), 443–449.

Fox, F.E., Morris, M., & Rumsey, N. (2007). Doing synchronous online focus groups with young people: Methodological reflections. *Qualitative Health Research* 17(4), 539–547.

Franklin, K.K., & Lowry, C. (2001). Computer-mediated focus group sessions: Naturalistic inquiry in a networked environment. *Qualitative Research* 1(2), 169–184.

Fraser, M., & Fraser, A. (2001). Are people with learning disabilities able to contribute to focus groups on health promotion? *Journal of Advanced Nursing* 33(2), 225–233.

Freire, P. (1970/1993). *Pedagogy of the oppressed.* New York: Continuum. (Original work published in 1970.)

Frey, J.H., & Fontana, A. (1993). The group interview in social research. In D.L. Morgan (ed.), *Successful focus groups: Advancing the state of the art* (pp. 20–34). Newbury Park, CA: Sage.

Frith, H. (1997). *Young women refusing sex: The epistemological adventures of a feminist.* PhD thesis, Loughborough University.

Frith, H. (2000). Focusing on sex: Using focus groups in sex research. *Sexualities* 3(3), 275–297.

Fuller, T.D., Edwards, J.N., Vorakitphokatorn, S., & Sermsri, S. (1993). Using focus groups to adapt survey instruments to new populations: Experience from a developing country. In D.L. Morgan (ed.), *Successful focus groups: Advancing the state of the art.* (pp. 89–104). Newbury Park, CA: Sage.

Gabard, D., & Martin, M. (2003). *Physical therapy ethics.* Philadelphia, PA: F.A. Davis.

Gaiser, T., & Schreiner, T. (2009). *A guide to conducting online research.* Thousand Oaks, CA: Sage.

Gaiser, T.J. (2008). Online focus groups. In N. Fielding, R.M. Lee, & G. Blank (eds.), *The Sage handbook of online research methods* (pp. 290–307). London: Sage.

Gamson, W.A. (1992). *Talking politics.* Cambridge: Cambridge University Press.

Gates, B., & Waight, M. (2007). Reflections on conducting focus groups with people with learning disabilities. *Journal of Research in Nursing* 12(2), 111–126.

Gibbs, G.R. (2007). *Analyzing qualitative data.* London: Sage.

Gibson, F. (2007). Conducting focus groups with children and young people: Strategies for success. *Journal of Research in Nursing* 12(5), 473–483.

Gilkes, C.T. (1994). 'If it wasn't for the women…': African American women, community work and social change. In M.B. Zinn & B.T. Dill (eds.), *Women of color in US society* (pp. 229–246). Philadelphia: Temple University Press.

Gilmore, G.D., & Campbell, M.D. (2005). *Needs and capacity assessment strategies for health education and health promotion,* 3rd edition. Sudbury, MA: Jones and Bartlett.

Giordano, F.G., Thumme, B., & Sierra, G.P. (2009). The hopes and dreams of Honduran women regarding their daughters' sexuality. *Qualitative Health Research* 19(7), 996–1009.

Glenn, E.N. (1986). *Issei, nisei, war bride: Three generations of Japanese American women in domestic service.* Philadelphia: Temple University Press.

Goffman, E. (1961). *Asylums: Essays on the social situation of mental patients and other inmates.* Chicago: Aldine.

Goffman, I. (1986). *Stigma: Notes on the management of spoiled identity.* New York: Touchstone.

Goldman, K.D., & Schmalz, K.J. (2001). Focus on focus groups! *Health Promotion Practice* 2(1), 14–15.

Goodman, C., & Evans, C. (2006). Using focus groups. In K. Gerrish & C. Lacey, C. (eds.), *The research process in nursing,* 5th edn (pp. 353–366). Oxford: Blackwell Publishing.

Goodman, K. (1998). Service user involvement. In M. Burton & J. Kellaway (eds.), *Developing and managing high quality services for people with learning disabilities* (pp. 257–269). Aldershot: Ashgate.

Grbich, C. (2007). *Qualitative data analysis: An introduction.* London: Sage.

Greenbaum, T.L. (2001). Online focus groups are no substitute for the real thing. *Groups Plus.* Retrieved on 24 July 2009, from www.groupsplus.com/pages/qmr0601.html

Greising, D. (1998). *I'd like the world to buy a Coke: The life and leadership of Robert Goizueta.* New York: Wiley.

Grunseit, A., Richters, J., Crawford, J., Song, A., & Kippax, S. (2005). Stability and change in sexual practices among first-year Australian university students (1990–1999). *Archives of Sexual Behaviour* 34(5), 557–568.

Ha, V.S. (2008). The harmony of family and the silence of women: Sexual attitudes and practices among rural married women in northern Viet Nam. *Culture, Health & Sexuality* 10(Supplement), S163–S176.

Halcomb, E.J., Gholizadeh, L., DiGiacomo, M., Phillips, J., & Davidson, P.M. (2007). Literature review: Considerations in undertaking focus group research with culturally and linguistically diverse groups. *Journal of Clinical Nursing* 16(6), 1000–1011.

Halkier, B. (2010). Focus groups as social enactments: Integrating interaction and content in the analysis of focus group data. *Qualitative Research* 10(1), 71–89.

Harding, S. (1987). *Feminism and methodology.* Bloomington, IN: Indiana University Press.

Hazel, N. (1996). Elicitation techniques with young people. *Social Research Update* 12. Retrieved on 26 March 2010, from http://sru.soc.surrey.ac.uk/SRU12.html

Hennessy, E., & Heary, C. (2005). Exploring children's views through focus groups. In S. Greene & D. Hogan (eds.), *Researching children's experience: Methods and approaches* (pp. 236–252). London: Sage.

Hennink, M.M. (2007). *International focus group research: A handbook for the health and social sciences.* Cambridge: Cambridge University Press.

Hennink, M.M. (2008). Language and communication in cross-cultural qualitative research. In P. Liamputtong (ed.), *Doing cross-cultural research: Ethical and methodological perspectives* (pp. 21–33). Dordrecht: Springer.

Hesse-Biber, S.N., & Leavy, P. (2010). *The practice of qualitative research,* 2nd edition. Thousand Oaks, CA: Sage.

Hill, M., Laybourn, A., & Borland, M. (1996). Engaging with primary-aged children about their emotions and well-being: Methodological considerations. *Children & Society* 10, 129–144.

Hinton, R., & Earnest, J. (2010). Stressors, coping, and social support among women in Papua New Guinea. *Qualitative Health Research* 20(2), 224–238.

Hodges, B.C., & Videto, D.M. (2005). *Assessment and planning in health programs.* Boston, MA: Jones and Bartlett.

Hollander, J. (2004). The social context of focus groups. *Journal of Contemporary Ethnography* 33, 602–37.

Holloway, W., & Jefferson, T. (2000). *Doing qualitative research differently: Free association, narrative and the interview method.* London: Sage.

Holmgren, K., & Dahlin Ivanoff, S. (2004). Women on sickness absence – Views of possibilities and obstacles for returning to work: A focus group study. *Disability and Rehabilitation* 26(4), 213–222.

Holstein, J.A., & Gubrium, J.F. (1995). *The active interview.* Thousand Oaks, CA: Sage.

Hopkins, P.E. (2007). Thinking critically and creatively about focus groups. *Area* 39(4), 528–535.

Hughes, J., & Lang, K.R. (2004). Issues in online focus groups: Lessons learned from an empirical study of peer-to-peer filesharing system users. *Electronic Journal of Business Research Methods* 2(2), 95–110.

Hyams, M. (2004). Hearing girls' silences: Thoughts on the politics and practices of a feminist method of group discussion. *Gender, Place & Culture* 11(1), 105–119.

Hyde, A., Howlett, E.H., Brady, D., & Drennan, J. (2005). The focus group method: Insights from focus group interviews on sexual health with adolescents. *Social Science and Medicine* 61(12), 2588–2599.

Hydén, L.-C., & Bülow, P.H. (2003). Who's talking? Drawing conclusions from focus groups – some methodological considerations. *International Journal of Social Research Methodology* 6(4), 305–321.

Im, E-O., & Chee, W. (2003). Feminist issues in e-mail group discussion among cancer patients. *Advances in Nursing Science* 26(4), 287–298.

Im, E-O., Page, R., Lin, L-C., Tsai, H-M., & Cheng, C-Y. (2004). Rigor in cross-cultural nursing research. *International Journal of Nursing Studies* 41, 891–899.

Israel, B.A., Eng, E., Schulz, A.J., & Parker, E.A. (2005). *Methods in community-based participatory research for health*. San Francisco: Jossey-Bass.

Irvine, F., Roberts, G., & Bradbury-Jones, C. (2008). The researcher as insider versus the researcher as outsider: Enhancing rigour through language and cultural sensitivity. In P. Liamputtong (ed.), *Doing cross-cultural research: Ethical and methodological perspectives* (pp. 35–48). Dordrecht, Netherlands: Springer.

Israel, M., & Hay, I. (2006). *Research ethics for social scientists: Between ethical conduct and regulatory compliance*. London: Sage.

Ivanoff, S.D., & Hultberg, J. (2006). Understanding the multiple realities of everyday life: Basic assumptions in focus-group methodology. *Scandinavian Journal of Occupational Therapy* 13(2), 125–132.

Jarrett, R.L. (1993). Focus group interviewing with low-income minority populations: A research experience. In D.L. Morgan (ed.), *Successful focus groups: Advancing the state of the art* (pp. 184–201). Newbury Park, CA: Sage.

Järviluoma, H., Moisala, P., & Vilkko, A. (2003). *Gender and qualitative methods*. London: Sage Publications.

Jefferson, G. (2004). Glossary of transcript symbols with an introduction. In C.H. Lemer (ed.), *Conversation analysis: Studies from the first generation* (pp. 13–23). Philadelphia: John Benjamins.

Jirojwong, S., Prior, J., & Wowan/Dululu Community Volunteer Group (2005). Chronic illnesses in Queensland rural and remote communities using two sampling units. *Southeast Asian Journal of Tropical Medicine & Public Health* 36(5), 1275–1282.

Johns, M.D., Chen, S.-L.S., & Hall, G.J. (eds.) (2004). *Online social research: Methods, issues, & ethics*. New York: Peter Lang.

Johnson, A. (1996). 'It's good to talk': The focus group and the sociological imagination. *Sociological Review* 44(3), 517–538.

Jones, A., Pill, R., & Adams, S. (2000). Qualitative study of views of health professionals and patients on guided self management plans for asthma. *British Medical Journal* 321(7275), 1507–1510.

Jonsson, I.M., Hallberg, L.R.-M., & Gustafsson, I.-B. (2002). Cultural foodways in Sweden: Repeated focus group interviews with Somalian women. *International Journal of Consumer Studies* 26(4), 328–339.

Joseph, J.G., Emmons, C.A., Kessler, R.C., Wortman, C.B., & O'Brien, K. (1984). Coping with the threat of AIDS: An approach to psychosocial assessment. *American Journal of Psychology* 39(11), 1297–1302.

Jowett, M., & O'Toole, G. (2006). Focusing researchers' minds: Contrasting experiences of using focus groups in feminist qualitative research. *Qualitative Research* 6(4), 453–472.

Jurkowski, J.M., Rivera, Y., & Hammel, J. (2009). Health perceptions of Latinos with intellectual disabilities: The results of a qualitative pilot study. *Health Promotion Practice* 10(1), 144–155.

Kamberelis, G., & Dimitriadis, G. (2008). Focus groups: Strategic articulations of pedagogy, politics, and inquiry. In N.K. Denzin & Y.S. Lincoln (eds.), *Collecting and interpreting qualitative materials*, 3rd edition (pp. 375–402). Thousand Oaks, CA: Sage.

Kapborg, I., & Bertero, C. (2002). Using an interpreter in qualitative interviews: Does it threaten validity? *Nursing Inquiry* 9(1), 52–56.

Kauser, F. (2001). *Maternal health care utilization among the urban poor of Maharashtra India*. PhD thesis, University of Southampton.

Kegler, M.C., Bird, S.T., Kyle-Moon, K., & Rodine, S. (2001). Understanding teen pregnancy from the perspective of young adolescents in Oklahoma City. *Health Promotion Practice* 2(3), 242–254.

Kennedy, C., Kools, S., & Krueger, R. (2001). Methodological considerations in children's focus groups. *Nursing Research* 50(3), 184–187.

Kenny, A.J. (2005). Interaction in cyberspace: An online focus group. *Journal of Advanced Nursing* 49(4), 414–422.

Khan, M.E., Anker, M., Patel, B.C., Barge, S., Sadhwani, H., & Kohle, R. (1991). The use of focus groups in social and behavioural research: some methodological issues. *World Health Statistics Quarterly* 44, 145–149.

Kieffer, E.C., Salabarria-Pena, Y., Odoms-Young, A.M., Willis, S.K., Baber, K.E., & Guzman, J.R. (2005). The application of focus group methodologies to community-based participatory research. In B.A. Israel, E. Eng, A.J. Schulz, & E.A. Parker (eds.), *Methods in community-based participatory research for health* (pp. 146–66). San Francisco: Jossey-Bass.

Kirby, D., Laris, B., & Rolleri, L. (2007). Sex and HIV education programs: Their impact on sexual behaviors of young people throughout the world. *Journal of Adolescent Health* 40, 206–217.

Kitzinger, J. (1994a). The methodology of focus groups: The importance of interaction between research participants. *Sociology of Health and Illness* 16(1), 103–121.

Kitzinger, J. (1994b). Focus groups: Method or madness? In M. Boulton (ed.), *Challenge and innovation: Methodological advances in social research on HIV/AIDS* (pp. 159–175). London: Taylor & Francis.

Kitzinger, J. (1995). Introducing focus groups. *British Medical Journal* 311(29 July), 299–302.

Kitzinger, J. (2005). Focus group research: Using group dynamics to explore perceptions, experiences and understandings. In I. Holloway (ed.), *Qualitative research in health care* (pp. 56–70). Maidenhead: Open University Press.

Kitzinger, J., & Barbour, R. (1999). Introduction: The challenge and promise of focus groups. In R. Barbour & J. Kitzinger (eds.), *Developing focus group research: Politics, theory and practice* (pp. 1–20). London: Sage.

Kitzinger, J., & Farquhar, C. (1999). The analytic potential of 'sensitive moments' in focus group discussions. In R.S. Barbour & J. Kitzinger (eds.), *Developing focus group research: Politics, theory and practice* (pp. 156–173). London: Sage.

Knodel, J., Havanon, N., & Pramualratana, A. (1984). Fertility transition in Thailand: A qualitative analysis. *Population and Development Review* 10(2), 297–315.

Knodel, J., Chamratrithirong, A., & Debavalya, N. (1987). *Thailand's reproductive revolution: Rapid fertility decline in a Third-World setting*. Madison: University of Wisconsin Press.

Kossak, S.N. (2005). Exploring the elements of culturally relevant service delivery. *Families in Society* 86(2), 189–195.

Kozol, J. (1985). *Illiterate America*. New York: Random House.

Kroll, T., Neri, M., & Miller, K. (2005). Using mixed methods in rehabilitation and disability research. *Rehabilitation Nursing* 30, 106–113.

Kroll, T., Barbour, R., & Harris, J. (2007). Using focus groups in disability research. *Qualitative Health Research* 17(5), 690–698.

Krueger, R.A. (1988). *Focus groups: A practical guide for applied research*. Newbury Park, CA: Sage.

Krueger, R.A. (1994). *Focus groups: A practical guide for applied research*, 2nd edition. London: Sage.

Krueger, R.A. (1998). *Analyzing and reporting focus group results*. London: Sage.

Krueger, R.A., & Casey, M.A. (2009). *Focus groups: A practical guide for applied research*, 4th edition. Thousand Oaks, CA: Sage.

Kvale, S. (2007). *Doing interviews*. London: Sage.

Lagerlund, M., Widmark, C., Lambe, M., & Tishelman, C. (2001). Rationales for attending or not attending mammography screening – A focus group study among women in Sweden. *European Journal of Cancer Prevention* 10(5), 429–442.

Lambert, S.D., & Loiselle, C.G. (2008). Combining individual interviews and focus groups to enhance data richness. *Journal of Advanced Nursing* 62(2), 228–237.

Landrine, H., Klonoff, E., & Brown-Collins, A. (1995). Cultural diversity and methodology in feminist psychology: Critique, proposal, empirical example. In H. Landrine (ed.), *Bringing cultural diversity to feminist psychology* (pp. 55–75). Washington, DC: American Psychological Association.

Lather, P., & Smithies, C. (1997). *Troubling the angels: Women living with HIV/AIDS*. Boulder, CO: Westview.

Laverack, G.R., & Brown, K.M. (2003). Qualitative research in a cross-cultural context: Fijian experiences. *Qualitative Health Research* 13(3), 333–342.

Leask, J., Hawe, P., & Chapman, S. (2001). Focus group composition: A comparison between natural and constructed groups. *Australian and New Zealand Journal of Public Health* 25(2), 152–154.

Lee, A.A., & Ellenbecker, C.H. (1998). The perceived life stressors among elderly Chinese immigrants: Are they different from those of other elderly Americans? *Clinical Excellence for Nurse Practitioners* 2, 96–101.

Lehoux, P., Poland, B., & Daudelin, G. (2006). Focus group research and 'the patient's view'. *Social Science and Medicine* 63(8), 2091–2104.

Lester, H., & Tritter, J.Q. (2005). 'Listen to my madness': Understanding the experiences of people with serious mental illness. *Sociology of Health & Illness* 27(5), 649–669.

Lettenmaier, C., Langlois, P., Kumah, O.M., Kiragu, K., Jato, M., Zacharias, J., Kols, A., & Piotrow, P.T. (1994). Focus-group research for family planning: Lessons learned in sub-Saharan Africa. *Health Transition Review* 4(1), 95–99.

Liamputtong, P. (ed.) (2006). *Health research in cyberspace: Methodological, practical and personal issues*. New York: Nova Science.

Liamputtong, P. (2007). *Researching the vulnerable: A guide to sensitive research methods*. London: Sage.

Liamputtong, P. (2009). *Qualitative research methods*, 3rd edition. Melbourne: Oxford University Press.

Liamputtong, P. (2010a). *Performing qualitative cross-cultural research*. Cambridge: Cambridge University Press.

Liamputtong, P. (2010b). The science of words and the science of numbers: Research methods as foundations for evidence-based practice in health. In P. Liamputtong (ed.), *Research methods in health: Foundations for evidence-based practice* (pp. 3–26). Melbourne: Oxford University Press.

Liamputtong Rice, P. (2000). *Hmong women and reproduction*. Westport, CT: Bergin & Garvey.

Liamputtong, P., & Jirojwong, S. (2009). Needs assessment of communities and populations. In S. Jirojwong & P. Liamputtong (eds.), *Population health, communities and health promotion: Assessment, planning, implementation and evaluation* (pp. 45–68). Melbourne: Oxford University Press.

Liang, W., Yuan, E., Mandelblatt, J.S., & Pasick, R.J. (2004). How do older Chinese women view health and cancer screening? Results from focus groups and implications for interventions. *Ethnicity & Health* 9(3), 283–304.

Lichtenstein, B. (2005). Domestic violence, sexual ownership, and HIV risk in women in the American deep south. *Social Science and Medicine* 60(4), 701–714.

Lichtenstein, B., & Nansel, T. (2000). Women's douching practices and related attitudes: Findings from four focus groups. *Women & Health* 31(2/3), 117–131.

Litosseliti, L. (2003). *Using focus groups in research*. London: Continuum.

Lloyd-Evans, S. (2006). Focus groups. In V. Desai & R.B. Potter (eds.), *Doing development research* (pp. 153–162). London: Sage.

Long, T. (2007). Review of 'Conducting focus groups with children and young people: Strategies for success'. *Journal of Research in Nursing* 12(5) 485–486.

Longhurst, R. (1996). Refocusing groups: Pregnant women's geographical experiences of Hamilton, New Zealand/Aotearoa. *Area* 28, 143–149.

Lopez, G.I., Figueroa, M., Connor, S.E., & Maliski, S.L. (2008). Translation barriers in conducting qualitative research with Spanish speakers. *Qualitative Health Research* 18(12), 1729–1737.

Lovering, K.M. (1995). The bleeding body: Adolescents talk about menstruation. In S. Wilkinson & C. Kitzinger (eds.), *Feminism and discourse: Psychological perspectives* (pp. 10–31). London: Sage.

Macdonald, R., & Wilson, G. (2005). Musical identities of professional jazz musicians: a focus group investigation. *Psychology of Music* 33(4), 395–417.

MacDougall, C., & Fudge, E. (2001). Planning and recruiting the sample for focus groups and in-depth interviews. *Qualitative Health Research* 11, 117–126.

MacLean, L.M., Meyer, M., & Estable, A. (2004). Improving accuracy of transcripts in qualitative research. *Qualitative Health Research* 14(1), 113–123.

Macnaghten, P., & Myers, G. (2004). Focus groups. In C. Seal, G. Gobo, J.F. Gubrium & D. Silverman (eds.), *Qualitative research practice* (pp. 65–79). London: Sage.

MacPherson, P., & Fine, M. (1995). Hungry for an us: Adolescent girls and adult women negotiating territories of race, gender, class and difference. *Feminism & Psychology* 5, 181–200.

Madriz, E. (1997). *Nothing bad happens to good girls: Fear of crime in women's lives*. Berkeley: University of California Press.

Madriz, E. (1998). Using focus groups with lower socioeconomic status Latina women. *Qualitative Health Research* 4, 114–128.

Madriz, E. (2000). Focus groups in feminist research. In N.K. Denzin & Y.S. Lincoln (eds.), *Handbook of qualitative research*, 2nd edition (pp. 835–850). Thousand Oaks, CA: Sage.

Madriz, E. (2003). Focus groups in feminist research. In N.K. Denzin & Y.S. Lincoln (eds.), *Collecting and interpreting qualitative materials*, 2nd edition (pp. 363–388). Thousand Oaks, CA: Sage.

Maiter, S., Simich, L., Jacobson, N., & Wise, J. (2008). Reciprocity: An ethic for community-based participatory action research. *Action Research* 6(3), 305–325.

Makhoul, J., & Nakkash, R. (2007). Understanding youth: Using qualitative methods to verify quantitative community indicators. *Health Promotion Practice* 10(1), 128–135.

Manderson, L., Bennett, E., & Andajani-Sutjahjo, S. (2006). The social dynamics of the interview: Age, class, and gender. *Qualitative Health Research* 16, 1317–1334.

Mann, C., & Stewart, F. (2000). *Internet communication and qualitative research: A handbook for researching online*. London: Sage.

Markham, A.N. (2008). The methods, politics, and ethics of representation in online ethnography. In N.K. Denzin & Y.S. Lincoln (eds.), *Collecting and interpreting qualitative materials*, 3rd edition (pp. 247–284). Thousand Oaks, CA: Sage.

Martin, D.M., Ror, A., Wells, M.B., & Lewis, J. (1997). Health gain through screening: Users' and carers' perspectives of health care: Developing primary health care services for people with an intellectual disability. *Journal of Intellectual & Developmental Disability* 22(4), 241–249.

Maynard, M., & Purvis, J. (1994). Doing feminist research. In M. Maynard & J. Purvis (eds.), *Researching women's lives from a feminist perspective* (pp. 1–9). London: Taylor & Francis.

Maynard-Tucker, G. (2000). Conducting focus groups in developing countries: Skill training for local bilingual facilitators. *Qualitative Health Research* 10(3), 396–410.

McClelland, G.T., & Newell, R. (2008). A qualitative study of the experiences of mothers involved in street-based prostitution and problematic substance use. *Journal of Research in Nursing* 13(5), 437–447.

McIntyre, A. (2008). *Participatory action research.* Thousand Oaks, CA: Sage.

Mead, G.H. (1934). *Mind, self and society.* Chicago: University of Chicago Press.

Melrose, M. (2002). Labour pains: Some considerations on the difficulties of researching juvenile prostitution. *International Journal of Social Research Methodology* 5(4), 333–351.

Merghati Khoei, E., Whelan, A., & Cohen, J. (2008). Sharing beliefs: What sexuality means to Muslim Iranian women living in Australia. *Culture, Health & Sexuality* 10(3), 237–248.

Merton, R. (1987). The focused group interview and focus groups: Continuities and discontinuities. *Public Opinion Quarterly* 51, 550–566.

Merton, R.K., & Kendall, P.L. (1946). The focused interview. *American Journal of Sociology* 51, 541–557.

Merton, R.K., Fiske, M., & Kendall, P.L. (1990). *The focused interview*, 2nd edition. New York: Free Press.

Mertz, N.T., & Anfara Jr., C.A. (2006). Conclusion: Coming full circle. In C.A. Anfara Jr. & N.T. Mertz (eds.), *Theoretical frameworks in qualitative research.* Thousand Oaks, CA: Sage.

Miller, W.L., & Crabtree, B.F. (2005). Clinical Research. In N.K. Denzin & Y.S. Lincoln (eds.), *The Sage handbook of qualitative research*, 3rd edition (pp. 605–639). Thousand Oaks, CA: Sage.

Minichiello, V., Aroni, R., & Hays, T. (2008). *In-depth interviewing: Principles, techniques, analysis*, 3rd edition. Frenchs Forest: Pearson Education Australia.

Minkler, M., & Wallerstein, N. (2008). *Community-based participatory research for health: From process to outcomes*, 2nd edition. San Francisco: Jossey-Bass.

Mmari, K., Michaelis, A., & Kiro, K. (2009). Risk and protective factors for HIV among orphans and non-orphans in Tanzania. *Culture, Health & Sexuality* 11(8), 799–809.

Moen, J., Antonov, K., Lars, J., Nilsson, G., & Ring, L. (2010). Interaction between participants in focus groups with older patients and general practitioners. *Qualitative Health Research* 20(5), 607–616.

Moezzi, S. (2007). *Combining personal perspectives and women's knowledge: Combining focus group and semi-structured interviews.* Poster presented at the 8th International, Interdisciplinary Advances in Qualitative Methods Conference, Banff, Canada.

Moloney, M.A., Dietrich, A.S., Strickland, O.L., & Myerburg, S. (2003). Using Internet discussion boards as virtual focus groups. *Advances in Nursing Science* 26(4), 274–286.

Montell, F. (1999). Focus group interviews: A new feminist method. *National Women's Studies Association Journal* 11(1), 44–71.

Moore, L.W., & Miller, M. (1999). Initiating research with doubly vulnerable populations. *Journal of Advanced Nursing* 30(5), 1034–1040.

Morgan, D.L. (1988). *Focus group as qualitative research.* Newbury Park, CA: Sage.

Morgan, D.L. (ed.) (1993). *Successful focus groups: Advancing the state of the art*. Newbury Park, CA: Sage.

Morgan, D.L. (1995). Why things (sometimes) go wrong in focus groups. *Qualitative Health Research* 5(4), 516–523.

Morgan, D.L. (1996). Focus groups. *Annual Review of Sociology* 22, 129–152.

Morgan, D.L. (1997). *Focus groups as qualitative research*, 2nd edition. Newbury Park, CA: Sage.

Morgan, D.L. (1998). *The focus group guidebook* (focus group kit, vol. 1). Thousand Oaks, CA: Sage.

Morgan, D.L. (2002). Focus group interviewing. In J.F. Gubrium & J.A. Holstein (eds.), *Handbook of interviewing research: Context & method* (pp. 141–159). Thousand Oaks, CA: Sage.

Morgan, D.L. (2010). Reconsidering the role of interaction in analyzing and reporting focus groups. *Qualitative Health Research* 20(5), 718–722.

Morgan, D.L., & Bottorff, J.L. (2010). Advancing our craft: Focus group methods and practice. *Qualitative Health Research* 20(5), 579–581.

Morgan, D.L., & Krueger, R.A. (1993). When to use focus groups and why. In D.L. Morgan (ed.), *Successful focus groups: Advancing the state of the art* (pp. 3–19). Newbury Park, CA: Sage.

Morgan, M., Gibbs, S., Maxwell, K., & Britten, N. (2002). Hearing children's voices: Methodological issues in conducting focus groups with children aged 7–11 years. *Qualitative Research* 2(1), 5–20.

Mosavel, M., Simon, C., van Stade, D., & Buchbinder, M. (2005). Community-based participatory research (CBPR) in South Africa: Engaging multiple constituents to shape the research questions. *Social Science and Medicine* 61(12), 2577–2587.

Munday, J. (2006). Identity in focus: The use of focus groups to study the construction of collective identity. *Sociology* 40(1), 89–105.

Murdoch, J., & Pratt, A.C. (1993). Rural studies: Modernism, postmodernism and the 'post-rural'. *Journal of Rural Studies* 8(2), 193–207.

Murphy, K., & Collins, M. (1997). Communication conventions in instructional electronic chats. *First Monday; A Peer Reviewed Journal on the Internet* 2(11). Retrieved February, 12, 2005 from www.firstmonday.org/issues/issue2_11/index.html

Murray, E.E. (1995). *Knowledge machines: Language and information in a technological society*. London: Longman.

Murray, P.J. (1997). Using virtual focus groups in qualitative research. *Qualitative Health Research* 7(4), 542–554.

Murray, S.A., Tapson, J., Turnbull, L., McCallum, J., & Little, A. (1994). Listening to local voices: Adapting rapid appraisal to assess health and social needs in general practice. *British Medical Journal* 308, 698–700.

Myers, G., & Macnaghten, P. (1999). Can focus groups be analysed as talk? In R. Barbour & J. Kitzinger (eds.), *Developing focus group research: Politics, theory, and practice* (pp. 173–85). London: Sage.

Napolitano, M., McCauley, L., Beltran, M., & Philips, J. (2002). The dynamic process of focus groups with migrant farmworkers: The Oregon experience. *Journal of Immigrant Health* 4(4), 177–182.

Nassar-McMillan, S., & Borders, D. (2002). Use of focus groups in survey item development. *The Qualitative Report* 7(1), 1–11. Retrieved on 3 February 2010, from www.nova.edu/ssss/QR/QR7-1/nassar.html

Ngo, A.D., McCurdy, S.A., Ross, M.W., Markham, C., Ratliff, E.A., & Pham, H.T.B. (2007). The lives of female sex workers in Vietnam: Findings from a qualitative study. *Culture, Health & Sexuality* 9(6), 555–570.

Norrick, N. (1993). *Conversational joking*. Bloomington: Indiana University Press.

Norris, J., Nurius, P.S., & Dimeff, L.A. (1996). Through her eyes: Factors affecting women's perception of and resistance to acquaintance aggression threat. *Psychology of Women Quarterly* 20(1), 123–145.

Nyamathi, A. (1998). Vulnerable populations: A continuing nursing focus. *Nursing Research* 47(2), 65–66.

O'Connor, H., & Madge, C. (2001). Cyber-mothers: Online synchronous interviewing using conferencing software. *Sociological Research Online* 5(4). Retrieved on 14 April 2009, from www.socresonline.org.uk/5/4/o'connor.html

O'Connor, H., & Madge, C. (2003). Focus groups in cyberspace: Using the Internet for qualitative research. *Qualitative Market Research: An International Journal* 6(2), 133–143.

O'Connor, H., Madge, C., Shaw, R., & Wellens, J. (2008). Internet-based interviewing. In N. Fielding, R.M. Lee & G. Blank (eds.), *The Sage handbook of online research methods* (pp. 271–298). London: Sage.

Oringderff, J. (2004). 'My Way': Piloting an online focus group. *International Journal of Qualitative Methods* 3(3). Article 5. Retrieved on 14 April 2009, from www.ualberta.ca/~iiqm/backissues/3_3/html/oringderff.html

Padgett, D.K. (2008). *Qualitative methods in social work research*, 2nd edition. Thousand Oaks, CA: Sage.

Padilla, R.V. (1993). Using dialogical research methods in group interviews. In D.L. Morgan (ed.), *Successful focus groups: Advancing the state of the art* (pp. 153–166). Newbury Park, CA: Sage.

Paradis, E.K. (2000). Feminist and community psychology ethics in research with homeless women. *American Journal of Community Psychology* 28(6), 839–858.

Parker, A., & Tritter, J. (2006). Focus group method and methodology: Current practice and recent debate. *International Journal of Research & Method in Education* 29(1), 23–37.

Patton, M. (2002). *Qualitative research and evaluation methods*, 3rd edition. Thousand Oaks, CA: Sage.

Peek, L., & Fothergill, A. (2009). Using focus groups: Lessons from studying daycare centers, 9/11, and Hurricane Katrina. *Qualitative Research* 9(1), 31–59.

Pendergrast, M. (1993). *For God, country and Coca-Cola: The unauthorized history of the world's most popular soft drink*. London: Weidenfeld & Nicolson.

Peterson-Sweeney, K. (2005). The use of focus groups in pediatric and adolescent research. *Journal of Pediatric Health Care* 19(2), 104–110.

Pfeffer, N. (2008). What British women say matters to them about donating an aborted fetus to stem cell research: A focus group study. *Social Science and Medicine* 66(12), 2544–2554.

Pini, B. (2002). Focus groups, feminist research and farm women: Opportunities for empowerment in rural social research. *Journal of Rural Studies* 18(3), 339–351.

Pitchforth, E., & van Teijlingen, E. (2005). International public health research involving interpreters: A case study from Bangladesh. *BMC Public Health*, 5, 71–78.

Pitts, V. (2004). Illness and internet empowerment: Writing and reading breast cancer in cyberspace. *Health* 8(1), 33–59.

Poland, B.D. (2002). Transcription quality. In J. Gubrium & J. Holstein (eds.), *Handbook of interview research: Context and method* (pp. 629–649). Thousand Oaks. CA: Sage.

Pollack, S. (2003). Focus group methodology in research with incarcerated women: Race, power, and collective experience. *Affilia* 18(4), 461–472.

Pösö, T., Honkatukia, P., & Nyqvist, L. (2008). Focus groups and the study of violence. *Qualitative Research* 8(1), 73–89.

Prandy, S.L., Norris, D., Lester, J., & Hoch, D.B. (2001). Expanding the guidelines for electronic communication with patients: Application to a specific tool. *Journal of the American Medical Informatics Association* 8(4), 344–348.

Propst, D.B., McDonough, M.H., Vogt, C.A., & Pynnonen, D.M. (2008). Roving focus groups: Collecting perceptual landscape data in situ. *International Journal of Qualitative Methods* 7(3), 1–14. Retrieved on 12 February 2010, from http://ejournals.library.ualberta.ca/index.php/IJQM/issue/view/352

Punch, S. (2002). Interviewing strategies with young people: The secret box, a stimulus material and task-based activities. *Children & Society* 16(1), 45–56.

Pyett, P. (2001). Innovation and compromise: Responsibility and reflexivity in research with vulnerable groups. In J. Daly, M. Guillemin & S. Hill (eds.), *Technologies and health: Critical compromises* (pp. 105–119). Melbourne: Oxford University Press.

Quest, T., & Marco, C.A. (2003). Ethics seminars: Vulnerable populations in emergency medicine research. *Academic Emergency Medicine* 10(11), 1294–1298.

Quine, S., & Cameron, I. (1995). The use of focus groups with the disabled elderly. *Qualitative Health Research* 5(4), 454–462.

Radway, J. (1991). *Reading the romance: Women, patriarchy, and popular literature.* Chapel Hill: University of North Carolina Press.

Ragnarsson, A., Onya, H.e., Thorson, A., Ekström, A.M., & Aarø, L.E. (2008). Young males' gendered sexuality in the era of HIV and AIDS in Limpopo Province, South Africa. *Qualitative Health Research* 18(6), 739–746.

Ramcharan, P. (2010). What is ethical research? In P. Liamputtong (ed.), *Research methods in health: Foundations for evidence-based practice* (pp. 27–41). Melbourne: Oxford University Press.

Ramji, H. (2008). Exploring commonality and difference in in-depth interviewing: A case-study of researching British Asian women. *British Journal of Sociology* 59(1), 99–116.

Rapley, T. (2007). *Doing conversation, discourse and document analysis.* London: Sage.

Ravenell, J.E., Johnson Jr., W.E., & Whitaker, E.E. (2006). African-American men's perceptions of health: A focus group study. *Journal of National Medical Association* 98(4), 544–550.

Reid, D.J., & Reid, F.J.M. (2005). Online focus groups An in-depth comparison of computer mediated and conventional focus group discussions. *International Journal of Market Research* 47(2), 131–162.

Reiger, K., & Liamputtong, P. (2010). Researching reproduction qualitatively: Intersections of personal and political. In I.L. Bourgeault, R. DeVries, & R. Dingwall (eds.), *The Sage handbook on qualitative health research* (pp. 641–657). London: Sage.

Reinharz, S., & Chase, S.E. (2002). Interviewing women. In J.F. Gubrium & J.A. Holstein (eds.), *Handbook of interview research: Context & method* (pp. 221–238). Thousand Oaks, CA: Sage.

Renzetti, C.M., & Lee, R.M. (eds.) (1993). *Researching sensitive topics.* Newbury Park, CA: Sage.

Rhodes, S.D., Hergenrather, K.C., Wilkin, A.M., & Jolly, C. (2008). Visions and voices: Indigent persons living with HIV in the southern United States use photovoice to create knowledge, develop partnerships, and take action. *Health Promotion Practice* 9(2), 159–169.

Roberts, C., Kippax, S., Waldby, C., & Crawford, J. (1995). Faking it: The story of 'ohh!'. *Women's Studies International Forum* 18(5/6), 523–532.

Robinson, J. (2009). Laughter and forgetting: Using focus groups to discuss smoking and motherhood in low-income areas in the UK. *International Journal of Qualitative Studies in Education* 22(3), 263–278.

Robson, K., & Williams, M. (2005). Researching online populations: The use of online focus groups for social research. *Qualitative Research* 5(4), 395–416.

Rodriguez, G. de Cortazar, A., Cabrera Leon, A., Hernan Garcia, M., & Manuel Jimenez Nunez, J. (2009). Attitudes of adolescent Spanish Roma toward noninjection drug use and risky sexual behavior. *Qualitative Health Research* 19(5), 605–620.

Romero-Daza, N., & Freidus, A. (2008). Female tourists, casual sex, and HIV risk in Costa Rica. *Qualitative Sociology* 31, 169–187.

Rubin, H.J., & Rubin, I.S. (1995). *Qualitative interviewing: The art of hearing data.* Thousand Oaks, CA: Sage.

Rubin, R. (2004). Men talking about Viagra: An exploratory study with focus groups. *Men and Masculinities* 7(1), 22–30.

Ruppenthal, L., Tuck, J., & Gagnon, A.J. (2005). Enhancing research with migrant women through focus groups. *Western Journal of Nursing Research* 27(6), 735–754.

Ryen, A. (2002). Cross-cultural interviewing. In J.F. Gubrium & J.A. Holstein (eds.), *Handbook of interview research: Context & method* (pp. 335–353). Thousand Oaks, CA: Sage Publications.

Salant, T., & Gehlert, S. (2008). Collective memory, candidacy, and victimization: Community epidemiologies of breast cancer risk. *Sociology of Health & Illness* 30(4), 599–615.

Salmon, A. (2007). Walking the talk: How participatory interview methods can democratize research. *Qualitative Health Research* 17(7), 982–993.

Sanders, T. (2004). Controllable laughter: Managing sex work through humour. *Sociology: The Journal of the British Sociological Association* 38(2), 273–291.

Sartorius, N., & Schulze, H. (2005). *Reducing the stigma of mental illness.* New York: Cambridge University Press.

Schilder, K., Tomov, T., Mladenova, M., Mayeya, J., Jenkins, R., Gulbinat, W., et al. (2004). The appropriateness and use of focus group methodology across international mental health communities. *International Review of Psychiatry* 16(1–2), 24–30.

Schlesinger, P., Dobash, R.E., Dobosh, R.P., & Weaver, C.K. (1992). *Women viewing violence.* London: British Film Institute.

Schulze, B., & Angermeyer, M.C. (2003). Subjective experiences of stigma: A focus group study of schizophrenic patients, their relatives and mental health professionals. *Social Science and Medicine* 56(2), 299–312.

Scott, S.D., Sharpe, H., O'Leary, K., Dehaeck, U., Hindmarsh, K., Moor, J.G., & Osmond, M.H. (2009). Court reporters: A viable solution for the challenges of focus group data collection? *Qualitative Health Research* 19(1), 140–146.

Selwyn, N., & Robson, K. (1998). Using e-mail as a research tool. *Social Research Update* 21. Retrieved on 25 November 2006, from www.soc.surrey.ac.uk/sru/SRU21.html

Seymour, J., Bellamy, G., Gott, M., Ahmedzai, S.H., & Clark, D. (2002). Using focus groups to explore older people's attitudes to end of life care. *Ageing & Society* 22, 517–526.

Seymour, J., Bellamy, G., Gott, M., Ahmedzai, S.H., & Clark, D. (2004). Planning for the end of life: The views of older people about advance care statement. *Social Science and Medicine* 59(1), 57–68.

Seymour, W. (2001). In the flesh or online? Exploring qualitative research methodologies. *Qualitative Research* 1(2), 147–168.

Shah, S. (2003). The researcher/interviewer in intercultural context: A social intruder. *British Educational Research Journal* 30(4), 549–575.

Shelton, A.J., & Rianon, N.J. (2004). Recruiting participants for a community of Bangladeshi immigrants for a study of spousal abuse: An appropriate cultural approach. *Qualitative Health Research* 14(3), 369–380.

Shklarov, S. (2007). Double vision uncertainty: The bilingual researcher and the ethics of cross-language research. *Qualitative Health Research* 17(4), 529–538.

Silva, M.C. (1995). *Ethical guidelines in the conduct, dissemination, and implementation of nursing research.* Washington, DC: American Nurses Publishing.

Sinha, S., Curtis, K., Jayakody, A., Viner, R., & Roberts, H. (2007). 'People make assumptions about our communities': Sexual health amongst teenagers from Black and minority ethnic backgrounds in East London. *Ethnicity & Health* 12(5), 423–441.

Skeat, J. (2010). Using grounded theory in health research. In Liamputtong, P. (ed.), *Research methods in health: Foundations for evidence-based practice* (pp. 106–122). Oxford University Press: Melbourne.

Skeggs, B., Moran, L., & Truman, C. (1998–2000). *Violence, security, space: A study of practical and policy context of substantive safe public space.* Lancaster University.

Smith, M.W. (1995). Ethics in focus groups: A few concerns. *Qualitative Health Research* 5(4), 478–486.

Smithson, J. (2000). Using and analysing focus groups: Limitations and possibilities. *International Journal of Social Research Methodology: Theory and Practice* 3(2), 103–119.

Smithson, J. (2008). Focus groups. In P. Alasuutari, L. Bickman & J. Brannen (eds.), *The Sage handbook of social research methods* (pp. 357–430). London: Sage.

Soydan, H. (1996). Using the vignette method in cross-cultural comparisons. In L. Hantrais & S. Mangen (eds.), *Cross-national research methods in the social sciences* (pp. 120–128). London: Pinter.

Sparks, R., Girling, E., & Smith, M.V. (2002). Lessons from history: Pasts, presents and futures of punishment in children's talk. *Children & Society* 16, 116–130.

Stanley, L. (1990). Feminist praxis and the academic mode of production: An editorial introduction. In L. Stanley (ed.), *Feminist praxis: Research, theory and epistemology in feminist sociology* (pp. 3–19). London: Routledge.

Stanley, L., & Wise, S. (1990). Method, methodology and epistemology in feminist research processes. In L. Stanley (ed.), *Feminist praxis: Research, theory and epistemology in feminist sociology* (pp. 20–60). London: Routledge.

Stevens, P.E. (1996). Focus groups: Collecting aggregate-level data to understand community health phenomena. *Public Health Nursing* 13(3), 170–6.

Stewart, D., Shamdasani, P., & Rook, D.W. (2009). Group depth interviews. In L. Bickman & D.J. Rog (eds.), *The Sage handbook of applied social research methods* (pp. 589–616). Thousand Oaks, CA: Sage.

Stewart, D.W., Shamdasani, P.N., & Rook, D.W. (2007). *Focus groups: Theory and practice,* 2nd edition. Sage: Thousand Oaks, CA.

Stewart, F., Eckerman, E., & Zhou, K. (1998). Using the Internet in qualitative public health research: A comparison of Chinese and Australia young women's perceptions of tobacco use. *Internet Journal of Health Promotion* December 29 [Online]. Retrieved on 10 March 1999 from: www.monash.edu.au/health/IJHP/1998/12 (no longer available online).

Stewart, K., & Williams, M. (2005). Researching online populations: The use of online focus groups for social research. *Qualitative Research* 5(4), 395–416.

Stokoe, E.H., & Smithson, J. (2002). Gender and sexuality in talk-in-interaction: Considering conversation analytic perspectives. In P. McIlvenny (ed.), *Talking gender and sexuality* (pp. 79–110). Amsterdam: John Benjamins.

Stone, T.H. (2003). The invisible vulnerable: The economically and educationally disadvantaged subjects of clinical research. *Journal of Law, Medicine and Ethics* 31(1), 149–153.

Strange, V., Forrest, S.A., Oakley, A., & the RIPPLE Study Team (2003). Mixed or single sex education: How would people like their sex education and why. *Gender and Education* 15(2), 201–214.

Strickland, C.J. (1999). Conducting focus groups cross-culturally: Experiences with Pacific Northwest Indian people. *Public Health Nurse* 16(3), 190–197.

Strickland, O.L., Moloney, M.F., Dietrich, A.S., Myerburg, S., Cotsonis, G.A., & Johnson, R.V. (2003). Measurement issues related to data collection on the World Wide Web, *Advances in Nursing Science* 26(4), 246–256.

Stycos, J.M. (1981). A critique of focus group and survey research: The machismo case. *Studies in Family Planning* 12(12), 450–456.

Tanjasiri, S.P., Kagawa-Singer, M., Nguyen, T.-U., & Foo, M.A. (2002). Collaborative research as an essential component for addressing cancer disparities among Southeast Asian and Pacific Islander women. *Health Promotion Practice* 3(2), 144–154.

Temple, B. (2002). Crossed wires: Interpreters, translators, and bilingual workers in cross-language research. *Qualitative Health Research* 12(6), 844–854.

Temple, B., & Edwards, R. (2002). Interpreters/translators and cross-language research: Reflexivity and border crossings. *International Journal of Qualitative Methods* 1(2). Article 1. Retrieved on 9 October 2005, from www.ualberta.ca/~ijqm

Thomas, A. (2008). Focus groups in qualitative research: Culturally sensitive methodology for the Arabian Gulf? *International Journal of Research & Method in Education* 31(1), 77–88.

Tilley, S.A. (2003). 'Challenging' research practices: Turning a critical lens on the work of transcription. *Qualitative Inquiry* 9(5), 750–773.

Toner, J. (2009). Small is not too small: Reflections concerning the validity of very small focus groups (VSFGs). *Qualitative Social Work* 8(2), 179–192.

Turnbull, B., Martínez-Andrade, G., Klünder, M., Carranco, T., Duque-López, X., Ramos-Hernández, R.I., Conzález-Unzaga, M., Flores-Hernández, S., & Martínez-Salgado, H. (2006). The social construction of anemia in school shelters for indigenous children in Mexico. *Qualitative Health Research* 16(4), 503–516.

Turney, L., & Pocknee, C. (2005). Virtual focus groups: New frontiers in research. *International Journal of Qualitative Methods* 4(2), Article 3. Retrieved on 12 April 2009, from www.ualberta.ca/~iiqm/backissues/4_2/pdf/turney.pdf

Twinn, S. (1998). An analysis of the effectiveness of focus groups as a method of qualitative data collection with Chinese populations in nursing research. *Journal of Advanced Nursing* 28(3), 654–661.

Umaña-Taylor, A.J., & Bámaca, M.Y. (2004). Conducting focus groups with Latino populations: Lessons from the field. *Family Relations* 53, 261–272.

Underhill, C., & Olmstead, M. G. (2003). An experimental comparison of computer mediated and face-to-face focus groups. *Social Science Computer Review* 21(4), 506–512.

Valaitis, R.K., & Sword, W.A. (2005). Online discussions with pregnant and parenting adolescents: Perspectives and possibilities. *Health Promotion Practice* 6(4), 464–471.

Valera, P., Gallin, J., Schuk, D., & Davis, N. (2009). 'Trying to Eat Healthy': A photovoice study about women's access to healthy food in New York City. *Affilia: Journal of Women and Social Work* 24(3), 300–314.

Vaughn, S., Schumm, J.S., & Sinagub, J. (1996). *Focus group interviews in education and psychology*. Thousand Oaks, CA: Sage.

Veale, A. (2005). Creative methodologies in participatory research with children. In S. Greene & D. Hogan (eds.), *Researching children's experience: Approaches and methods* (pp. 253–272). London: Sage Publications.

Vera, E.M., Reese, L.E., Paikoff, R.L., & Jarrett, R.L. (1996). Contextual factors of sexual risk-taking in urban African American preadolescent children. In B.J. Leadbeater & N. Way (eds.), *Urban girls: Resisting stereotypes, creating identities* (pp. 291–304). New York: New York University Press.

Vissandjée, B., Abdool, S.N., & Dupéré, S. (2002). Focus groups in rural Gujarat, India: A modified approach. *Qualitative Health Research* 12(6), 826–843.

Vo-Thanh-Xuan, J., & Liamputtong, P. (2003). What it takes to be a grandparent in a new country: The lived experiences and emotional well-being of Australian-Vietnamese grandparents. *Australian Journal of Social Issues, Refugees and Migrant Issues – Special issue* 38(2), 209–228.

Walston, J.T., & Lissitz, R.W. (2000). Computer mediated focus groups. *Evaluation Review* 24(5), 457–483.

Wang, C., & Burris, M.A. (1997). Photovoice: Concept, methodology and use for participatory needs assessment. *Health and Behaviour* 24, 369–387.

Wang, C.C. (2003). Using photovoice as a participatory assessment and issue selection tool: A case study with the homeless in Ann Arbor. In M. Minkler & N. Wallerstein (eds.), *Community based participatory research for health* (pp. 179–196). San Francisco: Jossey-Bass.

Warr, D.J. (2001). *The practical logic of intimacy: An analysis of a class context for (hetero)sex-related health issues.* PhD thesis, La Trobe University.

Warr, D.J. (2004). Stories in the flesh and voices in the head: Reflections on the context and impact of research with disadvantaged populations. *Qualitative Health Research* 14(4), 578–587.

Warr, D.J. (2005). 'It was fun…but we don't usually talk about these things': Analyzing sociable interaction in focus groups. *Qualitative Inquiry* 11(2), 200–225.

Warr, D.J., & Pyett, P.M. (1999). Difficult relations: Sex work, love and intimacy. *Sociology of Health & Illness* 21(3), 290–309.

Watkins-Mathys, L. (2006). Focus group interviewing in China: Language, culture, and sensemaking. *Journal of International Entrepreneurship* 4, 209–226.

Welch, C., & Piekkari, R. (2006). Crossing language boundaries: Qualitative interviewing in international business. *Management International Review* 46(4), 417–437.

Wellings, K., Branigan, P., & Mitchell, K. (2000). Discomfort, discord and discontinuity as data: Using focus groups to research sensitive topics. *Culture, Health and Sexuality* 2(3), 255–267.

Whitehead, L.C. (2007). Methodological and ethical issues in Internet-mediated research in the field of health: An integrated review of the literature. *Social Science and Medicine* 65(4), 782–791.

Whyte, W.F. (1943). *Street corner society: The social structures of an Italian slum.* Chicago: University of Chicago Press.

Whyte, W.F. (1955). *Street corner society: The social structure of an Italian slum.* Chicago: University of Chicago Press.

Wilkin, A., & Liamputtong, P. (2010). The photovoice method: Researching the experiences of Aboriginal health workers through photographs. *Australian Journal of Primary Health.*

Wilkinson, S. (1998). Focus groups in feminist research: Power, interaction, and the co-construction of meaning. *Women's Studies International Forum* 21, 111–125.

Wilkinson, S. (1999). How useful are focus groups in feminist research? In R.S. Barbour & J. Kitzinger (eds.), *Developing focus group research: Politics, theory and practice* (pp. 64–78). London: Sage.

Wilkinson, S. (2004). Focus groups: A feminist method. In S.N. Hesse-Biber & M.L. Yaiser (eds.), *Feminist perspectives on social research* (pp. 271–295). New York: Oxford University Press.

Wilkinson, S., & Kitzinger, C. (1996). *Representing the other.* London: Sage.

Williams, J., & Ayres, L. (2007). 'I'm like you': Establishing and protecting a common ground in focus groups with Huntington disease caregivers. *Journal of Research in Nursing* 12(6), 655–664.

Williams, M. (2003). *Virtually criminal: Deviance and harm within online environments.* Doctoral dissertation, University of Wales, Cardiff.

Williams, M., & Robson, K. (2004). Reengineering focus group methodology for the online environment. In M.D. Johns, S.-L.S. Chen & G.J. Hall (eds.), *Online social research: Methods, issues & ethics* (pp. 25–45). New York: Peter Lang.

Willis, E., Pearce, M. & Jenkin, T. (2005). Adapting focus group methods to fit Aboriginal community-based research. *Qualitative Research Journal* 5(2), 112–123.

Willis, J.W. (2007). *Foundations of qualitative research: Interpretive and critical approaches.* Thousand Oaks, CA: Sage Publications.

Willis, K., Green, J., Daly, J., Williamson, L., & Bandyopadhyay, M. (2009). Perils and possibilities: Achieving best evidence from focus groups in public health research. *Australian and New Zealand Journal of Public Health* 33(2), 131–136.

Winslow, W.W., Honein, G., & Elzubeir, M.A. (2002). Seeking Emirati women's voices: The use of focus groups with an Arab population. *Qualitative Health Research* 12(4), 566–575.

Wojcicki, J.M., & Malala, J. (2001). Condom use, power and HIV/AIDS risks: Sex-workers bargain for survival in Hillbrow/Joubert Park/Berea, Johannesburg. *Social Science and Medicine* 53(1), 99–121.

Wollersheim, D., Merkes, M., Shields, N., Liamputtong, P., Wallis, L., Reynolds, F., & Koh, L. (2010). Physical and psychosocial effects of wii video game use among older women. Paper submitted to *the International Journal of Emerging Technologies and Society (iJETS)*.

Yelland, J., & Gifford, S.M. (1995). Problems of focus group methods in cross-cultural research: A case study of beliefs about sudden infant death syndrome. *Australian Journal of Public Health* 19(3), 257–263.

Zaltman, G. (2003). *How customers think.* Boston, MA: Harvard Business School Press.

# INDEX